M000267495

"Benjamin Laird has written an insigh[...] the New Testament. Laird explains everything from ancient writing practices to book production and publication to letter writing in antiquity, as well as the origins and reception of Christian texts, and the importance of apostolic authority. A helpful read for anyone interested in the what and the how of the Bible."

Michael F. Bird, academic dean and lecturer in New Testament at Ridley College in Melbourne, Australia

"*Creating the Canon* is a dependable guide for the early formation of the New Testament. It not only introduces the major scholarly voices in the debate, it also is structured to answer several common questions regarding the composition, formation, and the authority of the New Testament. Though the questions are common, Laird does not merely offer simple answers; rather, his work engages insights from textual criticism and canon research to address the origin, extent, and authority of the canon. Accessible to the student, yet filled with insights for teachers and scholars, Laird's volume will be a helpful reference tool for many and provide a gateway into deeper canon studies for others—highly recommended!"

Darian R. Lockett, professor of New Testament at Talbot School of Theology, Biola University

"For those who wrestle with the nature and significance of the scriptural canon in modern Christianity and wonder about its ancient origins, Benjamin Laird's book cuts a lucid and engaging path through many aspects of the canon's composition, formation, and authority. Laird writes both as a historian and as a Christian, combining critical attention to sources and hermeneutics with a personal sense of the importance of these questions today."

Jane Heath, Durham University

"As one treks into the rugged terrain of New Testament canon studies, a daunting range of issues looms on the horizon. Benjamin Laird maps out the general contours of current scholarship and then proposes his own path forward. His study provides a panoramic view of canon-related considerations but also raises significant questions concerning the relationship between apostolicity and the ecclesial recognition of divinely inspired texts."

Paul A. Hartog, professor of theology at Faith Baptist Seminary

"The wonderful thing about studying the origins of the New Testament canon is that there's always more to discover. It seems like a well without a bottom. This new volume by Benjamin Laird exemplifies this reality. In this wide-ranging study, Laird not only revisits older questions but also explores newer ones, creating a fresh and helpful addition to the growing body of work on the origins of the canon."

Michael J. Kruger, president and Samuel C. Patterson Professor of New Testament at Reformed Theological Seminary in Charlotte, North Carolina

CREATING the CANON

Composition, Controversy, and the Authority of the New Testament

BENJAMIN P. LAIRD

ivp
Academic

An imprint of InterVarsity Press
Downers Grove, Illinois

InterVarsity Press
P.O. Box 1400 | Downers Grove, IL 60515-1426
ivpress.com | email@ivpress.com

InterVarsity Press® is the publishing division of InterVarsity Christian Fellowship/USA®. For more information, visit intervarsity.org.

All Scripture quotations, unless otherwise indicated, are taken from the *New American Standard Bible*®, copyright 1960, 1962, 1963, 1968, 1971, 1972, 1973, 1975, 1977, 1995 by The Lockman Foundation. Used by permission.

The publisher cannot verify the accuracy or functionality of website URLs used in this book beyond the date of publication.

Cover design: David Fassett
Interior design: Daniel van Loon
Cover image: Saint Jerome, detail de la main et du livre. Peinture de Pierre Subleyras (1699-1749). Pinacoteca di Brera, Milan. 481,1 Photo © Raffaello Bencini / Bridgeman Images

ISBN 978-1-5140-0110-3 (print) | ISBN 978-1-5140-0111-0 (digital)

Printed in the United States of America ∞

Library of Congress Cataloging-in-Publication Data
A catalog record for this book is available from the Library of Congress.

29   28   27   26   25   24   23 | 13   12   11   10   9   8   7   6   5   4   3   2   1

To Meredith, Jonathan, Lydia, Nora, and Charles

μειζοτέραν τούτων οὐκ ἔχω χαράν, ἵνα ἀκούω

τὰ ἐμὰ τέκνα ἐν τῇ ἀληθείᾳ περιπατοῦντα

CONTENTS

Acknowledgments—ix   *Abbreviations—xi*

Introduction *1*

PART ONE

Questions Relating to the Production of the New Testament Writings

1 The Composition of the New Testament Writings. *11*

2 The Original Autographs of the New Testament Writings *42*

3 The Original Readers of the New Testament Writings *65*

PART TWO

Questions Relating to the Formation of the New Testament Canon

4 Theological Controversies and the Formation of the
New Testament Canon. *87*

5 The Primary Witnesses to the Early State of the
New Testament Canon. *120*

6 The Canonical Subcollections and the Formation of the
New Testament Canon. *141*

PART THREE

Questions Relating to the Authority of the New Testament Canon

7 Apostolicity and the Formation of the New Testament Canon *177*

8 Apostolic Authorship and the Authority of the
New Testament Canon. *206*

Bibliography—237   *Name Index—253*

Scripture Index—255   *Ancient Writings Index—257*

ACKNOWLEDGMENTS

THE HISTORICAL BACKGROUND of the New Testament continues to be a subject of significant interest and curiosity. It would seem that the more we learn about the world of the first century and the background of the New Testament writings, the more areas of potential research emerge. I am grateful for the opportunity to take part in a small way in the ongoing discussion. It is my hope that the subjects that are explored in this volume will prompt fresh questions, encourage further dialogue, and provide clarity on a broad range of subjects that relate in one respect or another to the composition, publication, formation, and authority of the New Testament writings.

I have had the good fortune to work with an exceptional team at IVP Academic. From the beginning to the end of the process, I was in very capable hands! In addition to those who worked quietly "behind the scenes" on the preparation of the volume, I would like to thank two individuals in particular: Anna Mosely Gissing, for her initial interest in the project and for her assistance during the early stages of the writing process, and Rachel Hastings, who offered helpful guidance through the final stages of the project and saw the work to its completion.

I would also like to express my gratitude to my wife, Margaret, for her encouragement and support during a busy season of research and writing and to each of my children for the happiness they bring to our lives and the sacrifices that they have made for me to devote time to this project. It is my joy to dedicate this volume to them.

ABBREVIATIONS

MODERN SOURCES

AB	Anchor Bible Commentary
AnBib	Analecta Biblica
ANF	*The Ante-Nicene Fathers*
ASE	*Annali di Storia dell'Esegesi*
BBR	*Bulletin of Biblical Research*
BETS	*Bulletin of the Evangelical Theological Society*
BGBE	Beiträge zur Geschichte der biblischen Exegese
BMSEC	Baylor-Mohr Siebeck Studies in Early Christianity
BN	*Biblische Notizen*
BNTC	Black's New Testament Commentaries
BPC	Biblical Performance Criticism
BZNW	Beihefte zur Zeitschrift für die neutestamentliche Wissenschaft
CCT	Contours of Christian Theology
CLA	Christianity in Late Antiquity
ClQ	*Classical Quarterly*
ConJ	*Concordia Journal*
FRLANT	Forschungen zur Religion und Literatur des Alten und Neuen Testaments
HTR	*Harvard Theological Review*
ICC	International Critical Commentary
Int	*Interpretation*
JBL	*Journal of Biblical Literature*
JETS	*Journal of the Evangelical Theological Society*

JRS	*The Journal of Roman Studies*
JSNT	*Journal for the Study of the New Testament*
JSPL	*Journal for the Study of Paul and His Letters*
JTI	*Journal of Theological Interpretation*
JTS	*Journal of Theological Studies*
LEC	Library of Early Christianity
LNTS	Library of New Testament Studies
MJT	*Midwestern Journal of Theology*
NICNT	New International Commentary on the New Testament
NovT	*Novum Testamentum*
NovTSup	Novum Testamentum Supplements
NPNF	*The Nicene and Post-Nicene Fathers*
NTS	*New Testament Studies*
NTTSD	New Testament Tools, Studies, and Documents
PAST	Pauline Studies
PFES	Publications on the Finnish Exegetical Society
PRSt	*Perspectives in Religious Studies*
RB	*Revue biblique*
ResQ	*Restoration Quarterly*
RevExp	*Review and Expositor*
RevScRel	*Revue des sciences religieuses*
SBET	*Scottish Bulletin of Evangelical Theology*
SBJT	*Southern Baptist Journal of Theology*
SBR	Studies of the Bible and its Reception
SD	Studies and Documents
SNTSMS	Society for New Testament Studies Monograph Series
SSEJC	Studies in Scripture in Early Judaism and Christianity
STAC	Studien und Texte zu Antike und Christentum
StPatr	Studia Patristica
SVC	Supplements to Vigiliae Christianae
TENTS	Texts and Editions for New Testament Study
TJ	*Trinity Journal*
TRE	*Theologische Realenzyklopädie*

TSAJ	Texte und Studien zum antiken Judentum
TU	Texte und Untersuchungen
TynBul	*Tyndale Bulletin*
VC	*Vigiliae Christianae*
WBC	Word Biblical Commentary
WesTJ	*Wesleyan Theological Journal*
WTJ	*Westminster Theological Journal*
WUNT	Wissenschaftliche Untersuchungen zum Neuen Testament
ZNW	*Zeitschrift für die neutestamentliche Wissenschaft und die Kunde der älteren Kirche*

ANCIENT SOURCES

Athanasius	*Ep. fest.*	*Festal Letters*
Athenagoras	*Suppl.*	*Supplication for the Christians*
Augustine	*Doctr. chr.*	*Christian Instruction*
Cicero	*Att.*	*Epistles to Atticus*
	Fam.	*Epistles to Friends*
Clement of Alexandria	*Paed.*	*Christ the Educator*
	Protr.	*Exhortation to the Greeks*
	Strom.	*Miscellanies*
Clement of Rome	*1 Clem.*	*1 Clement*
Cyprian	*Test.*	*To Quirinius: Testimonies against the Jews*
Cyril of Jerusalem	*Lec.*	*Catechetical Lectures*
Epiphanius	*Pan.*	*Refutation of All Heresies*
Eusebius	*Hist. eccl.*	*Ecclesiastical History*
	Vit. Const.	*Life of Constantine*
Hippolytus of Rome	*Haer.*	*Refutation of All Heresies*
Ignatius	*Eph.*	*Epistle to the Ephesians*
	Magn.	*Epistle to the Magnesians*
	Rom.	*Epistle to the Romans*
Irenaeus	*Haer.*	*Against Heresies*
Jerome	*Epist.*	*Epistle*
	Vir. ill.	*On Illustrious Men*

Josephus	*Ag. Ap.*	*Against Apion*
	Ant.	*Jewish Antiquities*
	J.W.	*Jewish War*
Justin	*Dial.*	*Dialogue with Trypho*
Origen	*Comm. Matt.*	*Commentary on the Gospel of Matthew*
	Comm. Rom.	*Commentary on Romans*
	Hom. Luc.	*Homily on Luke*
Pliny the Younger	*Ep.*	*Epistle*
Polybius	*Polyb.*	*The Histories*
Polycarp	Pol. *Phil.*	*Epistle to the Philippians*
Tertullian	*De baptismo*	*Baptism*
	Marc.	*Against Marcion*
	Praescr.	*Prescription against Heretics*
	Pud.	*Modesty*
Theophilus	*Autol.*	*To Autolycus*

INTRODUCTION

We are witnessing a great increase in intelligent interest in the
New Testament, its origin, and its message. Many thoughtful
people are keenly interested in how the New Testament arose;
who selected the books, and on what grounds some were
chosen and others left out.

EDGAR GOODSPEED, *THE FORMATION OF THE NEW TESTAMENT*

THE WORDS ABOVE WERE WRITTEN NEARLY a century ago but
could have been written today. Even after many years of careful investigation into the background and early reception of the New Testament
writings, the question of how the New Testament canon was formed
remains a perennial interest among students, lay readers, and scholars
alike. Many remain curious about how the New Testament writings
were composed and published and how a relatively small number of
works eventually emerged to form a popular and influential collection
of sacred Scripture. Questions have also been raised about the legitimacy
of the canon and the basis of its authority. Do the canonical writings
bear inherent authority, or is their authoritative status something that
was merely conferred on them by those with significant influence during
a pivotal period of church history?[1] Should we think of the canonical

---

[1]Terms such as *canonical* and *noncanonical* will be used throughout the volume in reference to the
works that were either included or excluded from the established Christian canon. While several
contemporary scholars make a sharp distinction between Scripture and canon, there is clearly a
close connection between the two terms. Consequently, descriptions such as "authoritative Scripture" and "canonical" will often be used in similar ways, though the particular word choice is

writings as something like "classics" from the early church that were incorporated into the New Testament as a result of their popularity and influence, or are there certain attributes or qualities that belong to these writings alone? Fundamental questions such as these have been answered in a variety of ways and continue to garner significant interest.

There are perhaps several reasons for the continuing interest in the subject of the canon's origin and development. This may be partly due to little more than natural curiosity. The New Testament writings, after all, have arguably had a greater impact on religious thought than any other writings in human history and continue to be read and studied by millions around the world. This is clearly not just any collection of ancient texts but a collection of writings that remain deeply valued and influential. As a result of the profound influence of the New Testament throughout church history and in contemporary society, it is only natural for readers to question where the canonical writings came from, how they formed into a single collection, and if there is a possible basis for their ongoing authority.

In addition to this natural curiosity, interest in the canon may also be related to a number of developments that have taken place in the world of scholarship. The discovery of a large body of ancient writings at sites such as Oxyrhynchus, Nag Hammadi, and Qumran have greatly enhanced our understanding of the literary environment in which the New Testament writings were composed. In addition, the discovery of several notable biblical manuscripts over the last century in Egypt and elsewhere has provided valuable insight related to the early reception

---

often determined by the particular subject that is being considered. Generally speaking, the term *canonical* is typically used in reference to works that are part of the specific collection of writings that have been widely recognized by the church as the authoritative standard for doctrine and Christian living. In many cases, therefore, the term serves as an acknowledgment of the historical recognition of a work's authoritative status. The word *Scripture*, on the other hand, was often used in the early church as a general yet meaningful reference to works that were understood to be of divine origin or to function as authoritative guides to the church. Each of the canonical writings were widely recognized as Scripture long before there was widespread recognition of a definitive body of Christian writings. In addition, the term was occasionally used to describe works that were not recognized as part of the canon. As the scope of the canon became more widely recognized and defined, the terms *canonical* and *Scripture* became more closely related and applied to the same body of writings.

of the New Testament writings and introduced several new areas of potential research. It would seem that as new pieces of the puzzle of the canon's origin have been discovered and analyzed, interest in the puzzle itself has steadily increased.

Finally, it may be possible to attribute some of the recent interest in the canon to certain trends and developments that have taken place in contemporary culture. In the current intellectual climate, many have become dismissive or even suspicious of organized religion and have become reluctant to accept core doctrines at the heart of the Christian faith, the reality of supernatural events, and even God's providence in human history. Instead of a diminished interest in the canon, however, it would seem that these perspectives have actually led to a greater curiosity in the events that may have prompted the canon's formation, at least in some circles. In light of modern culture's interest in historical mysteries and the increasingly distrustful attitude toward religious institutions and political institutions, it is certainly understandable why many have become intrigued by the possibility that the formation of the New Testament canon may have been the result of political wrangling, secretive meetings, and calculated maneuvers designed to shape Christianity in a particular way. The popularity of Dan Brown's novel *The Da Vinci Code* bears evidence of this.[2] Understood from this perspective, the New Testament canon might be thought to be more reflective of the beliefs and practices of the church of the fourth and fifth centuries than of the church known to the apostles and the first generation of Jesus' followers.

Although the origin of the New Testament remains a subject of considerable interest among scholars and lay readers alike, I would suggest that there are a number of consequential subjects relating to the creation of the canon that have either been misunderstood or not fully explored. In fact, the more I discuss the subject of canon with students and lay people and engage in research of the subject, the more apparent it becomes to me that greater clarity and insight is needed with respect

---

[2]Dan Brown, *The Da Vinci Code* (New York: Anchor, 2009).

to our understanding of the process that led to the composition and
formation of the canonical writings and the basis of their authoritative
status. In light of this reality, I wrote this book in order to tell the story—
so far as we are able—of the process that led to the canon's composition
and formation, to address certain subjects related to the study of canon
that have been largely overlooked or misunderstood, and finally, to
reflect on the question of the canon's authority, a practical matter that
is often a source of confusion among contemporary readers. My intention is for this volume to serve as an accessible guide to those with
limited prior study of the background of the New Testament writings
while encouraging further dialogue in the scholarly community about
specific subjects that have not been adequately explored or possibly
even misunderstood.

Although the topics addressed in this volume are wide ranging, the
objective here is not to offer a comprehensive introduction to the
subject of canon—several excellent introductions have been published
in recent years—but to address specific subjects that relate to the composition, formation, or authority of the New Testament that have received only limited attention or have been misconstrued in some way.[3]
Our investigation will begin with an exploration of various subjects
that relate to the composition of the writings and will then transition
to an assessment of the likely process that led to the creation of discrete canonical collections, a process that eventually led to the establishment and recognition of a single collection known today as the

---

[3]Some of the more thorough introductions published over the last forty years include the follow-
ing: Lee Martin McDonald, *The Biblical Canon: Its Origin, Transmission and Authority* (Peabody,
MA: Hendrickson, 2007), and *The Formation of the Biblical Canon*, vol. 2, *The New Testament
Canon: Its Authority and Canonicity* (London: T&T Clark, 2021); Bruce Metzger, *The Canon of the
New Testament: Its Origin, Development, and Significance* (Oxford: Clarendon, 1987); F. F. Bruce,
The Canon of Scripture (Downers Grove, IL: InterVarsity Press, 1988); Harry Y. Gamble, *The New
Testament Canon: Its Making and Meaning* (Philadelphia: Fortress, 1985); Arthur G. Patzia, *The
Making of the New Testament* (Downers Grove, IL: InterVarsity Press, 1995). Older introductions
and studies that have made a significant contribution to scholarship on the canon include
B. F. Westcott, *A General Survey of the History of the Canon of the New Testament*, 7th ed. (London:
Macmillan, 1896); Theodor Zahn, *Geschichte des Neutestamentlichen Kanons*, 2 vols. (Erlangen:
Deichert, 1888–1892), and *Grundriss der Geschichte des Neutestamentlichen Kanons* (Leipzig: De-
ichert, 1901); Adolf von Harnack, *The Origin of the New Testament and the Most Important Consequences of the New Creation*, trans. J. R. Wilkinson (New York: Macmillan, 1925).

New Testament. We will thus consider the larger story of the creation of the canon, a story that includes the composition of the individual writings and ends with the widespread recognition of a particular collection of sacred works. It is my hope that the subjects addressed in this volume will offer readers a more informed understanding of how a particular body of writings that were composed by multiple authors, in different times, in different locations, and in response to different concerns, may have been composed, how they ultimately came to be recognized as a single collection, and why these writings should be regarded as authoritative Scripture today.

Before setting out on this journey, it will be helpful to briefly outline how the volume is organized. Each chapter in the volume will address a specific question that relates in some way to the composition, formation, or authority of the New Testament canon. The first three chapters address subjects that relate to the composition of the New Testament writings. Several of the subjects explored in these chapters have received only limited attention in the scholarly world but promise to offer valuable insight relating to the composition of the writings and their initial distribution. As will be seen, advancements in our knowledge of ancient literary conventions may call into question some of the prevailing assumptions about the composition and early distribution of the New Testament writings and offer fresh insight about the manner in which literary works were often composed and collected during the first century. The first chapter considers the collaborative nature of first-century writing and explores how the composition of the canonical writings often involved a large number of individuals who played an important role at some point in the process. The chapter focuses largely on the role of secretaries, letter carriers, and those who served in one capacity or another in the production and initial distribution of the canonical writings. The second chapter challenges the common assumption that the composition of each of the biblical writings culminated with the production of a single original autograph. It will be suggested that it is best to think in terms of something like an original edition of each work rather than a single manuscript that was dispatched to the intended readers. Building on this subject, the third chapter challenges common perceptions related to the initial readers of the New Testament and considers the possibility that the biblical authors often wrote for the benefit of multiple audiences rather than a single "original audience."

The three chapters in the second major unit of the volume address essential questions related to the canon's formation. The fourth chapter evaluates the common assumption that the canon's initial formation was prompted by theological controversies such as the threat of Marcion during the second century or by one or more developments or events that took place during the reign of Constantine in the fourth century. Marcion is not as well-known to lay readers but is often understood by church historians and biblical scholars to have played a significant role in provoking the leadership of the greater church to recognize a specific body of writings as authoritative Scripture. Others have assumed that Constantine was largely responsible for creating the necessary conditions for the church to reach an agreement on the scope of the canon. Chapter five offers a concise overview of some of the most important witnesses to the early state of the canon such as canonical lists, Greek manuscripts, and the writings of early Christian writers. This is then followed in the sixth chapter with an attempt to account for the process that ultimately led to the widespread recognition of a specific set of twenty-seven canonical writings. Building on several recent studies, the chapter emphasizes the role that the canonical subcollections played in the development of the New Testament canon. Rather than a sudden creation of a single collection of writings that was sanctioned by powerful figures at some point in church history, it is argued that the consensus regarding the extent of the New Testament canon naturally followed the establishment of widely recognized canonical subcollections—the fourfold Gospel, Acts, the Catholic Epistles, the Pauline Epistles, and Revelation. In other words, what came to be regarded as the New Testament might be understood simply as the amalgam of the various canonical subcollections of authoritative Scripture that initially circulated independently.

Finally, the third major unit of the volume takes up the important question of the canon's authority. In chapter seven we consider how the emphasis placed on apostolic instruction and testimony appears to have influenced the reception of a number of writings and the canonical process itself. The final chapter will then offer an assessment of some of the prevailing assumptions and viewpoints about the canon's legitimacy and authority and consider the possible basis for its ongoing authority.

The study of canon is one of most challenging yet rewarding areas of research in the broader field of New Testament studies. Among other things, it involves the investigation of a diverse body of ancient witnesses (e.g., biblical manuscripts, canonical lists, and the writings of ancient writers) and ancient literary conventions; an evaluation of the possible influence of several historical figures, events, and developments; and the consideration of a number of important theological matters. Given the complexities of the subject, it is of little surprise that there are a wide range of opinions relating to the circumstances that may have prompted the composition of the biblical writings, the process that led to the formation of the canon, the role of the canon in biblical hermeneutics, and even the legitimacy of the canon's authority! No single volume is capable of fully examining each of these major issues or of settling all debate and this volume is certainly not intended to serve as the final word on these matters. Nevertheless, it is my hope that the following chapters will enable readers from a variety of backgrounds to arrive at a more informed understanding of all that was involved in the process of creating the canon, from the initial composition of the writings to the establishment of a widely recognized canonical collection.

PART ONE

QUESTIONS RELATING to the PRODUCTION of the NEW TESTAMENT WRITINGS

THE COMPOSITION OF THE
NEW TESTAMENT WRITINGS

How would the New Testament authors have gone about the task of composing their writings?

The New Testament is a gift from the East. We are accustomed to read it under our Northern sky, and though it is by origin an Eastern book, it is so essentially a book of humanity that we comprehend its spirit even in the countries of the West and North. But details here and there, and the historical setting, would be better understood by a son of the East, especially a contemporary of the evangelists and apostles, than by us.

Adolf Deissmann, *Light from the Ancient East*

When we think about the composition of the New Testament writings, we often envision an aged man with a large white beard hovering over a wooden table carefully dipping his quill in a bottle of ink as he pensively writes by candlelight. Such is the image portrayed by several prominent artists such as Rembrandt and Jan Lievens in their portraits of the apostle Paul, one of the more well-known writers of Scripture. Behind these depictions is the underlying assumption that writing in the ancient world typically took place in quiet and isolated places, and that it was fairly similar to writing in the modern age, apart, of course, from the more primitive materials that were used. If Paul were writing today, we might expect him to flip a light switch before settling in at his desk to work from his computer, but the solitary nature of the work would remain unchanged. It is certainly understandable why this assumption of writing in the ancient world remains common. The study of ancient book culture and literary conventions are heavily specialized academic fields that are largely unfamiliar to contemporary readers of the Bible. Other than a small handful of postgraduate students and academics who have the patience and inclination to study technical works that address obscure literary practices from antiquity, few contemporary readers are familiar with the basic process by which ancient works were commonly composed, assembled, and distributed.

While our knowledge of ancient literary practices is far from complete, a number of significant discoveries of ancient manuscripts over the last few centuries have yielded fresh insights on a host of issues related to writing in the Greco-Roman world. We now have a much greater understanding of the features and characteristics of various literary genres, the materials that were often used to produce literary works, the manner in which writings were often disseminated and preserved, and the role that written texts played in society. The material discovered at sites such as Oxyrhynchus and Nag Hammadi include several early biblical manuscripts (e.g., the Bodmer Papyri and Chester Beatty Papyri)[1] and other early Christian writings (e.g., early noncanonical works such as the *Gospel of Thomas*), as well as a large trove of personal letters, business documents, and religious texts that were used throughout the Mediterranean world. Naturally, much of the attention has focused on what these writings may reveal about the culture in which they were written, though they also provide significant insight about the role of literary works and documents in ancient society, the physical features and characteristics of ancient writings, and a host of related matters. Despite the significant attention that has been given to

---

[1] For background regarding the discovery of several biblical papyri, see Brent Nongbri, *God's Library: The Archaeology of the Earliest Christian Manuscripts* (New Haven, CT: Yale University Press, 2018).

what people were reading and the role of literature in ancient society, surprisingly little attention has been given to the simple question of how writers went about their work. There cannot be a simple answer to this question, of course, as each literary genre is unique, as were the circumstances facing each individual author. A letter to a colleague about a particular matter of business or a personal letter between a husband and a wife was typically a more straightforward process than the production of a philosophical or religious treatise, a historical work, or other types of literature that were intended to circulate among larger audiences.

The study of how writings were composed and produced in the Greco-Roman world is of particular interest to the study of the background of the New Testament. While Christians were certainly not the only members of ancient society who made significant use of literature, their affinity for written texts was one of their defining characteristics. As Larry Hurtado explains, "Reading, writing, copying, and dissemination of texts had a major place—indeed, a prominence—in early Christianity that, except for ancient Jewish circles, was unusual for religious groups of the Roman era."[2] There were certainly a number of written accounts that describe the origin and exploits of various deities or address one aspect or another of ancient worship. For the most part, however, written texts appear to have played a less foundational role in Greco-Roman religion than in Jewish and Christian circles. Most people did not attend a weekly study on writings about Poseidon, for example, or carefully scrutinize a collection of religious texts for instruction pertaining to the proper worship of a Roman emperor. In many contexts, religious activity appears to have been largely cultic in nature with a focus on external acts of worship, with most people simply paying their respects to various deities when, where, and how it was deemed appropriate in their particular environment.

In light of the unique role that written texts have played in Christianity for two millennia, it will be helpful to briefly consider what may

---

[2]Larry W. Hurtado, *Destroyer of the Gods: Early Christian Distinctiveness in the Roman World* (Waco, TX: Baylor University Press, 2016), 105-6.

be determined regarding the manner in which the biblical authors composed and distributed their works.[3] Our concern in this volume, after all, is not limited to how and why certain writings were recognized as part of New Testament. These matters are certainly of great importance and will be taken up more directly in subsequent chapters. Ultimately, we are interested in the broader story that began with the composition of individual texts and ultimately culminated with the establishment of a widely recognized collection of canonical works. Before we entertain questions relating to the formation and authority of the canon, it will be beneficial to briefly consider how the biblical authors likely went about the task of composition, and even how they "published" their completed material. Although it is important to carefully assess and evaluate *what* the biblical authors wrote and *why* they wrote it, it is also helpful to consider *how* the biblical authors went about their work. When Luke set out to compose his Gospel, for example, what would have been involved in the process of creating his unique account of Christ's life, teaching, and salvific work? Did he simply patch together existing traditions that had circulated orally or in a number of existing literary sources, perhaps adding his own literary touch and historical insights along the way? What were the sources of the unique material contained in his Gospel? Did he rely on works that are no longer extant for this information? What about the apostle Paul and those responsible for the Epistles contained in the New Testament? Did they simply receive reports about a particular situation

---

[3]For further background relating to the composition of the New Testament writings, see George W. Houston, *Inside Roman Libraries: Book Collections and Their Management in Antiquity* (Chapel Hill: University of North Carolina Press, 2014); David E. Aune, *The New Testament in its Literary Environment*, LEC 8 (Philadelphia: Westminster, 1987); Hans-Josef Klauck, *Ancient Letters and the New Testament: A Guide to Context and Exegesis* (Waco, TX: Baylor University Press, 2006); Stanley K. Stowers, *Letter Writing in Greco-Roman Antiquity*, LEC 5 (Philadelphia: Westminster, 1986); Harry Y. Gamble, *Books and Readers in the Early Church* (New Haven, CT: Yale University Press, 1995); M. Luther Stirewalt, *Paul, the Letter Writer* (Grand Rapids, MI: Eerdmans, 2003); E. Randolph Richards, *Paul and First-Century Letter Writing: Secretaries, Composition and Collection* (Downers Grove, IL: InterVarsity Press, 2004); Richards, "Reading, Writing, and Manuscripts," in *The World of the New Testament: Cultural, Social, and Historical Contexts*, ed. Joel B. Green and Lee Martin McDonald (Grand Rapids, MI: Baker Academic, 2013), 345-66; David Trobisch, *The First Edition of the New Testament* (New York: Oxford University Press, 2000); Pieter J. J. Botha, *Orality and Literacy in Early Christianity*, BPC 5 (Eugene, OR: Cascade, 2012).

and then retreat to their private quarters to compose written instructions and admonitions in response to the matters at hand? In short, what can we conclude about the actual composition of the New Testament writings and their initial distribution?

A fundamental characteristic of the composition of the New Testament writings that is often overlooked is its collaborative nature. As the content and features of ancient writings are examined, it becomes increasingly apparent that writing in the Greco-Roman world often involved significant collaboration between an author and a number of individuals, each of whom served a specific role during the compositional process. While the biblical writers were ultimately responsible for the content of their writings, the evidence would suggest that they worked directly with a number of individuals who contributed in one way or another to the composition, publication, and distribution of their writings. In what follows, we will briefly consider some of the primary ways in which individuals appear to have assisted the New Testament authors. We will begin with a brief overview of the role of secretaries and letter carriers before looking into some of the ways that the canonical authors may have benefited from their collaboration with their partners and colleagues.

SECRETARIES

For many individuals living during the first century, the composition of a personal letter, business or legal document, or virtually any type of literary work involved direct collaboration with a trained secretary, or amanuensis, as they are often called.[4] Those who were illiterate—the majority of the population by most estimates—had no practical means of communicating with others from a distance other than to hire a

---

[4]For background relating to the role of secretaries in the compositional process of the New Testament writings, see Richards, *Paul and First-Century Letter Writing*; Steve Reece, *Paul's Large Letters: Paul's Autographic Subscriptions in the Light of Ancient Epistolary Conventions*, LNTS 561 (London: T&T Clark, 2017); Richard N. Longenecker, "Ancient Amanuenses and the Pauline Epistles," in *New Dimensions in New Testament Study*, ed. Richard N. Longenecker and Merrill C. Tenney (Grand Rapids, MI: Zondervan, 1974), 281-97; Klauck, *Ancient Letters and the New* Testament, 55-60; Jerome Murphy-O'Connor, *Paul the Letter Writer* (Collegeville, MN: Liturgical, 1995), 1-41.

secretary to produce a letter or to request assistance from a friend or acquaintance who possessed the skills and means to do this for them.[5] Many of the letters that were discovered at Oxyrhynchus, for example, were everyday letters and business documents that were composed by secretaries on behalf of their clients.[6] It was not just the illiterate who made use of secretaries, however. In addition to the fact that writing in the ancient world was less convenient than it is for modern writers who benefit from the use of computers and other electronic devices, many authors preferred to work directly with a secretary because of their expertise and convenience. In addition to maintaining the necessary writing materials, secretaries were capable of composing documents in a variety of literary genres and in a style that was typically more efficient, rhetorically effective, and pleasing to the eye.

Composing documents by hand was not something that most people engaged in on a frequent basis. Those who were literate might jot notes on a *tabula* (wax tablet) or write short pieces for their personal use. However, when it came to the production of official documents, literary pieces, letters, or other types of literature that were of any significant length or designed to be read by multiple readers, enlisting the services of a secretary was the widely preferred practice. We might compare the services offered by a secretary to those today who mow grass, change the oil of a car, or file taxes on behalf of their clients. Many individuals are capable of completing these tasks on their own

---

[5]A wide range of estimates have been offered regarding the literacy rates during the first century, though scholars generally agree that it was very low. As Craig Evans explains, "Most agree that literacy rates were somewhere between 5 and 10 percent (and that most of the literate were males), with perhaps somewhat higher rates among the Jewish people." *Jesus and His World: The Archaeological Evidence* (Louisville, KY: Westminster John Knox, 2012), 66. Some such as William Harris have suggested a higher literacy, while others such as Catherine Hezser have concluded that literacy rates were likely even lower. William Harris, *Ancient Literacy* (Cambridge, MA: Harvard University Press, 1991); Catherine Hezser, *Jewish Literacy in Roman Palestine*, TSAJ 81 (Tübingen: Mohr Siebeck, 2001). The low literacy rate would have necessitated the need for the oral proclamation of the New Testament writings. We find evidence for this in passages such as Col 4:16; 1 Thess 5:27; 1 Tim 4:13. Also of interest is Jesus' interaction with various individuals. In the Sermon on Mount, for example, the phrase "you have heard" is recorded five times (Mt 5:21, 27, 33, 38, and 43). When speaking to the religious authorities, however, Jesus questioned if they had read (Mt 12:3; 21:16; 22:31; Lk 10:26).

[6]For further insight regarding the scribal features of this literature, see William A. Johnson, *Bookrolls and Scribes in Oxyrhynchus* (Toronto: University of Toronto Press, 2004).

but prefer to hire someone for the sake of convenience or because of the known quality of an individual's work. Those of the upper classes were even known to enlist a trained slave to serve as their personal secretary. A famous example of a slave who possessed considerable literary abilities and training was Tiro, who served the Roman philosopher and statesman Cicero. When Cicero determine to write a letter, he did not sit down with pen and ink and compose the document by hand as he worked in solitude. Instead, it appears to have been his common practice to dictate his writings to Tiro or one of his other trained secretaries. From Cicero's large corpus of extant writings we learn not only that he commonly dictated his writings to secretaries such as Tiro, but that he often maintained copies of his writings (see, e.g., *Att.* 16.5.5 and *Fam.* 7.25.1).[7] As will be seen later in our study, the fact that secretaries often produced copies of the documents they composed for both their client and the intended recipient(s) is of special relevance to our understanding of the early formation of the Pauline letter corpus.

When composing letters, individuals would often stipulate key items to a secretary that he or she wished to communicate to their intended reader(s). The secretary would then craft the document according to this instruction. In many cases, we might suspect that the secretary would have recorded various notes from his conversation with the author on a tablet and would then use this information to compose the written work. On other occasions, individuals may have taken a more involved role, working carefully with the secretary throughout the process. Authors were known, for example, to dictate their writings directly to a scribe. On one occasion Cicero explains that his practice was to dictate his work to his slave Tiro, who, "usually takes down whole periods at a breath." He also refers to another assistant named Spintharus who was apparently not as skilled. When working with him, Cicero explains that he was forced to dictate his work "syllable by

---

[7] This also appears to have been the case with Pliny the Younger. In his letter to Septittus (*Ep.* 1.1), Pliny refers to copies of his letters that were in his possession and suggests that he had marked some of these for public circulation.

syllable."[8] Regardless of whether an author carefully dictated a text to his secretary or simply delineated the most pertinent information that was to be included in the document, it appears to have been a common practice for secretaries to present the completed work to the author for his or her approval prior to dispatch. If the client was literate, this might involve a careful reading of the written document. On other occasions, the scribe might simply read the completed text back to the individual. Once the author was satisfied, a note of authentication was often placed at the end of the writing, and arrangements were then made for its dispatch and/or public circulation.

Although it does not appear to be the case that the New Testament authors were independently wealthy or that they enjoyed the conveniences afforded to figures such as Cicero, it is unnecessary to assume that they composed each of their writings on their own or without the use of a trained secretary. In light of the fact that Paul and the other New Testament writers were well connected to Christian communities throughout the Roman world, it may have very well been the case that a number of individuals offered their time and expertise to assist them with the composition of their writings. In fact, we learn in Romans 16:22 that an individual by the name of Tertius served as Paul's secretary. It is unclear if he assisted Paul with other writings, but we can be certain that he served as Paul's secretary during the composition of Romans, an event that most likely took place during Paul's stay in Corinth near the end of the third missionary journey. Because the word order of the Greek text is flexible, it is possible for his greeting to be understood in different ways. Translations such as "I, Tertius, who wrote this letter, greet you in the Lord" are common in modern English versions as most scholars understand the prepositional phrase ἐν κυρίῳ (*en Kyriō*) as modifying ἀσπάζομαι ὑμᾶς (*aspazomai hymas*) rather than ὁ γράψας (*ho grapsas*). Understood in this sense, it was Tertius's greeting that was "in the Lord." It is possible, however, to understand the phrase "in the Lord" in connection to the writing itself, resulting in a translation such

---

[8]Cicero, *Att.* 13.25. Translation from *Letters of Cicero: The Whole Extant Correspondence in Chronological Order*, trans. Evelyn S. Shuckburgh (London: George Bell and Sons, 1908–1909).

as "I, Tertius, who wrote this epistle in the Lord, greet you." If this was indeed the sense in which the greeting was intended to be understood, Tertius's brief interjection may offer a subtle hint that he offered his services to Paul free of charge in order to order to advance his mission.

LETTER CARRIERS

In a world that did not have an organized postal system available to the general public or an electronic means of communication, authors often had little option but to entrust their associates or personal slaves with the task of delivering their writings.[9] While there is evidence that letters were commonly delivered by strangers traveling from one location to another, this mode of delivery was certainly not ideal. Who could ensure that the letter would actually make its way to the intended readers and not be tampered with or read? Considering the amount of time and resources that went into the composition of their writings and the importance of the content they contained, we may safely assume that authors such as Paul relied primarily and possibly even exclusively on trusted colleagues and associates to deliver their writings to their intended recipients. M. Luther Stirewalt is likely correct in his conclusion that Paul "did not depend on hired carriers or slaves, nor upon the chance journeying of friends or strangers" and that he instead "relied on people who shared his work and therefore had an investment in the communications necessitated by his circuit-riding ministry."[10] At times the letter carrier may have been a trusted companion who

---

[9]Recent studies of the role of letter carriers in the Greco-Roman world include Richards, *Paul and First-Century Letter Writing*, 171-209; Stirewalt, *Paul, the Letter Writer*, 9-19; Murphy-O'Connor, *Paul the Letter Writer*, 37-41; Margaret M. Mitchell, "The New Testament Envoys in the Context of Greco-Roman Diplomatic and Epistolary Conventions: the Example of Timothy and Titus," *JBL* 111 (1992): 641-62; Eldon J. Epp, "New Testament Papyrus Manuscripts and Letter Carrying in Greco-Roman Times," in *The Future of Early Christianity: Essays in Honor of Helmut Koester*, ed. B. A. Pearson, et al. (Minneapolis, MN: Fortress, 1991): 35-56; Klauck, *Ancient Letters*, 43-66; Peter M. Head, "Letter Carriers in the Ancient Jewish Epistolary Material," in *Jewish and Christian Scripture as Artifact and Canon*, ed. Craig A. Evans and H. D. Zacharias, SSEJC 13 (London: T&T Clark, 2009), 203-19; Head, "Named Letter-Carriers Among the Oxyrhynchus Papyri," *JSNT* 31 (2009): 279-99; Matthew S. Harmon, "Letter Carriers and Paul's Use of Scripture," *JSPL* 4 (2014): 129-48; Stephen Llewelyn, "Sending Letters in the Ancient World: Paul and the Philippians," *TynBul* 46 (1995): 337-56.

[10]Stirewalt, *Paul, the Letter Writer*, 19.

ministered alongside the author in a given location, while on other occasions the author may have entrusted this task to an individual from the community in which he wrote. Epaphroditus, for example, may have been entrusted to deliver the epistle to the Philippians on his return to Philippi after ministering to Paul.

Because illiteracy was rather high in the first century and access to written texts was often limited, we can safely assume that it was customary for the New Testament writings to be publicly read to the original recipients and other audiences shortly after their initial composition. In fact, instruction for the public reading of Paul's writings or Scripture in general may be found in passages such as Colossians 4:16, 1 Thessalonians 5:27, and 1 Timothy 4:13. Similarly, Luke 4:14-30, Acts 15:21, and 2 Corinthians 3:15 refer to the traditional Jewish practice of the reading of Scripture in the synagogue. The public reading of texts was not limited to the works of Scripture, however. As several scholars have noted, public-reading events were quite common in the Greco-Roman world.[11] Brian Wright has recently observed that the works of a variety of ancient authors such as Josephus, Philo, Celsus, Seneca, Strabo, Ovid, Quintilian, and Dio Chrysostom were often read in this fashion. These public-reading events enabled individuals to become familiar with a variety of writings even if they were illiterate or did not have access to a copy. This might be compared to the modern practice of listening to audiobooks, albeit these readings took place in public gatherings. It has also been noted that the public reading of a text often played a role in preserving a reliable textual tradition. As people became familiar with a writing through public reading, faulty and heavily redacted readings could more easily be identified and eliminated.[12]

---

[11]For background related to the practice of public reading of texts in the Roman world, see T. P. Wiseman, *The Roman Audience: Classical Literature as Social History* (New York: Oxford University Press, 2015); William A. Johnson, *Readers and Reading Culture in the High Roman Empire: A Study of Elite Communities* (New York: Oxford University Press, 2010); Brian Wright, *Communal Reading in the Time of Jesus: A Window into Early Christian Practices* (Minneapolis, MN: Fortress, 2017).

[12]For further discussion, see Timothy Mitchell, "Exposing Textual Corruption: Community as a Stabilizing Aspect in the Circulation of the New Testament Writings during the Greco-Roman Era," *JSNT* 43 (2020): 266-98.

Based on what may be established regarding the literary culture of the first-century Roman world and the role that public-reading events served, we might conclude that a significant number of early Christians would have encountered Scripture primarily through public-reading events rather than from reading texts in private settings. With regard to the New Testament writings, we may safely assume that in many cases the dispatched copy would have been read to the intended audience soon after it was delivered. While it is unclear how often letter carriers were charged with publicly reading the letters to the intended recipients, a number of extant writings from around the first century indicate that letter carriers often provided additional clarification and supplemental information regarding the content of the writings they delivered.[13] In many cases, an elder of a church or other designated individual may have read the text during a public gathering, though there may have also been occasions in which the letter carrier personally read the text to the intended audience. Regardless of who read the letter, the letter carrier would have often been available to offer clarification on key points and to offer additional insight on various subjects addressed in the text. We might imagine Tychicus (see Col 4:7-9), for example, offering clarification on certain topics addressed in Paul's epistle to the Colossians that may have been initially unclear after the initial reading in Colossae. In light of the reality that "some things [in Paul's letters are] hard to understand" (2 Pet 3:16), it is possible that Paul's letter carriers often provided the original readers with clarity and additional insight when needed. As Peter Head observes, Paul's letter carriers appear to have served "as personal mediators of Paul's authoritative instruction to his churches, and as the earliest interpreters of the individual letters."[14] This particular responsibility would have necessitated that letter carriers work closely with the author prior to setting off on their journey. We might

---

[13]See Head, "Named Letter-Carriers," for a number of primary sources which refer to the role which letter carriers played in providing readers with clarity and additional insight.

[14]Head, "Named Letter-Carriers," 298. See also, William Doty, *Letters in Primitive Christianity* (Minneapolis, MN: Fortress, 1973), 45-46; Stirewalt, *Paul, the Letter Writer*, 13-18.

speculate, for example, that Paul discussed several of the major themes addressed in his epistle to the Colossians with Tychicus prior to the dispatch of the writing in order to ensure that Tychicus correctly understood Paul's primary concerns and the arguments he sought to make.

THE BIBLICAL WRITERS AND THEIR COLLEAGUES

As we examine the New Testament writings and other extant literature from this general period, it becomes apparent that the New Testament authors worked closely not only with those who served as secretaries and letter carriers but also with a number of colleagues and acquaintances who could offer valuable guidance, suggestions, and useful information during the compositional process. Information was obviously much more difficult to acquire in the first century, a reality that often necessitated collaboration with those who possessed firsthand testimony about past events (e.g., a miracle of Jesus) or recent developments that took place in a particular community (e.g., the factions and controversies in Corinth). On other occasions, writers may have simply sought the advice of colleagues on how to address a particular situation or subject matter most effectively. Several of the writings in the New Testament contain accounts of events that the author did not personally witness or instruction relating to situations in communities that were a considerable distance from the author. There are reasons to assume, therefore, that regardless of their literary abilities, the authors of the New Testament are likely to have worked closely with a number of individuals during the compositional process. While a full discussion of this subject cannot be taken up here, it will be helpful to make a few observations regarding the background of the Gospels and the Pauline Epistles and the extent to which the authors of the canonical writings may have collaborated with various colleagues.

The composition of the Gospels. Much attention has been placed in recent scholarship—Gospel studies in particular—on the various sources that may have been familiar to the canonical authors. For many years, scholars have carefully scrutinized and compared the text of each Gospel in order to establish what sources may have been available to each evangelist (source criticism), the original form of the literary units contained in the Gospels (form criticism), and how the evangelists may have adopted, used, and arranged their existing sources to fulfill their particular objectives (redaction criticism). What has not been as widely discussed is the manner in which the Gospel writers may have gone about the daunting task of composing their written accounts of the life and teaching of Christ. This subject is relevant to the study of the Gospels given that our understanding of this process will naturally inform our perception of foundational subjects such as authorship, the historical reliability of the Gospel accounts, and the particular objectives of each author.

We might first observe that the study of the sources available to each Gospel writer and the process by which each of the Gospel writers went about their task are not entirely unrelated. If the sources available to a given author were primarily literary accounts, a case could be made that the Gospel writers worked independently throughout much of the compositional process, working with no more than a secretary and perhaps a few colleagues who may have provided assistance with the acquisition of sources and other practical tasks. However, if the author drew from eyewitness testimony, it would have been necessary to consult with one or more individuals who could provide firsthand information regarding the events that were recorded. In light of the practical implications of our understanding of the background of the Gospels, it will be helpful to briefly outline some of the traditional theories regarding the sources available to the Gospel writers. This will enable us to better assess how they may have gone about their work of compiling reliable accounts about the life of Christ and some of the ways that they may have been assisted by their colleagues.

A mere casual reading of the four canonical Gospels reveals a number of similarities between each writing, particularly among the Synoptic Gospels. While there is certainly unique content in each Gospel, it is clear that they record a number of the same events and conversations, that these accounts are often presented in a similar manner and described with similar language, and that the Gospel writers often arrange their material in a similar fashion. For some, these similarities are the inevitable result of the overlapping objectives of each writer or the inspiration of the Holy Spirit. If each of the Gospel writers wrote under the Spirit's guidance and sought to describe several of the major events that took place in the life of Christ, should we not expect a significant degree of similarity? While this type of explanation may seem reasonable, biblical scholars from a variety of backgrounds have concluded that the large number of similarities between the Gospel accounts are best explained by one theory or another that involves literary dependence—that is, the viewpoint that the Gospel writers were familiar with one or more previously written accounts of the life of Christ.[15] As Francis Watson explains, the "Gospels are interconnected, with later ones always directly or indirectly dependent on their predecessors, and this dependence may be expressed in a variety of ways: word-for-word copying, minor interpretive clarifications, stylistic improvements, changes of sequence, insertion of new narrative material to fill perceived gaps, and so on."[16] While we might quibble with Watson's portrayal of certain differences between the Gospels as "improvements," it is certainly the case that compelling arguments have been made for the conclusion that the Gospel writers wrote with an awareness of other sources when they produced their written accounts of the life and teaching of Christ.[17]

Although there are convincing reasons to affirm that the Gospel writers were familiar with previously written accounts about the life and teaching of Jesus, a case could be made that it was not written

---

[15]The question of the so-called Synoptic problem and the background of the canonical writings are typically discussed in graduate-level introductions to the New Testament and the Gospels. In addition to introductory volumes, readers may find it beneficial to consult the following multi-view volumes that provide a defense of various positions: Stanley E. Porter and Bryan Dyer, eds., *The Synoptic Problem: Four Views* (Grand Rapids, MI: Baker Academic, 2016); Robert Thomas, ed., *Three Views on the Origins of the Synoptic Gospels* (Grand Rapids, MI: Kregel, 2002).

[16]Francis Watson, *Gospel Writing: A Canonical Perspective* (Grand Rapids, MI: Eerdmans, 2013), 604.

[17]It should be observed that the writing style of each individual is unique, that there are often a variety of ways to express a single thought in the Greek language, and that our estimation of literary style tends to be quite subjective in nature. We might have a greater appreciation for one style over another, but it would be unfounded in my view to conclude that each of the differences between the canonical Gospels point to corrections or improvements.

sources alone that were consulted by the Gospel writers. Scholars such as Martin Dibelius (1883–1947) and Rudolf Bultmann (1884–1976) have famously argued that a large number of sayings of Jesus and traditions related to Jesus' life and ministry circulated for many decades in oral form before they were collated by the Gospel writers and incorporated into their written accounts.[18] Dibelius and Bultmann were pioneers of what has come to be referred to as form criticism, a method originally applied to the study of the Old Testament before it was later adopted by New Testament scholars during the early twentieth century. According to proponents of this method, the traditions that eventually found their way into the Gospels would have included accounts of Jesus' miracles, his encounters with various individuals, and key events such as his birth, baptism, and resurrection. In addition to several oral traditions about Jesus' life and ministry, a body of *logia*—that is, sayings of Jesus—are also thought to have circulated independently for some time in oral form. This would have included pronouncements against his opponents as well as several prophecies, parables, teaching discourses, and other types of speech material. Many biblical scholars assume that these early sayings and traditions about the life of Christ were quite malleable and that they were subject to frequent modification as various communities adopted them for their own purposes and as early Christians became increasingly drawn to the Christ of faith rather than the Jesus of history, to use the language of Martin Kähler and others.

Although many scholars remain convinced that oral accounts of the life and teaching of Jesus served as a foundational source of information for the Gospel writers, some scholars have begun to emphasize the value that ancient writers appear to have placed on eyewitness testimony. Rather than a patchwork of uncorroborated oral traditions that were later reworked by the authors for their purposes, it has become more widely accepted that the Gospel writers often relied on

---

[18]Two of the primary works in the early history of the movement included Martin Dibelius, *Die Formgeschichte des Evangelium*, 3d ed., ed. Günter Bornkamm (Tübingen: J. C. B. Mohr, 1919), and Rudolf Bultmann, *The History of the Synoptic Tradition*, rev. ed. (Peabody: MA: Hendrickson, 1994).

living eyewitness testimony.[19] As Richard Bauckham concludes in his well-known study of the subject, the abundance of specific details in the Gospel accounts is consistent with what one would expect of eyewitness testimony. The writers share intimate firsthand knowledge of the political and cultural landscape of the land of Israel and often record specific information such as particular topological features, the names of individuals, and other details that would have been unfamiliar to those who did not observe the events themselves or consult directly with living eyewitnesses. As a matter of observation, many of the specific details contained in the canonical Gospels are absent from the later noncanonical writings. The *Gospel of Thomas*, for example, contains a collection of 114 *logia* while offering very few descriptions of particular events and historical details that might be expected of a work that derived directly from eyewitness testimony.[20]

For those who recognize the traditional authors of the Gospels, it is only natural to conclude that Matthew and John would have included a significant amount of firsthand testimony in their accounts. As disciples of Jesus, Matthew and John would have personally witnessed many of the events they recorded. While it is unnecessary to conclude that they relied solely on their own experiences, it is certainly reasonable to assume that they drew on their own recollections when describing the events which they personally witnessed. On the other hand, Mark and Luke were relatively obscure figures in the early Christian movement and did not personally witness the majority of the events they described. What might we assume about their sources of information? Did they simply compile various traditions of unknown origin about Jesus that had circulated in Christian communities or draw on various written accounts that fit their purposes?

According to early tradition, Mark's Gospel was based on the eyewitness testimony that Peter recounted prior to his martyrdom in

---

[19]Richard Bauckham, *Jesus and the Eyewitnesses*, rev. ed. (Grand Rapids, MI: Eerdmans, 2017).
[20]For further comparison of the noncanonical and canonical Gospels, see Simon Gathercole, *The Gospel and the Gospels: Christian Proclamation and Early Jesus Books* (Grand Rapids, MI: Eerdmans, 2022); Darrell L. Bock, *The Missing Gospels: Unearthing the Truth behind Alternative Christianities* (Nashville: Thomas Nelson, 2006).

Rome.[21] If these early traditions provide reliable information, Mark would not have been limited to an eclectic assortment of written and oral accounts about the life of Jesus. He would have served, rather, as the "interpreter" (ἑρμηνευτής; *hermēneutēs*) of the apostle Peter. This would indicate that Mark was not simply a close colleague of Peter but that he was responsible for recording summaries of Peter's teaching, which he then compiled, arranged, and edited in a manner he deemed to be appropriate for his intended audience.

In addition to Mark, we might also question how Luke acquired the information that became the basis for his two major works. Fortunately, the Prologue of his Gospel (Lk 1:1-4) provides a basic picture of how he understood his role as a writer. From this brief passage, we find evidence that Luke regarded himself as a responsible historian who sought to provide reliable testimony about the life and teaching of Christ.[22] Of interest is his reference to "those who from the beginning were eyewitnesses" (οἱ ἀπ' ἀρχῆς αὐτόπται; *hoi ap archēs autoptai*). The term αὐτόπτης (*autoptēs*) is particularly significant. Although this word does not appear in the New Testament outside of this passage, its meaning is not difficult to discern. Etymologically, the term is a compound of αὐτός (*autos*) and ὁράω (*horaō*) and thus carries the sense of one who has seen something with his own eyes, hence one with firsthand knowledge of an event.[23] A number of those who had personally witnessed the events related to the life of Christ, Luke notes, "handed down" (Lk 1:2) their firsthand knowledge regarding "the things accomplished among us" (Lk 1:1).[24] The implication is that the story of Jesus was not lost to history, and that many who had personally encountered

---

[21]See, for example, the early testimony of Papias recorded by Eusebius (*Hist. eccl.* 3.39.15) and other early sources such as Justin Martyr (*Dial.* 106) and Irenaeus (*Haer.* 3.1.1).

[22]In addition to technical commentaries on Luke's Gospel, additional insight regarding the Prologue of Luke and what it reveals about the historical nature of Luke-Acts include Osvaldo Padilla, *The Acts of the Apostles: Interpretation, History and Theology* (Downers Grove, IL: InterVarsity Press, 2016), 76-88; Bauckham, *Jesus and the Eyewitnesses*, 116-24; and Loveday Alexander, *The Preface to Luke's Gospel*, SNTSMS 78 (Cambridge: Cambridge University Press, 1993).

[23]The word is used in this sense by ancient authors such as Polybius (*Polyb.* 3.4; 10.11; 12.4, 28) and Josephus (*Ant.* 18.9.5; 19.1.15; *J.W.* 3.9.5; 6.2.5; *Ag. Ap.* 1.10).

[24]Luke uses the verb παραδίδωμι (*paradidōmi*) to describe the "handing down" of eyewitness tradition. This verb appears frequently in the New Testament in reference to the handing down of

Jesus and were familiar with his life and ministry had passed along their testimony to others. From the very beginning of the Christian movement, believers were convinced that God had performed miraculous acts of eschatological significance in time and space and that these events could be corroborated by those who witnessed them. Paul, for example, refers to "more than five hundred brethren" who observed the resurrected Christ (1 Cor 15:6), while John frequently makes use of language that is reflective of eyewitness testimony, referring, for example, to "what we have heard, what we have seen with our eyes, what we have looked at and touched with our hands" (1 Jn 1:1). The language used by Luke likewise indicates that the events he describes were based on the firsthand testimony of eyewitnesses. As Bauckham explains, Luke's assertion should be understood as "a claim that the eyewitnesses had been present throughout the events from the appropriate commencement of the author's history onward."[25]

Some may object that it would be a stretch to conclude that Luke consulted living eyewitnesses given that he does not specify the sources that served as the basis for his Gospel. The language of "handing down," for example, might be taken as a reference to various oral traditions or written accounts rather than direct eyewitness testimony. Even if we were to grant that many of these traditions originated with eyewitnesses, what is there to indicate that the content that was handed down from one individual to the next did not evolve in significant ways by the time Luke composed his Gospel?

Many students have at one time or another participated in the so-called telephone game. After many years, I can still vividly recall one of my elementary school teachers whispering a short story in the ear of a student and directing the class to circulate the story from one student to the next as we sat together in a circle. Needless to say, once the message had made its way around the circle and returned to the student who originally received the message, the story was drastically different.

---

tradition or doctrine from one party to another (see, for example, Mk 7:13; Acts 6:14; Rom 6:17; 1 Cor 11:2; 15:3; 2 Pet 2:21; Jude 3).

[25]Bauckham, *Jesus and the Eyewitnesses*, 119.

Naturally, we were all humored and a bit surprised by how many of the details of the story were lost at some point along the way and how even the basic plot had been significantly distorted. While we might find the results of a game such as this to be amusing, what it suggests about the nature of communication often becomes etched in our minds. The impression is given that oral communication between individuals is inherently unreliable. It certainly does not take much reflection to recognize how negative perceptions of oral transmission might cause individuals to question the reliability of the New Testament writings. The stories and accounts contained in the Bible may certainly be based on actual events that occurred, it might be reasoned, but how confident can we be in their accuracy if they are the product of unknown accounts that were passed down from one community or individual to the next before they were eventually adopted by later authors who wrote with particular theological objectives?[26]

Obviously, the telephone game is hardly a scientific method of assessing the accuracy of the transmission of information in predominantly oral cultures. Even though there are reasons to assume that the transmission of oral traditions in ancient cultures was more reliable than is typically imagined, it is important to note that Luke seems to suggest that he was able to personally consult a number of the *autoptai* (αὐτόπται). This would have clearly been the most reliable way for him to investigate the events that occurred "from the beginning" (Lk 1:3). If he came across a tradition regarding an encounter between Jesus and another individual, for example, how might he confirm that the event actually took place and that the various details of the tradition were accurate? He could certainly compare and assess the available accounts

---

[26]The degree to which oral transmission was reliable cannot be taken up in this chapter. Readers interested in pursuing the subject in greater detail may wish to consult recent works such as Samuel Byrskog, *Story as History—History as Story: The Gospel Tradition in the Context of Ancient Oral History*, WUNT 123 (Tübingen: Mohr Siebeck, 2000); Birger Gerhardsson, *The Reliability of the Gospel Tradition* (Grand Rapids, MI: Baker Academic, 2001); James D. G. Dunn, *The Oral Gospel Tradition* (Grand Rapids, MI: Eerdmans, 2013); Eric Eve, *Behind the Gospels: Understanding the Oral Tradition* (Minneapolis, MN: Fortress, 2014); Werner Kelber and Samuel Byrskog, eds., *Jesus in Memory: Traditions in Oral and Scribal Perspectives* (Waco, TX: Baylor University Press, 2018).

that describe the same incident in order to establish common features and points of agreement, but the most reliable method of validating the accuracy of these accounts would be to personally consult with those who experienced the events firsthand, something that in many cases would have still been possible during his lifetime.

In light of the value that was placed on eyewitness testimony in the ancient world and what Luke reveals about his approach and objectives, a plausible case could be made that he interacted directly with a number of individuals who personally heard Jesus' teaching and witnessed his miracles. As a close associate of Paul, we may infer that he had opportunities to interact directly with the living apostles, though we need not limit Luke's interaction to the apostolic circle. It is certainly possible that he interacted with a number of witnesses, some well-known and some who were more obscure or who are unknown to us today. We may suspect, for example, that many of the unique details and accounts in Luke's birth narrative (Lk 1:5–2:52) derived from Mary, the mother of Jesus. Who better to provide information about the events surrounding Jesus' birth than her? The unique material relating to the life and ministry of Jesus is unlikely to have been limited to the first few chapters of his Gospel, of course. In addition to consulting with Mary, it is possible that Luke personally interviewed individuals such as Zaccheus (Lk 19:1-10) and one or both of the disciples on the road to Emmaus (Lk 24:13-49), just to name a few. For a writer such as Luke, composition appears to have involved much more than simply compiling written sources and providing supplemental information from various traditions that had circulated orally. While Luke was clearly familiar with a number of sources, it does not appear that he relied solely on secondhand information. He appears, rather, to have personally interacted with a number of individuals who were capable of providing eyewitness testimony related to the events he described.

In addition to consulting with various eyewitnesses, it is also possible that the Gospel writers, and perhaps some of the other New Testament authors, consulted with other colleagues and acquaintances during the time leading up to the initial circulation of their works.

Among other things, ancient authors were known to make all or a portion of their completed work available to close friends and acquaintances who could offer suggestions for improvement prior to the public release of the writing. Raymond Starr's description of this process is helpful:

> Once a work was drafted, authors commonly sent a copy to a close friend for comments and criticism. . . . Once the author had received his friend's comments and initially revised the draft, he slightly widened the circle to which his work was accessible. This could be done by sending draft copies, again made in his home by slaves at his expense, to several more friends. He could also invite a few friends to his home and recite the work to them in order to elicit their comments and reactions. . . . These first readings were entirely closed. The audience would naturally discuss the work during and after the recitation, but the text itself did not circulate. . . . The work remained entirely in the control of the author, who could decide whether it would ever reach a wider public either in further recitations or in written form.[27]

Although there were surely variations in the precise manner in which ancient writings were prepared (e.g., slaves producing copies and the public reading offered in one's own home), Starr's description helpfully identifies several of the important steps that often took place prior to the public release of a literary work. As he observes, an author might provide a close circle of his friends with an initial draft of his work for them to review, or he could offer a public reading (*recitatio*) of all or a portion of his work to a small number of trusted friends and family.[28] In both cases, authors tended to welcome recommendations for improvement and honest reflections. This often led to a period of revision that eventually culminated in the work's public release—what we might describe as its "publication."

What we mean by "publication" today is much different in several respects to the process that led to the dissemination of literary works

---

[27]Raymond J. Starr, "The Circulation of Literary Texts in the Roman World," *ClQ* 37 (1987), 213-14.
[28]Gamble, *Books and Readers*, 83-84.

during the first century. Rather than submit a finished manuscript to a publisher, who then makes arrangements for the work to be printed in large quantities and sold to various venders, literary works produced during the first century were produced exclusively by hand. Making matters even more challenging, there were no copyright laws to protect individuals from reproducing the work or from making changes to the text. As Eric Turner explains, the ancient equivalent of publication took place when "the work in question was available for consultation and presumably for copying." It was "'published' in the sense that its existence became known and that it was 'issued' to readers."[29]

With regard to the collaborative nature of disseminating ancient writings, Timothy Mitchell observes that the process leading to a work's publication often "involved some of the author's closest associates, who gave constructive criticism, suggested changes, and at times used the services of a scribe or secretary to copy down dictation." After this process was completed, "the piece was finished by releasing the work to be copied and circulated through networks of friends and acquaintances, sending the work to a dedicatee, reciting the piece to the community, or by sending a copy to a bookseller or library."[30] Once the work was released to the public, it became very difficult for revisions to take place, especially if numerous copies were already produced. Consequently, authors often sought feedback from a number of individuals prior to the public distribution of their work.

One of the better-known examples of this process is the famous Roman poet Virgil's personal reading of portions of the *Aeneid* to a live audience before it was released to the public. According to a later work on the life of Virgil by the fourth-century grammarian Aelius Donatus, Virgil spent considerable time refining his work before personally reading three of its books to Augustus and members of the royal family. If the account of Donatus is to be trusted, the reading left quite an

---

[29]Eric G. Turner, *Greek Papyri: An Introduction* (Oxford: Oxford University Press, 1968), 112-13.
[30]Timothy Mitchell, "Myths about Autographs: What They Were and How Long They May Have Survived," in *Myths and Mistakes in New Testament Textual Criticism*, ed. Elijah Hixson and Peter Gurry (Downers Grove, IL: InterVarsity Press, 2019), 35.

impact on the family. In fact, Octavia, the sister of Augustus, is said to have become so overcome by a reference to her son Marcellus that she fainted! Additional readings to larger audiences later took place as Virgil continued to refine and revise his monumental work.[31]

Although certain conclusions are difficult to maintain, we might speculate that a similar process took place during the composition of several of the biblical writings. In addition to consulting with various eyewitnesses, it is possible that one or more of the four evangelists may have read their work before a smaller audience prior to the public release of their finished work, inviting feedback on specific ways in which they might present a more effective and memorable presentation of their material. It is helpful to remember that the New Testament writings were designed to be heard by the intended recipients.[32] Reading a completed work to a live audience would have been particularly helpful as it would have provided the authors an opportunity to receive honest reflections about the rhetorical effectiveness of their work. Perhaps John offered a personal reading of his Gospel to those in Ephesus before it began to circulate. Another possibility is that Luke offered a reading of some or all of his Gospel before Theophilus and a small audience of friends and family members at some point before it was released to the public.

Finally, we should not overlook the fact that the distribution of a work such as one of the four Gospels would have been a substantial undertaking. Following the initial publication of the Gospels, there would have been a significant need for additional manuscripts to be copied, without which the writings would have had only a limited influence and would have ultimately been lost to history, much like several of the noncanonical gospels. The reproduction of Christian texts would have likely been accomplished in a number of ways. As a consequence of the popularity of the New Testament writings and the expense associated with reproducing writings and acquiring personal

---

[31] Aelius Donatus, *Life of Virgil* 31-34.
[32] This topic is explored in the recent work, Paul Borgman and Kelly James Clark, *Written to be Heard: Recovering the Messages of the Gospels* (Grand Rapids, MI: Eerdmans, 2019).

copies, we might assume that a number of early Christians took part in reproducing these works. In some cases, individuals may have reproduced texts for their own use, while on other occasions wealthy Christians may have instructed their slaves or hired professional scribes to duplicate writings. These were not uncommon practices in antiquity. As George Houston observes, Galen and individuals known to Fronto personally reproduced writings for their own use while Cicero and his friend Atticus are known to have instructed their slaves to make copies of certain works.[33] The number of wealthy Christian slave owners in the first century does not appear to have been great, but it is certainly possible that some of the early canonical writings were reproduced by those who served in Christian households in major cities such as Rome, Corinth, Ephesus, and Thessalonica. We may also assume that individuals who were experienced in reproducing texts occasionally volunteered their services on a pro bono basis, assisting authors with either the original composition of the writings or with the early production of copies. As noted above, Tertius may have served Paul in both of these ways.

Another possibility is that individuals such as Theophilus (Lk 1:3; Acts 1:1) served as what might be described as literary patrons. In this role, individuals may have used their wealth and influence to promote and finance the production of the canonical writings in the period immediately following their composition. In some cases, they may have provided the necessary funds to hire professionally trained scribes to assist with the reproduction of texts or instructed their slaves to produce copies. A writer's colleagues—especially those who were affluent and well connected—might also assist with the distribution of the finished work. As Loveday Alexander explains, wealthy and influential patrons "could offer a social framework for scholarly communication" while also offering "an author an entree into a different social network of the patron's own peers, whether by oral performance within the patron's house, or by the deposition of a

---

[33]Houston, *Inside Roman Libraries*, 14-16.

presentation copy of a book in the patron's private library." Once the author was satisfied with his work and was prepared for its release, it would often be made "available to any of the patron's friends who wished to read or copy it."[34] It is certainly possible, therefore, that Theophilus arranged for his copy of Luke's Gospel to be available to his circle of friends, who could then take part in its wider distribution. If Theophilus was an official of some type—a plausible deduction given Luke's reference to him as "most excellent"—he and members of his social network may have had the means to ensure that numerous copies were produced. Those who served in this type of role might be compared to those today who donate a large sum of money to a particular ministry in order for certain materials to be produced and disseminated around the world.

The composition of the Epistles. Having discussed a number of literary practices that relate primarily to the composition of the Gospels, we may also briefly address a few matters that relate more specifically to the Epistles of the New Testament. Our brief comments in this section will focus primarily on the Pauline writings, though the practices that will be addressed may also relate to the composition of the Catholic Epistles. As his own writings and the various narratives contained in Acts make evident, Paul worked closely with dozens of individuals throughout his years as an apostle and missionary. In his effort to advance the gospel message and establish vibrant local churches, Paul traveled and ministered alongside a large number of individuals and maintained contact with Christians throughout the Roman world.[35] As F. F. Bruce observes, "there are about seventy people mentioned by name in the New Testament of whom we should never have heard were

---

[34]Loveday Alexander, "Ancient Book Production and the Circulation of the Gospels," in *The Gospels for All Christians: Rethinking the Gospel Audiences*, ed. Richard Bauckham (Grand Rapids, MI: Eerdmans, 1998), 98.

[35]Paul's missionary strategies have been helpfully explored in a number of recent studies. See, for example, Eckhard Schnabel, *Paul the Missionary: Realities, Strategies and Methods* (Downers Grove, IL: InterVarsity Press, 2008); Robert L. Plummer and John Mark Terry, eds., *Paul's Missionary Methods: In His Time and Ours* (Downers Grove, IL: InterVarsity Press, 2012). These works build on the earlier publication of works such as Ronald Allen, *Missionary Methods: St. Paul's or Ours?* (Grand Rapids, MI: Eerdmans, 1962).

it not for their association with Paul, and over and above these there is a host of unnamed friends."[36]

Paul's collaboration with his colleagues and believers throughout the Roman world was not limited to his work of evangelism, teaching, and other ministries that took place in local communities. In addition to this, it would appear that he often worked closely with a number of individuals when composing his epistles, a conclusion that is consistent with what is known of ancient letter writing in general as well as the fact that his epistles are occasional in nature. Even his most sophisticated and theologically developed epistles (e.g., Romans and 1–2 Corinthians) were written not as theological treatises for general audiences or as comprehensive treatments of Christian doctrine but in response to the particular concerns and challenges facing those in specific communities.

When writing to churches that he was unable to personally visit, Paul would have had need of reliable sources of information about the recent developments that had taken place in their communities and the nature of the conflicts, struggles, and questions that had become a cause of controversy or confusion. We find evidence in his writings that communities often contacted him with specific concerns and questions about a host of subjects. Much of the content in 1 Corinthians, for example, appears to have been written in response to questions that the Corinthians had sent to Paul either in written form or through various emissaries. We find that members of Chloe's household provided information to Paul while he was in Ephesus (1 Cor 1:11). Perhaps one or more members of the family, broadly defined in the first century to include one's slaves, were sent to Ephesus by Chloe to complete some type of business. While in the city, they may have met up with Paul and provided him with news regarding the recent developments in Corinth.[37] On other occasions,

---

[36]F. F. Bruce, *The Pauline Circle* (Eugene, OR: Wipf & Stock, 2006), 9.

[37]The fact that these individuals may have been slaves is not surprising in light of the large number of slaves in the first-century Roman world. It may even be possible that Chloe was not a believer but that some of her slaves had converted to the faith.

Paul appears to have sent his own trusted associates to minister to believers in specific locations. On their return, they would have then provided a report to Paul on recent developments.

Evidence that Paul regularly collaborated with various individuals during the composition of his epistles may be observed in the greetings and other locations of his writings. In fact, the opening greeting of eight of Paul's epistles includes a reference to one or more of his associates:

- 1 Corinthians   Our brother Sosthenes

- 2 Corinthians   Timothy our brother

- Galatians   All the brothers with me

- Philippians   Timothy

- Colossians   Timothy our brother

- 1 Thessalonians   Silvanus and Timothy

- 2 Thessalonians   Silvanus and Timothy

- Philemon   Timothy our brother

It is sometimes assumed that on certain occasions Paul included the names of his associates in the greetings of his letters simply as a polite gesture or for the purpose of strengthening the authority of his instruction. This understanding, however, has been challenged in recent decades.[38] Harry Gamble, for example, has concluded that this practice "was probably not a formality but a reflection of the involvement of his associates in the conception, if not in the composition, of many of the letters."[39] Gamble's conclusion is consistent with none other than

---

[38]See, for example, Richards, *Paul and First-Century Letter Writing*, 33-34. Jerome Murphy-O'Connor provides examples from Cicero's writings of family members who were in fact included in the opening greeting of his epistles. He is correct in his conclusion that "the relevance of these parallels to Paul's epistles is severely diminished by the fact that both recipients are especially significant members of Cicero's household. The Pauline letters are addressed to communities. They belong to a different category from Cicero's highly personal letters to his wife and valued associate." He also observes that Cicero "mentions *all* those with him who have a relationship to the recipient." See "Co-Authorship in the Corinthian Correspondence," *RB* 100 (1993), 563.

[39]Gamble, *Books and Readers*, 99.

Origen, who many centuries ago made passing reference to Paul's associates in his commentary on Matthew's Gospel. In his remarks, Origen referred to the composition of Paul's epistles to the Corinthians, writing, "Two made a symphony [συνεφώνησαν; *synephōnēsan*], Paul and Sosthenes, when writing the first epistle to the Corinthians; and after this Paul and Timothy when sending the second epistle to the same. And even three made a symphony when Paul and Silvanus and Timothy gave instruction by letter to the Thessalonians."[40] For Origen, the reference to Sosthenes and Timothy in the greetings of the Corinthian epistles was not the simple equivalent of a modern "hello" but an acknowledgment of their involvement in one form or another in the epistle's composition.

In his research on first-century letter writing, E. Randolph Richards observed that there were only rare occasions in antiquity in which more than one author was cited in the greeting of an epistle.[41] Occasionally, a formal grievance or appeal to an individual of high authority was sent from a specific group or party. In such cases, a collective title or description of the group may have been used to identify the senders. In addition, there were also instances in which a husband's and wife's names were mentioned together in the greeting. This use, however, typically took place in private letters between individuals rather than in material written to an entire community. Richards notes that while Paul's letters differed in certain respects from other letters in antiquity, no coauthors can be found in the works of notable writers as Seneca or Pliny the Younger. In addition, only six of the 645 private letters from Oxyrhynchus include coauthors in the greeting.[42]

Because of the fact that names were not typically placed in the greetings of letters simply as a kind gesture, we may assume that each of the individuals who appear in the greetings of Paul's writings were

---

[40]Origen, *Comm. Matt.* (*ANF* 9:495).
[41]See Richards, *Paul and First-Century Letter Writing*, 33-36. For additional treatment, see Sean A. Adams, "Paul's Letter Opening and Greek Epistolography: A Matter of Relationship," in *Paul and the Ancient Letter Form*, ed. Stanley E. Porter and Sean A. Adams, PAST 6 (Leiden: Brill, 2010), 40-44.
[42]Richards, *Paul and First-Century Letter Writing*, 34.

well positioned to provide Paul with relevant insight or information that enabled him to provide timely and appropriate instruction. They may have recently ministered in the communities to which Paul wrote or had at least acquired reliable information that made them helpful conversation partners during the composition process. One can imagine, for example, Paul discussing the concerns of the Corinthians with Sosthenes as they walked the city streets of Ephesus or shared a meal together.[43] Paul clearly recognized his apostolic authority, but this did not preclude him from working closely with other believers, many of whom he seems to have regarded as close partners in his apostolic ministry. Missionary activity for Paul was a collaborative effort, not an independent venture.

In addition to working closely with Sosthenes on at least one occasion, we may assume that Paul often collaborated with close companions such as Timothy and Silas as he corresponded with various communities. We know from Luke's account that after Paul was forced to abruptly leave Thessalonica, that Timothy and Silas remained in the nearby town of Berea for some time before making the journey south where they eventually reunited with Paul in Corinth (Acts 17:14; 18:5). We may infer that Paul spent considerable time with Timothy and Silas discussing the situation in Thessalonica during his lengthy stay in Corinth and that they offered him several suggestions and insights as he composed his epistles to the Thessalonians. Having recently departed from Macedonia, they would have had a keen understanding of a number of practical matters that needed to be addressed in Paul's written instruction as well as several theological subjects that continued to trouble or confuse those in Thessalonica and the surrounding region.

---

[43]According to Acts, an individual named Sosthenes served as the ruler of the synagogue in Corinth and was beaten by an angry crowd following Paul's appearance before the proconsul Gallio (Acts 18:17). If this is indeed the same individual referred to in the greeting of 1 Corinthians, it may be possible that he converted to the faith during Paul's ministry in the city and later traveled to Ephesus where he met of up with Paul. As a former leader of a Jewish synagogue in Corinth, he certainly would have been familiar with the recent events that had transpired in the city and would have been well-known to the Corinthian believers.

The use of first-person plural verbs and pronouns in some of the Pauline writings is occasionally taken as evidence that Paul was not the sole author of certain works.[44] For some, these plural forms would be unexpected or unnatural if Paul wrote independently or if he was the lone author. In some of Paul's writings such as the epistles to the Corinthians, Philippians, and Philemon, there is little evidence outside of the greeting that the work is the product of joint authorship. On the other hand, epistles such as 1 and 2 Thessalonians include a considerable number of first-person plural pronouns and verbs, an indication to some that Timothy and Silas may have played a significant role in the composition of these writings. References such as a letter "from *us*" (2 Thess 2:2, 15) and "*our* instruction" (2 Thess 3:14) might be taken as evidence for some type of mutual effort in the letter-writing process. In response, it might be observed that singular verbs and pronouns appear frequently throughout the Pauline writings and that there are several literary features that may often be observed in multiple epistles. The fact that there is a discernible style that may often be observed throughout the Pauline writings would suggest that Paul was the primary mind and authority behind each of the writings that bore his name. Although the evidence is not particularly compelling that Paul's companions served as coauthors in the sense that they personally penned portions of the epistles, it would seem plausible that they provided him with useful information that enabled him to address specific matters in his writings with greater insight and effectiveness.

Conclusions

Our brief survey of the literary environment of the first century has revealed that the composition of the New Testament writings was likely a much more collaborative process than is often assumed. The circumstances facing each author would have naturally differed, though it

---

[44]Several articles were written during the late nineteenth century through the mid-twentieth century on the alternation between the first-person singular and plural pronouns in Paul's epistles. For a more recent treatment of this subject, see Murphy-O'Connor, *Paul the Letter Writer*, 16-31.

appears likely that the production of many of the biblical writings involved collaboration between the author and a number of individuals who served in various capacities. In light of what may be determined about the manner in which ancient writings were composed and how authors acquired relevant information, it is plausible that many of the biblical writers consulted with those who could provide eyewitness testimony of certain events or insight related to recent developments or subjects that needed to be addressed. It would also seem that writers such as Paul worked closely with secretaries who could assist with the actual production of the writing, letter carriers who were responsible for delivering the writings to their intended destination, and several friends and colleagues who could assist in one way or another with the early transmission and distribution of their works.

THE ORIGINAL AUTOGRAPHS
OF THE NEW TESTAMENT
WRITINGS

WAS THERE A SINGLE "ORIGINAL AUTOGRAPH" OF EACH NEW TESTAMENT WRITING?

The question of "original text" in the New Testament is not only complex and tangled, but is also an issue that confronts one with increased intensity and urgency in this generation when, quite understandably, ambiguity is pervasive and multiple meanings are endemic to this multicultural world.

ELDON J. EPP, *PERSPECTIVES ON NEW TESTAMENT TEXTUAL CRITICISM*

CONTINUING OUR TREATMENT OF THE COMPOSITION of the canonical writings, we now turn our attention to the concept of an "original autograph." It is widely assumed that the textual history of each New Testament writing began with a single autograph that was dispatched to the intended readers shortly after composition. None of the autographs have survived, of course, as they were eventually lost, discarded, or worn out after a period of use.[1] All that remains are early

---

[1]Scholars generally assume that the original autographs survived only a short time. Craig Evans has recently suggested, however, that it was not uncommon for manuscripts in the ancient world to be in use for two centuries or even longer. Evans reasons that if the autographs of the New Testament writings were in fact in use for an extended period, they may have played a role in regulating

copies of these writings. Some of the early textual witnesses to the New Testament contain readings that are clearly quite primitive, yet no surviving manuscript can lay claim with any verifiable evidence to preserve a text that is an undisputed and flawless replication of the original composition of one or more of the canonical writings.

The traditional objective of text critics—those who specialize in the study of the textual transmission of the canonical writings throughout history—has been to ascertain, so much as may be determined, the most probable text of the original autographs. Scholars have not always shared the same degree of optimism about the prospect of fulfilling this objective and have held to a variety of competing theories, approaches, and methodologies. The primary goal of many text critics, however, has been to establish the most probable reading of the "original autographs" of the canonical writings.[2] With so much focus on reconstructing the probable content of the autographs, it is worth considering how our knowledge of first-century literary practices may inform our understanding of the nature of these elusive autographs. As will be suggested, a more nuanced perspective of the nature of the original autographs may offer a possible explanation for the origin of alternative readings in the biblical text that have proven difficult to explain.

---

the transmission of the text in the second and third centuries. See "How Long Were Late Antique Books in Use? Possible Implications for New Testament Textual Criticism," *BBR* 25 (2015): 23-37.

[2]Those familiar with the current state of New Testament textual criticism will recognize that not all text critics share this objective. For some, the early textual witnesses are too diverse, too limited in number, and were produced too late to determine with any degree of certainty the precise wording and material contained in the original autographs. In short, the traditional objective is untenable. For those who share this perspective, the goal of determining the "original text" has largely been replaced by one of two objectives. For some, the primary objective is to reconstruct the text of the canonical writings during a period subsequent to their initial composition, a text that might be described as the earliest discernible form of the New Testament writings that served as the basis of future copies. This is often referred to in contemporary scholarship as the *Ausgangstext*, or the "initial text." Others such as Bart Ehrman have suggested that the focus of the discipline should be placed on what competing readings of certain passages—particularly those of theological significance—may reveal about the state of early Christianity. For a summary of his position, see Bart D. Ehrman, "The Text as Window: New Testament Manuscripts and the Social History of Early Christianity," in *The Text of the New Testament in Contemporary Research*, ed. Bart D. Ehrman and Michael W. Holmes, rev. ed., NTTSD 42 (Leiden: Brill, 2013), 803-30. For a defense of the traditional objective of textual criticism, see Daniel Wallace, "Challenges in New Testament Textual Criticism for the Twenty-First Century," *JETS* 52 (2009): 79-100; Abidan Paul Shah, *Changing the Goalpost of New Testament Textual Criticism* (Eugene, OR: Wipf & Stock, 2020).

Common Assumptions Regarding the Concept of the "Original Autographs"

It is commonly assumed that the composition of each of the canonical writings culminated in a single "original autograph" that became the basis for all future copies. It might be supposed, for example, that Paul dispatched the original manuscript of Romans to the community of believers in Rome, where it was first read and where copies were then produced. While the manuscript delivered to those in Rome has not survived, it is thought that copies of the text would have been produced by local believers and that these copies began to circulate in Christian communities throughout the Mediterranean world. Understood in this manner, the extant Greek witnesses to the text of Romans ultimately derive from the original autograph delivered to Rome nearly two millennia ago.

It is certainly reasonable to assume that many of Paul's initial readers would have made arrangements for the epistles they received to be reproduced, especially when they were regarded as theologically significant or of practical importance. But what is the probability that there was a single "original autograph" of each writing that was dispatched to the intended readers that later became the basis for all subsequent copies? As a matter of scholarly interest, this question has received surprisingly little attention over the years. Scholars have engaged in extensive debate about the text of the New Testament, but only moderate attention has been given to the concept and precise meaning of terms such as *original autograph* and *original text*. As Eldon J. Epp has rightly noted, the complexities of the subject have undoubtedly played a role in discouraging scholarly reflection. As he observes, scholars began raising questions about the nature of the original text and its relationship to the original autographs as early as the nineteenth century, though terms such as *original autograph*, *original text*, and *canonical text* continue to be used interchangeably with little distinction or specificity regarding their precise meaning.[3]

---

[3]For further insight relating to the various ways that text critics have understood the term *original text* and the primary task of the discipline, see Eldon J. Epp, "The Multivalence of the Term 'Original Text,'" in *Perspectives on New Testament Textual Criticism: Collected Essays, 1962–2004*,

As he writes, "Over several generations the New Testament textual critics have been socialized into thinking of a single original text as its object."[4] What is needed, Epp's treatment illustrates, is a more nuanced understanding of the original text and its relationship to the original autographs. If the ultimate purpose, or at least a primary purpose, of the discipline of textual criticism is to reconstruct the text of the "original autographs," a precise understanding of the term is obviously important.

While some may be inclined to assume that questions relating to the composition of the canonical writings are of little relevance, it should be recognized that the manner in which the doctrines of inspiration and inerrancy have been understood and articulated is often predicated on a particular understanding of the nature of the "original autographs."[5] As Timothy Mitchell observes, "The limitation of inspiration and inerrancy to the 'autographs' of Scripture has been a central component of the doctrine of Scripture in America, at least since before the American Civil War, and was incorporated into many doctrinal statements of the twentieth century and has continued so into the present day."[6] Similarly, John H. Walton and D. Brent Sandy explain that "within evangelical circles discussing inerrancy and authority, the common affirmation is that the text is inerrant in the original autographs. This qualification allowed the recognition that scribes copying the text from generation to generation made errors in the copying

---

NovTSup 116 (Leiden: Brill, 2005), 554-62; Michael W. Holmes, "From 'Original Text' to 'Initial Text': The Traditional Goal of New Testament Textual Criticism in Contemporary Discussion," in *The Text of the New Testament in Contemporary Research*, ed. Bart D. Ehrman and Michael W. Holmes, rev. ed., NTTSD 42 (Leiden: Brill, 2013), 637-88.

[4] Epp, "The Multivalence of the Term 'Original Text,'" 589.

[5] Timothy Mitchell, "What Are the NT Autographs? An Examination of the Doctrine of Inspiration and Inerrancy in Light of Greco-Roman Publication," *JETS* 59 (2016), 292. See also Mitchell, "Myths about Autographs: What They Were and How Long They May Have Survived," in *Myths and Mistakes in New Testament Textual Criticism*, ed. Elijah Hixson and Peter Gurry (Downers Grove, IL: InterVarsity Press, 2019), 26-47; Mitchell, "Where Inspiration is Found: Putting the New Testament Autographs in Context," *SBJT* 24 (2020): 83-101.

[6] Mitchell, "What Are the NT Autographs?" 290. As Mitchell explains, the attribution of inerrancy to the original autographs may be observed in the mid-eighteenth century with the writings of John Adger and shortly thereafter in the writings of the Princetonian scholars Charles Hodge, Archibald Hodge, and Benjamin Warfield.

process. Therefore, since all copies were not pristine, inerrancy could only be connected to the putative originals."[7]

Rather than arguing for the existence of a single surviving manuscript that is flawless and free of corruption, it is often explained that the "original autographs" were inerrant and that the diligence of text critics has enabled us to recover with reasonable confidence the probable text of these manuscripts, at least in the vast majority of instances.[8] We might also point out that this understanding of the autographs is not limited to the New Testament writings. Despite the unique issues that must be explored when assessing the textual history of Old Testament literature, many remain convinced that inerrancy is to be attributed only to the original manuscripts rather than to the subsequently produced copies, regardless of a writing's location in the biblical canon. Reflecting this viewpoint, Wayne Grudem writes, "It is extremely important to affirm the inerrancy of the original documents, for the subsequent copies were made by human beings with no claim or guarantee by God that these copies would be perfect."[9]

In addition to various works written by evangelical scholars, reference to a single inerrant autograph may be observed in a number of doctrinal statements associated with modern organizations and ministries. Perhaps the most well-known statement on the subject is the *Chicago Statement on Biblical Inerrancy*, a document signed by over two hundred evangelical scholars and pastors in 1979. Article 10 of the statement is of special interest to our discussion, and states in part, "We affirm that inspiration, strictly speaking, applies only to *the autographic text* of Scripture, which in the providence of God can be ascertained from

---

[7] John H. Walton and D. Brent Sandy, *The Lost World of Scripture: Ancient Literary Culture and Biblical Authority* (Downers Grove, IL: InterVarsity Press, 2013), 66.

[8] It should be emphasized that the affirmation of the divine inspiration of Scripture does not rise or fall on a particular understanding of the nature of first-century autographs. One may certainly affirm the divine qualities of Scripture while maintaining one of a number of perspectives on the precise manner in which the New Testament writings were originally composed and disseminated. What is challenged here is not the attribution of divine inspiration to the original autographs but common perceptions about the nature of the autographs.

[9] Wayne Grudem, *Systematic Theology: An Introduction to Biblical Doctrine*, rev. ed. (Grand Rapids, MI: Zondervan, 2020), 93.

available manuscripts with great accuracy. We further affirm that copies and translations of Scripture are the Word of God to the extent that they faithfully represent the original" (italics added). Similar affirmations may be observed in the following statements published by various ministries and organizations (italics added):

> The Bible alone, and the Bible in its entirety, is the Word of God written and is therefore inerrant in *the autographs*.[10]

> We believe that God has spoken in the Scriptures, both Old and New Testaments, through the words of human authors. As the verbally inspired Word of God, the Bible is without error in *the original writings*, the complete revelation of His will for salvation, and the ultimate authority by which every realm of human knowledge and endeavor should be judged. Therefore, it is to be believed in all that it teaches, obeyed in all that it requires, and trusted in all that it promises.[11]

> We believe that God has inspired the words preserved in the Scriptures, the sixty-six books of the Old and New Testaments, which are both record and means of his saving work in the world. These writings alone constitute the verbally inspired Word of God, which is utterly authoritative and without error in *the original writings*, complete in its revelation of his will for salvation, sufficient for all that God requires us to believe and do, and final in its authority over every domain of knowledge to which it speaks.[12]

> We believe the Scriptures, errorless in *the original documents*, are divine authority in all matters which they address.[13]

Interestingly, reference to the original autographs is not limited to evangelical ministries and denominations. The *Dei Verbum*, a theological treatise overwhelmingly approved by the Second Vatican Council (1965), adopted similar language: "But since the word of God should be

---

[10]See the "Doctrinal Basis" of the Evangelical Theological Society. See https://www.etsjets.org/about/constitution#A3.

[11]See the "Statement of Faith" of the Evangelical Free Church of America, www.efca.org/resources/document/efca-statement-faith.

[12]See the "Confessional Statement" of the Gospel Coalition, www.thegospelcoalition.org/about/foundation-documents/#confessional-statement.

[13]See the "Articles of Faith" of the Fellowship of Evangelical Churches, https://fecministries.org/about/our-beliefs/articles-faith/.

accessible at all times, the Church by her authority and with maternal concern sees to it that suitable and correct translations are made into different languages, especially from *the original texts* of the sacred books."[14]

ANCIENT LITERARY CONVENTIONS AND
THE ORIGINAL AUTOGRAPHS OF THE NEW TESTAMENT

If a primary objective of the discipline of textual criticism is to establish the text of the original autographs, and if it is the autographs that are to be understood as divinely inspired, our perception about the nature of the "autographs" is of obvious importance. What some may regard as a rather straightforward and simple subject, however, is in many ways a difficult and complicated issue. Much of the challenge in establishing what constitutes the "original autographs" stems from the fact that there were several stages in a writing's development that may potentially be identified as the beginning of its "literary existence," to use the language of Epp.[15] As men of their time who would have produced works in a similar fashion as other first-century writers, we may assume that the New Testament authors completed a series of drafts and made several edits before the text was eventually finalized. This is the normal process of writing, and there is no reason to assume that it was any different for the biblical authors. This leads to some complicated questions, however. When we refer to an original autograph, are we referring to the initial draft of a work, a later revision or expansion, the edition that first began to circulate, or to the state of the writing at some later stage in the compositional process? In light of all that was involved in ancient writing, establishing the precise moment in which a work become the authoritative text that served as the basis for subsequent copies may not be immediately obvious. Some have even questioned the notion that there even was anything that resembled a finished text and that writings remained "textually fluid"![16]

---

[14]Italics added. The complete statement may be found at www.vatican.va/archive/hist_councils /ii_vatican_council/documents/vat-ii_const_19651118_dei-verbum_en.html.

[15]Epp, "The Multivalence of the Term 'Original Text,'" 577.

[16]See, for example, Matthew Larsen, "Accidental Publication, Unfinished Texts and the Traditional Goals of New Testament Textual Criticism," *JSNT* 39 (2017): 362-87.

Although the composition of the New Testament writings would have involved many phases, it would seem most appropriate to identify the original autograph of a work not as the initial draft but as the final state of the writing that the author had reviewed and approved for public circulation.[17] This basic understanding of the original autographs will likely seem reasonable to many, but what are its possible implications? In addition to arriving at a more nuanced perspective of the nature of the original autographs, we must also consider a few thorny questions that have largely been overlooked: First, how many of the manuscripts produced by the author or his scribe at this particular point in the compositional process may be properly classified as originals? Second, if multiple copies were produced, where were they sent and what was their purpose? Finally, does the doctrine of inerrancy become more difficult to maintain if it is determined that multiple manuscripts were produced that could legitimately be described as "original autographs?"

As noted earlier in the volume, it was fairly common for copies of a writer's work to be produced at the end of the compositional process. As Gamble explains, "Ancient writers often kept copies of their private letters even when no particular literary merit or topical importance [was] attached to them; and copies of instructional, administrative letters were all the more likely to be kept. In antiquity, collected editions of letters were nearly always produced by their author or at their author's behest, often from copies belonging to the author."[18] The probability of an author or his secretary producing one or more duplicate copies would have been especially high if the author envisioned an eventual circulation of a formal collection of his works, when he or she considered the work to be of relevance to a broad audience, or when the document contained some type of important personal information.

---

[17]Mitchell offers a similar definition: "the completed authorial work which was released by the author for circulation and copying, not earlier draft versions or layers of composition." Mitchell, "What are the NT Autographs?" 287.

[18]Harry Y. Gamble, *Books and Readers in the Early Church* (New Haven, CT: Yale University Press, 1995), 101.

As a consequence of this practice, we must determine not only the particular point of the compositional process that an author's work contained the original text but the possible implications of there being multiple copies of an author's work produced around this time. If multiple copies of a biblical text was produced, would each copy have been identical? If not, is it more likely that the earliest textual witnesses to the New Testament writings derived from the copies retained by the authors or their companions or from those that were dispatched to the intended recipients?

In order to address these difficult questions, it will be helpful to make a few observations about the formation of literary collections in the Greco-Roman world. To be sure, the background of each writing and each literary collection was unique, and we should not assume that there was a single and consistent process that led to the formation of each collection. It would seem, however, that there were certain literary practices that were widely observed during the general period in which the New Testament writings were composed that may help us to address these issues.

Recent scholarly attention related to the formation and circulation of ancient literary collections has yielded several valuable insights related to the process that was often involved in the formation of ancient collections—collections of epistolary literature in particular.[19] Examples include the massive collection of letters composed by the Roman statesman and philosopher Cicero, a collection which

---

[19]Among the recent scholarship on ancient epistolography, four works should be briefly mentioned. First, Bronwen Neil and Pauline Allen of Australian Catholic University have edited a volume that includes a dozen essays, each of which examine a particular collection from the first six centuries of the Christian era or a subject germane to the study of ancient literary collections. In addition, Cristiana Sogno, Bradley Storin, and Edward Watts have recently edited a large compilation of essays which examine the formation of numerous letter collections from antiquity and late antiquity. In addition, George Houston's study on book production in antiquity provides a wealth of insight regarding the ways in which literary collections were assembled, acquired, and maintained. Finally, Roy Gibson has written an insightful article that offers helpful information about ancient letter collections, particularly how the material was arranged. Bronwen Neil and Pauline Allen, eds., *Collecting Early Christian Letters: From the Apostle Paul to Late Antiquity* (Cambridge: Cambridge University Press, 2015); Cristiana Sogno, Bradley Storin, and Edward Watts, eds., *Late Antique Letter Collections: A Critical Introduction and Reference Guide* (Oakland: University of California Press, 2017); George W. Houston, *Inside Roman Libraries: Book Collections and Their Management in Antiquity* (Chapel Hill, NC: University of North Carolina Press, 2014); Roy Gibson, "On the Nature of Ancient Letter Collection," *JRS* 102 (2012): 56-78.

appears to have been assembled by later admirers who organized his extant letters into four discrete subcollections based on the recipients (i.e., *Epistulae ad Atticum*, *Epistulae ad Brutum*, *Epistulae ad Familiares*, and *Epistulae ad Quintum Fratrem*). While not nearly as extensive as the collections of Cicero, and written for very different purposes, the collection of epistles attributed to Ignatius of Antioch serves as an additional example of an early literary collection. On his voyage to Rome where he suffered martyrdom, the elderly bishop is known to have penned letters to Christian communities in Ephesus, Magnesia, Tralles, Rome, Philadelphia, and Smyrna. A personal letter to Polycarp was also produced. At some time following the death of Ignatius, the copies of these epistles would have been prepared for circulation, presumably by one of his close associates such as Polycarp.[20] A collection of several dozen letters of Cyprian, the third-century theologian and bishop of Carthage, appears to have been preserved and assembled in a similar manner. Because these writings were addressed to a large number of recipients, they were not divided into subcollections, as is the case with the letters of Cicero, but are simply numbered in modern editions.

Not all ancient letter collections appear to have been assembled by an author's associates or later admirers. In some cases, the authors seem to have played a direct role in preserving, arranging, editing, and circulating their own writings. The first-century Roman philosopher Seneca is a noteworthy example of this. The content of his letters and some of the passing references he makes to their composition and early use indicate that he maintained a direct interest in the preservation of his extant works. Rather than writing for the sole benefit of those addressed in his writings, he seems to have envisaged his works circulating in the public sphere and playing an important role in solidifying his reputation as a statesman, writer, and philosopher. As Michele Renee Salzman observes, the extant letters of Seneca demonstrate "clear signs of intentional editing, which most scholars would take as an

---

[20]Eusebius provides a brief overview of the martyrdom of Ignatius and the composition of his writings in *Hist. eccl.* 3.36.

indication that the collection was likely published by Seneca himself."[21] In addition to the fact that some ancient authors played a role in editing their writings and preparing their collections for circulation, we may also conclude that the personal copies in the possession of authors or their close companions often served as the basis of literary collections. It would be difficult to imagine Seneca, for example, attempting to acquire copies of his letters from those he wrote throughout his career in order to publish a collection of his works. Although our knowledge of the formation of early literary collections remains limited, it would seem that collections of writings such as the Pauline corpus are likely to have formed in much the same way as other epistolary collections from the time—that is, by simply preparing the copies that were in the possession of the author or his or her close circle of companions.

Despite the observations that can be made about the formation of various literary collections from the Greco-Roman world and the evidence that secretaries often made multiple copies of the works they produced, it remains widely assumed that there was a single original autograph of each New Testament writing. It is interesting to observe how this assumption is largely limited to the composition of the biblical writings. Historians recognize, for example, that no less than a dozen copies of the Magna Carta were produced in or around the year AD 1215, four of which remain extant. Some have even suggested that as many as three dozen copies or more may have been produced at the time the document was ratified by King John. While there is dispute as to the precise number of manuscripts that were produced and when this took place, there were several manuscripts that could arguably be classified as "originals." This conclusion is not difficult to make given that a small number of these writings remain extant. When it comes to the New Testament writings, however, none of the original manuscripts have survived, making it less obvious that there may have been multiple copies of each writing produced at the end of the compositional process.

---

[21]Michele Renee Salzman, "Latin Letter Collections before Late Antiquity," in *Late Antique Letter Collections*, 25.

If it was indeed the case that multiple copies of several of the New Testament writings were produced when the authors were fully satisfied with the state of the text and were prepared for their work to enter into circulation, it would be more difficult to affirm that each of the extant Greek witnesses can be traced back to a single "original autograph." While one completed manuscript obviously had to be produced first—unless there was a very talented scribe capable of producing two manuscripts at once (perhaps one with each hand!)—it is probable that multiple copies were produced within a short time of one another, often by the same individual (e.g., a secretary such as Tertius) or group (e.g., a small number of Paul's friends and associates who were with him at the time of composition). As a consequence, it is perhaps best to put aside our concept of a single "original autograph" that was dispatched to a distant location with something more like an initial edition that involved the production of multiple copies.

But this leads to another difficult question. If multiple copies of a writing were produced at the end of the compositional process, is it possible that there were slight differences between them? While we can only speculate, it should probably be assumed that in some instances each of the copies produced at the end of the compositional period were not identical in every detail. After all, each copy would have been produced for different readers. A copy of an epistle that Paul kept for himself, for example, might have differed in certain respects from a copy that was produced for those in his vicinity or for those who were the primary recipients. Perhaps there were references or instructions to those in one location that were not relevant to those in others, resulting in some copies being a bit longer than others. Because the copies maintained by ancient authors typically served as the basis of future epistolary editions and essentially functioned as part of a literary archive, we might suspect that the copies maintained by authors such as Paul were complete and served as the basis for future literary collection, whereas those produced for those in the immediate vicinity or elsewhere may have omitted certain sections or contained other minor differences. It may thus be helpful to distinguish between what might be described as an authorial edition (the author's copy) and the other copies that would have been produced around the same time, even those that were dispatched to the initial recipients.

In sum, it is a realistic possibility that the majority of ancient witnesses to the New Testament writings, the epistles in particular, can be traced back to the copies maintained by the author or his companions—that is, to the "authorial editions" rather than to the manuscripts that were sent to the intended recipients or to other communities. While these manuscripts would become the primary basis of future literary collections, it is also reasonable to conclude that copies of the New Testament writings were reproduced throughout the Roman world and that they circulated for some time in various communities or regions. If this was indeed the case, we might suspect that alternative versions of some works were in circulation, at least for a period of time. It does not appear to have been long, however, before the larger subcollections of the canonical writings such as the fourfold Gospel and the Pauline Epistles began to circulate, the result of which would have been a steady decrease in demand for copies of single works that could not be traced back to the "authorial editions."[22] We might imagine, for example, that the two epistles dispatched by Paul to Thessalonica may have circulated on their own, or perhaps alongside a work like Philippians, for a period of time in Macedonia. Once larger editions of the Pauline corpus that were based on the manuscripts in Paul's possession began to circulate, however, these smaller collections would have begun to circulate much less frequently.

The Original Autographs and the Ending of Romans

To this point of the chapter we have considered the possibility that multiple copies of several of the New Testament writings were produced at the end of the compositional process. In what follows, we will consider how the production of several copies, each of which might be described as "original autographs," may possibly account for some of

---

[22]The emergence of the canonical subcollections will be explored in the sixth chapter.

the textual differences that appear in early witnesses to the canonical writings. Some readers may be inclined to dismiss the significance of the possibility that ancient authors such as Paul or Seneca may have produced multiple copies of their letters. Why does it ultimately matter if there was a single autograph from which all subsequent copies later derived or if multiple manuscripts were produced by the author or his associates? None of the originals have survived, so why speculate as to their precise nature or how many copies of a given work may have been produced? In the end, our focus must remain on what has survived, it might be suggested, not on speculative theories regarding their early production. As we will see, however, the recognition that multiple copies of a given work were likely produced at the time of composition may provide significant insight relating to the manner in which the earliest collections of biblical writings may have emerged and may even help account for the origin of various discrepancies in the text of the earliest witnesses. Although scholarship relating to ancient literary practices has advanced, the implications of these findings for our understanding of the textual transmission of the New Testament have not been fully explored.

Those familiar with the textual history of the New Testament will be aware of the major textual issues that have led to a number of questions relating to the original content and form of the canonical writings. By "major" we are referring not to passages in which there is dispute about a single word or phrase—as significant as these minor differences may be to the meaning of a passage—but to passages in which there are questions about the inclusion or omission of a major unit of text. Perhaps the most notable examples include the ending of Mark's Gospel (Mk 16:9-20) and the *Pericope Adulterae* (Jn 7:53–8:11). For some, the textual issues related to these and other passages may serve as evidence that the Gospels underwent significant revisions over the centuries as manuscripts were damaged or as scribes added, omitted, and rearranged material for various reasons.

Notable textual issues are not limited to the Gospels, however. With respect to the Pauline Epistles, Gamble observes in his major study of the textual history of Romans that "it has been a strong and growing conviction among many critics that the transmitted texts of at least some of the letters of Paul do not correspond in form to the letters actually written by Paul, but are to be regarded as 'editorial products,' in which originally independent pieces of Paul's correspondence are conflated."[23] Scholars have espoused a wide array of opinions regarding the degree to which the extant witnesses likely differ from the original compositions of the Pauline writings and the likely cause of several of the major textual variants that appear in the ancient witnesses. As an illustration of the possible insight that our knowledge of ancient literary conventions may contribute to our understanding of the early transmission of the New Testament writings, we will briefly consider a well-known textual issue in the final chapters of Paul's most famous epistle.[24] In this case, the recognition that several manuscripts of Romans were likely produced at the end of the compositional process may offer a potential explanation for the emergence of some significant differences in the text of the early Greek witnesses.

One of the most challenging textual problems in the Pauline Epistles relates to the location of the doxology that typically appears in English translations at the end of Romans.[25] Those acquainted with the epistle will be familiar with the final three verses:

> Now to Him who is able to establish you according to my gospel and the preaching of Jesus Christ, according to the revelation of the mystery which has been kept secret for long ages past, but now is manifested, and by the Scriptures of the prophets, according to the commandment of the eternal God, has been made known to all the nations, leading to obedience of faith; to the only wise God, through Jesus Christ, be the glory forever. Amen. (Rom 16:25-27)

---

[23]Harry Y. Gamble, *The Textual History of the Letter to the Romans*, SD 42 (Grand Rapids, MI: Eerdmans, 1979), 11.

[24]For background and treatment on this textual issue, see Gamble, *The Textual History of Romans*; Larry W. Hurtado, "The Doxology at the End of Romans," in *New Testament Textual Criticism: Its Significance for Exegesis. Essays in Honor of Bruce M. Metzger*, ed. Eldon J. Epp and Gordon Fee (Oxford: Clarendon, 1981), 185-99; I. Howard Marshall, "Romans 16:25-27: An Apt Conclusion," in *Romans & the People of God: Essays in Honor of Gordon D. Fee on the Occasion of His 65th Birthday*, ed. Sven Soderlund and N. T. Wright (Grand Rapids, MI: Eerdmans, 1999), 170-84.

[25]A shorter doxology also appears in a large number of witnesses at the end of Romans 15.

The most prominent location of the doxology in the Greek witnesses is where one may expect it: at the very end of the epistle. English translations follow these witnesses and likewise place the doxology at the end of the writing (Rom 16:25-27) just after a short benediction (Rom 16:24) that appears in only a relatively small number of the early manuscripts.[26] Although several witnesses include the doxology at the end of the epistle, it is occasionally placed at the end of chapter fourteen or even at the end of chapter fifteen.[27] To make the subject even more perplexing, some witnesses include the doxology at the end of chapter fourteen *and* at the end of chapter sixteen while others omit the doxology altogether![28] A comparison of the earliest Greek witnesses to Romans makes clear that there was significant divergence with respect to the inclusion of the benediction and the placement of the doxology. As one might suspect, scholars have offered several explanations and developed a number of theories related to these difficult textual issues. In particular, a variety of conclusions have been made about the three fundamental issues that pertain to the doxology and the original form of the epistle: (1) whether the doxology was original to Paul, (2) the overall length of the original edition of the epistle, and (3) the best explanation for the various placements of the doxology in the extant witnesses.

One of the more popular theories among critical scholars is that the original composition of Romans only included the text contained in the first fourteen or fifteen chapters and that additional material was

---

[26]The earliest witness that contains the short benediction in 16:24 is Codex Claromontanus (D 06), a manuscript that also includes the doxology. Many early witnesses do not include this particular benediction but do include a shorter and arguably earlier benediction that appears in verse 20. Significant textual witnesses that place the doxology at the end of the epistle include 𝔓[61], Codex Sinaiticus (א 01), Codex Vaticanus (B 03), Codex Ephraemi Rescriptus (C 04), and Codex Claromontanus (D 06). With the exception of Claromontanus, these manuscripts do not include the benediction typically placed at 16:24 in English translations.

[27]Manuscripts that place the doxology at the end of Romans 14 are generally dated later and include Codex Athous Laurae (Ψ 01), Codex Angelicus (L 020), Uncial 0209, and Minuscules 181, 326, 330, 451, 460, and 614. Interestingly, Papyrus 46 (𝔓[46]) places the doxology at the end of Romans 15.

[28]Manuscripts that place the doxology after Rom 14:23 and at the end of the epistle include Codex Alexandrinus (A 02), Codex Porphyrianus (P 025), Uncial 0150, and several later minuscules. The doxology is omitted entirely in Codex Augiensis (F 010) as well as in Codex Boernerianus (G 012). For a more comprehensive overview of the location of the doxology in the Greek witnesses, see Gamble, *Textual History*, 131.

added a short time later. This position has been advocated by scholars such as Kirsopp Lake who concluded that "it is very unlikely that this [the doxology] was originally anywhere else than the end of the Epistle, wherever that was."[29] He found it improbable that the longer recension (Rom 1–16) was shortened and that the doxology was simply moved to the end of a shorter edition. It is more plausible, he reasoned, that Romans was originally designed as a circular letter and that it did not originally include the references to those in Rome (e.g., Rom 1:7) or much of the material at the end of the epistle that may not have been regarded as relevant to some readers. Lake assumed that the personal greetings at the end of the epistle were added when an edition was later prepared for those in Rome, an addition that would have prompted some scribes to relocate the doxology to what is now the end of the writing. According to this viewpoint, the textual issues related to this passage can be accounted for by the recognition that scribes did not consistently place the doxology at the end of the longer recension after an expanded edition of Romans was created. As Lake explains, "If we assume that the doxology really belonged originally to the shorter recension, or to one form of the short recension, and the long recension had no doxology at all, but ended with 'Grace' . . . the textual history seems to admit of a reasonable reconstruction, as the result of attempts of scribes to combine these two forms."[30]

A similar solution has been proffered by T. W. Manson. On the basis of the strong external evidence and his judgment that the text "imperatively demands a particular reference to a well-known community not founded by Paul or hitherto visited by him," Manson argued that "Paul prepared a letter (Rom 1–15) and sent it to Rome" and that "at the same time a copy was prepared to be sent to Ephesus" along with material now contained in Romans 16.[31] Many of the subsequent copies produced in places like Egypt then began to combine this material, thus

[29]Kirsopp Lake, *The Earlier Epistles of St. Paul: Their Motive and Origin* (London: Rivingtons, 1919), 343.

[30]Lake, *The Earlier Epistles of St. Paul*, 344-45.

[31]T. W. Manson, "St. Paul's Letter to the Romans," in *The Romans Debate*, ed. Karl Donfried (Grand Rapids, MI: Baker Academic, 1991), 6, 13.

creating the sixteen-chapter epistle that eventually became the standard. While Lake and Manson disagree on the original destination of the epistle, they share the opinion that the original composition did not include the material contained in all sixteen chapters and that the doxology was placed at the end of the epistle only after the longer recension first emerged.

Not all scholars agree that the best explanation for the multiple locations of the doxology in early witnesses is that the original epistle was later expanded, a development that would have caused the doxology to eventually be shifted from what was the original ending at the end of Romans 14 or Romans 15, to the end of what is now Romans 16. Some have argued for the alternative theory that the original form of Romans included the content contained in the final two chapters and that the epistle was later shortened. Those who hold this basic perspective often differ as to what may have led to the omission of the final portion of the epistle at some time subsequent to its composition. One possible explanation is that the text was shortened by Marcion or someone within his community during the second century in order to avoid the stronger Jewish elements contained in the final two chapters (e.g., the affirmation that Christ served the Jewish people in Romans 15:8 or the greetings to many Jewish believers in Romans 16). It is thought that the doxology was then added to the end of the shortened edition as well as to subsequent copies of the longer edition of the epistle. In agreement with this perspective, Robert Jewett writes, "The widely accepted hypothesis is that some branch of the church that was using Marcion's fourteen-chapter version of Romans added the doxology, which probably had been used in that church's liturgy in some other context."[32] Elsewhere he posits that the doxology was likely added in order to emphasize the "supersession of Jewish prerogatives"; the result, he argues, was "a new form of mission that entailed cultural

---

[32]Robert Jewett, "Fourth Sunday of Advent, Year B," in *The Lectionary Commentary: Theological Exegesis for Sunday's Texts, the Second Readings: Acts and the Epistles*, ed. Roger E. Van Harn (Grand Rapids, MI: Eerdmans, 2001), 143.

and theological domination and a destructive legacy of anti-Semitism."[33] James Dunn shares a similar viewpoint, contending that the shortened recension was the result of an effort to distance the Christian gospel from its Jewish foundations. As he writes, the doxology was "first added to an abbreviated (Marcionite) version of the letter (= 1:1–14:23), then incorporated into the longer original."[34]

Other scholars who have concluded that material from a longer original was eventually omitted include J. B. Lightfoot, who suggested that scribes later omitted material in the epistle that would have been relevant only to those in Rome and that the shorter edition was designed to serve a more universal audience.[35] As Nils Dahl explained, many early readers would have struggled to ascertain "why letters written to particular churches on particular occasions should be regarded as canonical and read in all churches." With respect to the Pauline Epistles, Dahl noted that their chief concern "was not their plurality, but their particularity."[36] If a writing was composed for the benefit of a specific audience and was designed to address particular concerns, how relevant could it be to those far removed from this original context? In response to these matters, it has been suggested that scribes engaged in a deliberate effort to remove references that may have seemed relevant only to the initial readers or to specific audiences. In the case of Romans, it is thought that this would have involved the intentional omission of a significant portion of the text contained in the final two chapters, much of which is comprised simply of greetings to individuals in the Roman church.

Gamble's major study makes essentially the same conclusion. He argues that the original composition dispatched to Rome included the material found in all sixteen chapters and that the material contained at the end of the epistle was omitted shortly thereafter in order to provide readers with an edition deemed more appropriate for a

---

[33]Robert Jewett, *Romans: A Commentary*, Hermeneia (Minneapolis, MN: Fortress, 2006), 1014.

[34]James D. G. Dunn, *Romans 9–16*, WBC 38B (Waco, TX: Word, 1988), 912.

[35]J. B. Lightfoot, *Biblical Essays* (London: Macmillan, 1893), 315-19.

[36]Nils A. Dahl, "The Particularity of the Pauline Epistles as a Problem in the Ancient Church," in *Neotestamentica et Patristica*, NovTSup 6 (Leiden: Brill, 1962), 261.

universal audience. Gamble suggests that the doxology, however, was likely a post-Pauline addition that was first placed at the end of Romans 14 after the epistle was shortened by scribes. It was not long, however, before the doxology began to be placed at the end of manuscripts that include longer recension—that is, in manuscripts that contain the material of all sixteen chapters. Interestingly, Gamble concludes that the benedictions found in Romans 16:20 and Romans 16:24 are both likely original but that the latter began to be omitted when the doxology was added to the end of chapter sixteen. Gamble's understanding of these textual issues is similar in important respects to what was articulated by Jewett and Dunn, not least in its assumption that the doxology was not original. However, he points to a different impetus for the shorter versions of the epistle and offers an alternative explanation for how the doxology came to be placed in different locations.

The "Original Autographs" and the Discipline of Textual Criticism

Despite the significant scholarly attention that has been given to the textual issues relating to the ending of Romans, a number of questions remain about the original content of the writing and how the different editions likely emerged. Even if it may be reasonably determined that the original composition included the material contained in Romans 15–16, a plausible explanation would still be needed for the various locations in which the doxology appears in the textual witnesses and how we might account for the origin of the shorter recension.

One possible solution to the difficult textual issues relating to the ending of Romans is that the alternative readings emerged not from a scribe who expanded or reduced the length of the epistle at some point after the text entered circulation but from the differences between the copies of the epistle that were produced at the end of the compositional process. As suggested above, it is a strong possibility that at least three copies of the text of Romans were produced at the end of the compositional process: one for the Romans, one for those in Corinth, and one for Paul and/or his associates. If this was indeed the case, it may be possible that the manuscripts produced for those in Rome and for Paul included the longer recension—that is, the material included in Romans 15–16—while at least one other manuscript, perhaps one produced for the local believers in Corinth, omitted much of the content of the final chapters. Perhaps Tertius or another early copyist in Corinth determined that much of the content contained in the final two chapters of the epistle was of limited value to those in the Corinthian community and decided not to include it. When this material was omitted, the doxology may have then been retained and simply placed at the end of the shorter version. This would explain both the origin of the shorter and longer recensions as well as the alternative locations of the doxology. As noted above, early Greek witnesses containing the shorter recension of Romans are not as well attested. This is what we might expect if the major editions of the Pauline letter collection that circulated in early Christianity derived from the copies maintained by Paul or his associates and if the circulation of the shorter recensions were fairly limited to particular areas such as Corinth.

One possible objection to this hypothesis is that Marcion was charged by some in the early church with omitting the ending of Romans. In fact, Origen specifically claimed that Marcion removed the final portion of the epistle along with the final benediction contained in Romans 16:24.[37] Consistent with this claim is the fact that there are no references to Marcion's interpretation of the final portions of Romans in Tertullian's massive work, *Against Marcion*. If Marcion was in fact guilty of this charge, it would certainly seem reasonable that the shorter recensions that began to circulate were the result of his heavy-handed editorial activity. As attractive as the Marcionite hypothesis may be as a solution to the textual issues surrounding the ending of Romans, it is not without its share of difficulties. We might observe, for example, that the multiple placements of the doxology in the earliest textual witnesses are more likely to have developed during the initial

---

[37] Origen, *Comm. Rom.*

phase of the writing's circulation than during the mid-second century when Marcion was allegedly active editing and circulating various writings. Gamble is certainly correct in his estimation that "the shorter forms of Romans could have arisen only during the early period, when the Roman letter circulated independently."[38]

Although a number of scholars remain convinced that the textual issues related to the doxology of Romans are best explained by the omission of the final portion of Romans by Marcion or by unknown scribes who sought to universalize the text for a broad audience, the awareness that multiple "autographs" were produced at the end of the compositional process may best account for these difficult issues. This theory enables us to account for the emergence of alternative readings early in the transmissional process while eliminating the difficulty of explaining why later scribes determined either to omit significant portions of the epistle or add supplemental material that would have undoubtedly seemed less relevant to later readers.

In our age of academic specialization, the study of the canonical development of the New Testament and the textual history of the New Testament writings are often practiced in isolation of one another. It should be kept in mind, however, that one's understanding of how the biblical writings were likely composed and disseminated may provide useful insight not only for how works were assembled and collected but how alternative readings of a given writing may have been introduced. In his reflections of the textual issues surrounding Romans, Gamble is certainly correct in his observation that "no strict separation can or should be made between the history of the formation of the *Corpus* and the history of the text of Paul's letters."[39]

CONCLUSIONS

This chapter has sought to provide clarity regarding the nature of the "original autographs" of the New Testament writings. In contrast to the common assumption that a single autograph of each writing was

---

[38]Gamble, *The Textual History of Romans*, 141.
[39]Gamble, *The Textual History of Romans*, 140.

produced and dispatched soon thereafter to the intended readers, it has been suggested that multiple copies of several of the canonical writings were likely produced at the end of the compositional process. In addition to the copy that was dispatched to the intended readers, there may have been occasions in which copies were produced for the author, his companions, and those in distant locations. Rather than assume that the compositional process of the canonical writings culminated with the production of a single "original autograph," it is therefore best to think of something that might be described as an original edition. As we have suggested, this awareness may provide clues relating to some of the thorny textual issues such as the ending of Romans. It is possible that the fluid placement of the epistle's doxology and some of the other textual issues associated with the ending of the epistle may have resulted from the differences between the initial manuscripts that were produced at the end of the compositional process. As suggested, it is possible that a shorter edition of Romans was produced for local believers in Corinth, while copies containing the full letter were made for Paul and the community in Rome.

THE ORIGINAL READERS
OF THE NEW TESTAMENT
WRITINGS

WHO EXACTLY WERE THE "ORIGINAL READERS" OR THE
"ORIGINAL AUDIENCE" OF THE NEW TESTAMENT WRITINGS?

*Interpreters must learn to interpret Paul's rhetoric in terms
of multiple audiences that include a letter's origin as well
as its destination, plus presumably its receptions en route,
if these can be determined.*

DOUGLAS CAMPBELL, *FRAMING PAUL*

BIBLICAL SCHOLARS HAVE LONG RECOGNIZED the importance
of carefully establishing, so far as can be determined, the historical
context in which each of the canonical writings were composed. Emphasis is often placed on the immediate circumstances and pressing
concerns facing the author, the factors that may have prompted the
author to write, and what may be known of the situation facing the
original readers. As challenging as it may be to reach firm conclusions
about the background of the canonical writings, the fact that each of the
writings contained in the New Testament were written in order to fulfill
particular objectives and to address particular issues facing a specific
group of readers should not be overlooked. In their discussion of the
hermeneutical insight that might be gleaned from our knowledge of the

original readers, the authors of a recent introductory volume on hermeneutics helpfully remind us that "knowing about the recipients—their
characteristics, circumstances, and community—sheds light on the
passage, particularly how and why the writer develops specific subjects."[1]

Despite the emphasis that is often placed on the situation facing the
original audience of the biblical writings, scholars have struggled to
reach a consensus regarding the identity of the intended readers of each
work. In fact, there is not even agreement as to whether there even was
a specific community that certain writings were originally designed to
reach! In recent decades, for example, some have suggested that the
Gospels were written primarily for a universal audience,[2] while others
maintain that each writing was composed primarily for a more specific
community (e.g., those in Rome, Ephesus, or Antioch). Between these
two basic perspectives is the understanding that each Gospel writer
may have had a general type of readership in mind (e.g., Jewish or
Greek readers), but perhaps not a specific community, at least not one
that can be determined with any degree of certainty.[3] It might be said,
for example, that the Gospel of Matthew was written for a predominately Jewish audience with the objective of presenting Jesus as the
rightful king of Israel who fulfilled various prophecies contained in the
Law and the Prophets (cf. Mt 5:17). The Gospels of Mark and Luke, on
the other hand, have been widely understood to have been written with
a predominately Gentile audience in view. Finally, some have concluded that the Gospel of John was likely written for a more universal
audience that included Gentiles and a considerable number of Jews
living in the Diaspora.

Questions related to the intended recipients of the biblical writings
are not limited to the canonical Gospels. There are even questions

---

[1]William Klein, Craig Blomberg, and Robert Hubbard, *Introducing Biblical Interpretation*, 3rd ed.
(Grand Rapids, MI: Zondervan, 2017), 322.

[2]See, for example, Richard Bauckham, ed., *The Gospel for All Christians: Rethinking the Gospel Audiences* (Grand Rapids, MI: Eerdmans, 1998).

[3]For a helpful overview of the debate on this subject, see Richard Burridge, "Who Writes, Why,
and for Whom?" in *The Written Gospel*, ed. Markus Bockmuehl and Donald Hagner (Cambridge:
Cambridge University Press, 2005), 99-115.

about the original readers of several of the Epistles in the canon. Scholars have debated at length, for example, the identity of the Galatians, specifically whether Paul used this designation with reference to an ethnic people group living in the more remote regions farther north in Asia Minor or to those living in the areas to the south where he visited during the first missionary journey. Significant debate has also centered around the identity of the recipients of the epistle referred to as Ephesians. In addition to the traditional viewpoint that it was written to the Christian community in the city of Ephesus,[4] others have suggested that it may have originally been intended for those in a different location such as Laodicea[5] or that it was originally written as a circular letter to several Christian communities in a larger region, only to become directly associated with the city of Ephesus at some point subsequent to its composition.[6]

Despite some lingering questions about the specific communities that were originally addressed by the canonical writers, it is widely recognized that each of the New Testament writings was composed in order to address specific subjects that the author considered to be relevant to specific readers. For this reason, we might think of the Epistles, not as theological treatises on theological subjects that were of interest to the authors, but as apostolic instruction and exhortation designed to address particular concerns of those in specific communities. When Paul wrote to the church in Philippi, for example, he addressed matters that were related not only to his own situation (e.g., his imprisonment and the arrival of Epaphroditus) but those that were of relevance to Christians living in Philippi. The content of the epistle indicates that the saints in Macedonia were threatened by false teaching (see Phil 3:2-3, 18-19) and that they were suffering from internal division. So

---

[4]This conclusion is well-supported by early Christian testimony, the widespread presence of the title ΠΡΟΣ ΕΦΕΣΙΟΥΣ in Greek manuscripts, as well as the words ἐν Ἐφέσῳ (*en Ephesō*) in some of the early Greek witnesses that contain the text of Eph 1:1.

[5]This was apparently the understanding of Marcion during the second century, a viewpoint that was vehemently rejected by Tertullian. See *Marc.* 5.17.1.

[6]As F. F. Bruce contends, Ephesians "might be called a general letter to Gentile Christians, more particularly in the province of Asia." *The Epistles to the Colossians, to Philemon, and to the Ephesians*, NICNT (Grand Rapids, MI: Eerdmans, 1984), 230.

destructive were these divisions that Paul determined to directly exhort two members of the community, Euodia and Syntyche, to be of the same mind (Phil 4:2). We should note, of course, that the occasional nature of the Epistles does not diminish their universal significance. Although biblical authors such as Paul addressed a number of specific issues that were of special importance to the original readers, the universal relevance of their instruction has long been recognized. In fact, a case could be made that the universal relevance of the canonical writings is a major reason they were preserved in the first place.

Despite the significant attention often placed on the identity of the intended recipients of the biblical writings, surprisingly little critical reflection has been given to the precise meaning of commonly used terms such as "original audience," "original readers," "original recipients," "intended audience," and so on. These types of descriptions are often used with the presumption that each author had a single audience in mind at the time of composition and that this audience was, quite naturally, the first to read the work after it was composed. In some cases, the assumed original audience may have consisted of those living in a specific city (e.g., believers in the cities of Rome or Corinth), while on other occasions it is thought to have included those in a wider region (e.g., believers living throughout Galatia). With respect to the Epistles, it is often assumed that the original audience would have simply been those who were referred to in the greetings, and, in the case of the Pauline Epistles, those who were addressed in the letter titles.[7]

This basic perspective on the identity of the original readers of the New Testament documents may seem quite obvious to contemporary readers, due in part perhaps to the influence of modern writing practices. When letters or messages are sent out in today's world, the author

---

[7]The titles of the Pauline Epistles are unique in that they identify the recipients of each writing rather than the author. For a study of the emergence of the letter titles of the Pauline Epistles, see David Trobisch, *The First Edition of the New Testament* (New York: Oxford University Press, 2000), 38-44; Benjamin P. Laird, "Early Titles of the Pauline Letters and the Publication of the Pauline Corpus," *BN* 175 (2017): 55-81; Laird, *The Pauline Corpus in Early Christianity: Its Formation, Publication, and Circulation* (Peabody, MA: Hendrickson, 2022), 73-89. For a study of the titles of the Gospels, see Simon Gathercole, "The Titles of the Gospels in the Earliest New Testament Manuscripts," *ZNW* 104 (2012): 33-76.

simply sends the completed text directly to a specific individual or organization. This most commonly takes place electronically and is a rather straightforward process. Because of our familiarity with this type of communication, we might find little reason to assume that the identification of an epistle's author or the original readers involves anything more than simply consulting the greeting or the title that became associated with the writing. As will be suggested in this chapter, however, a case could be made that the original readers of some of the New Testament writings encompassed a wider body of individuals than those who are explicitly cited in the greeting or title of a given text. In some cases, those who first encountered a canonical writing may not have been those directly addressed in the text but those who were a part of the Christian community in the author's immediate vicinity. There may have even been times in which the New Testament authors addressed specific matters or used certain language that would have been of special significance not just to those who were directly addressed in their work but to those in the author's surrounding area. While such a scenario could have been the case with several of the canonical writings, we will focus our attention in this chapter on the background of some of the Pauline Epistles.

THE "ORIGINAL AUDIENCE" OF THE PAULINE EPISTLES IN RECENT SCHOLARSHIP

Scholars such as Charlotte Hartwig and Douglas Campbell have suggested that on some occasions the first to read or hear Paul's writings would have been those in his immediate vicinity rather than the specific individual(s) directly addressed in the greeting.[8] It is certainly no stretch to assume that there would have been occasions in which the Christians living and ministering around Paul were aware of his

---

[8]Charlotte Hartwig, "Die korinthische Gemeinde als Nebenadressat des Römerbriefes. Eine Untersuchung zur Wiederaufnahme von Themen aus dem 1. Korintherbrief im Römerbrief" (PhD diss., University of Heidelberg, 2001). A summary of her study was cowritten with Gerd Theissen in "Die Korinthische Gemeinde als Nebenadressat des Römerbriefs," *NovT* 46 (2004): 229-52. Douglas Campbell's treatment of this subject may be found in his work *Framing Paul: An Epistolary Biography* (Grand Rapids, MI: Eerdmans, 2014).

literary activities. If this were indeed the case, we might further assume that there were instances in which believers in his present location would have been the first to hear or read a writing before it was dispatched to those in a distant location. As Hartwig and Campbell have suggested, an epistle's *Nebenadressat*—that is, those who were essentially a secondary or nearby audience—may provide insight relating to the inclusion of certain material in Paul's epistles and help explain why certain subjects are emphasized to a greater extent than might otherwise be expected. In what follows, we will briefly discuss the recent attention given to the subject of the *Nebenadressat* of the Pauline writings and consider some of its possible hermeneutical and historical implications.

In her study, Hartwig contends that some of the content of Romans appears to have been designed to address a number of issues and subjects that would have been of special relevance to the Corinthian community.[9] As she observes, Paul's instruction to the Corinthian church was not limited to his personal interaction during his visits to Corinth or even to the written instruction that was part of the Corinthian correspondence. In addition to these primary mediums, Hartwig suggests that Paul may have communicated indirectly to the Corinthians through his epistle addressed to those in Rome. In some cases, the believers in Corinth may have actually been better suited to understand and appreciate the content of the epistle than those who were part of the church at Rome, a community of believers with which Paul was not particularly well acquainted.[10]

Hartwig draws attention to several thematic parallels between Romans and the Corinthian epistles in support of her thesis that the Corinthians were the *Nebenadressat* of Paul's epistle to the Romans. As

---

[9]A variety of proposals for the provenance of Romans have been offered, though many details in Acts and the final chapter of Romans appear to support the conclusion that the epistle was written from Corinth shortly before Paul traveled to Jerusalem at the conclusion of the third missionary journey.

[10]For a treatment of what may be known of Paul's relationship with those in Rome, see Peter Lampe, *From Paul to Valentinus: Christians at Rome in the First Two Centuries* (Minneapolis, MN: Fortress, 2003), 153-83.

she observes, one need not read past the initial passages in Romans before encountering certain references that would have been especially meaningful to those in Corinth. We find, for example, a parallel between his calling to proclaim the gospel "both to the wise and the foolish" (Rom 1:14) and his previous references to those who were "wise" among the Corinthians (e.g., 1 Cor 1:20-21; 2:6). Hartwig also identifies several references to theological and ethical matters discussed throughout Romans that were also treated in the Corinthian correspondence. These references, she contends, suggest that Paul may have included certain material in Romans to serve, at least in part, as a reminder to the Corinthians of matters that he had previously addressed. Some of the more notable subjects treated in Romans that were also addressed in Paul's previous instructions to the Corinthians include:

- The judgment resulting from human rejection of divine wisdom (cf. Rom 1:18–2:16; 1 Cor 1:18–2:5).

- The practice of homosexuality (Rom 2). This subject may have been addressed in part as a result of its widespread practice in Corinth (1 Cor 6:9).

- The ethical implications of baptism in Christ (Rom 6:1-11). This instruction may have been included as a result of the divisions that had formed in Corinth that were related in some way to the practice of baptism (1 Cor 1:11-17).

- The charge of antinomianism (cf. Rom 7). Paul's denial of the accusation that he was opposed to the law may have been prompted, at least in part, to recent accusations levied against him by his critics in Corinth who challenged his teaching and apostolic credentials.

- Practical instruction in Romans 14–15 relating to situations involving the "strong" and the "weak." The treatment on this subject may have been designed to reinforce previous teaching that was previously given to the Corinthians (1 Cor 8–9). Paul's response to the question of meat sacrificed to idols would have certainly been of interest to those in both Rome and Corinth.

Another intriguing possibility is that Paul's brief reference to the relief offering was included, at least in part, for the benefit of the Corinthians. Near the end of Romans, Paul makes reference to his forthcoming journey to Jerusalem (Rom 15:25-32), a reference Hartwig suggests would have served as a fitting final word to the Corinthians before his departure to Jerusalem. It is interesting that Paul praises the church in Macedonia and Achaia for their generous contribution to the relief offering. They thought it good (εὐδόκησαν; *eudokēsan*) to participate in the collection, Paul writes (Rom 15:26). Nowhere in these brief remarks is there an indication that the Corinthians were reluctant to make a contribution. In contrast to the favorable description of the Achaeans' participation in the relief offering that appears in Romans, the Corinthian epistles indicate that those in Corinth were in need of additional encouragement and admonishment to follow through with their initial commitment (see, e.g., 1 Cor 16:1-4; 2 Cor 8–9).

This rather negative assessment of the Corinthians' involvement contained in 2 Corinthians makes the more favorable description of the Achaeans' contribution to the offering in Romans 15:26 somewhat unexpected. How might these references be reconciled? One possible explanation is that the Corinthians had followed through with Paul's instructions and made a generous contribution to the collection by the time he penned Romans near the end of the third missionary journey. This would provide a plausible and straightforward explanation for why he praised the generosity of those in Corinth and the broader region in Romans 15:26.[11] It is difficult, however, to determine whether the collection had already been taken up at the time Paul offered his praise. On that Paul began to encourage the Corinthians to contribute to the offering when he first arrived in the city, but that many of them had still not done so by the time he composed Romans. If this was indeed the case, Paul's reference in Romans 15:26 to the willingness of the Achaeans to take part in the relief offering may have been designed, at least in part,

---

[11]This is the conclusion reached by David J. Downs in his study of Paul's relief offering in *The Offering of the Gentiles: Paul's Collection for Jerusalem in Its Chronological, Cultural, and Cultic Contexts* (Grand Rapids, MI: Eerdmans, 2016), 53.

to place public pressure on the Corinthians to follow through with their initial commitment. If they became hesitant to give financially to the Jewish believers in another part of the empire—something that was a very real possibility—they may have at least been stirred by a desire to maintain the honor that stemmed from Paul's public praise. In either scenario, the reference to the offering would have been of special interest to those in Paul's immediate vicinity.

In addition to a number of references in Romans to subjects that would have been of special interest to believers in Corinth, it is also apparent that the Christians in this area would have been aware that Paul was writing the epistle during his stay there. As noted in the first chapter, Paul worked directly with Tertius, an individual who apparently resided in Corinth or perhaps in a nearby location such as Cenchreae. Tertius, it will be recalled, identified himself as the amanuensis of the epistle (Rom 16:22) and would have obviously had firsthand knowledge of its content. An awareness of Paul's correspondence to the Romans would have also been known to individuals such as Phoebe, who, on the basis of Paul's commendation in Romans 16:1-2, is often thought to have been responsible for delivering the letter, and Gaius, whom Paul identifies as his host (Rom 16:23).

In view of the fact that a number of individuals in Corinth worked either directly with Paul during the composition of Romans or would have at least been aware of the writing, it may be safely assumed that it was public knowledge among the Christians in the area that he had composed a substantial epistle to the church in Rome. Consequently, it is quite difficult to imagine that those in Corinth would have received access to the epistle only after copies made their way back to Achaia at some point after the writing first arrived in Rome. It would have only been natural for at least one copy of the epistle to have been produced for those in the local area before it was dispatched to Rome. It may also be possible that the text was read in local churches in the area shortly after it was composed. In either case, it is entirely plausible, even likely, that Christians in Corinth were the first to either hear or read the text of Romans.

Despite the possible implications of this understanding of the composition of Romans, few scholars have sought to investigate the ideas explored by Hartwig. One of the few to interact with her work is Douglas Campbell, author of numerous scholarly works related to the theology of Paul and the background of his writings. In his work *Framing Paul*, Campbell considers the possible *Nebenadressat* of several of the Pauline Epistles in order to ascertain why Paul may have addressed certain subjects in his writings and presented certain arguments in a particular manner. As he explains, interpreters must "learn to interpret Paul's rhetoric in terms of multiple audiences that include a letter's origin as well as its destination, plus presumably its receptions en route, if these can be determined."[12] In addition to how these considerations might inform our reading of Paul's writings, Campbell also considers what our knowledge of the secondary audiences of Paul's letters may reveal about their provenance and dating and when he may have traveled to various locations.

To cite but one example, Campbell examines the notoriously difficult question of the background of Galatians by evaluating various clues in the text that may provide insight into the situation facing Paul's *Nebenadressat*, information that may prove useful in establishing the provenance of the writing. Many scholars have concluded that Paul wrote from Jerusalem, Antioch of Syria, or another location in this general region (proposals that are typically more prevalent among proponents of the South Galatian theory), while others have suggested that he more likely wrote from one of the cities he visited during a subsequent missionary journey (a viewpoint more favorable to the North Galatian theory).

For Campbell, some of the material contained in Galatians may not have been especially relevant to Jewish Christians. He points to the vice list contained in Galatians 5:19-21 as an example. Although sexual immorality, idolatry, sorcery, and drunkenness were practices that were of concern to Christians throughout the Greco-Roman world, these vices would have arguably been a more pressing matter to those living in a location such as Corinth than to those in the smaller cities spread

---

[12]Campbell, *Framing Paul*, 55.

throughout Asia Minor. As Campbell explains, "There have been no hints in the letter thus far that the Galatians are sexually immoral, idolatrous, or drunken. Worse than this, however, one would hardly expect a community being tempted primarily by Judaizing to be suffering from these sins."[13] He further observes that Galatians places a strong emphasis on the importance of Christian unity (Gal 3:26-29), a subject Paul strongly emphasizes in 1 Corinthians (1 Cor 1:11-17; 12:12-26).

On the basis of these observations, Campbell concludes that Paul likely wrote Galatians from Corinth during his stay in the city around AD 51–52, a visit which he believes occurred shortly after the composition of the Corinthian epistles. Consequently, Campbell finds it plausible that Paul may have made certain references and incorporated various ethical teachings into his vice list for the benefit of those in the Corinthian community who had recently converted to Christianity from paganism. As he suggests, recognition of the Corinthians as the *Nebenadressat* of Galatians helpfully accounts for the inclusion of the somewhat unexpected instruction about these vices while providing possible clues relating to the epistle's provenance.

Although there is certainly value in recognizing that Paul often wrote for the benefit of multiple audiences, a word of caution is necessary. In many cases, a possible *Nebenadressat* of Paul's writings is difficult to determine. This may be the result of a disputed provenance or simply because there is little information pertaining to the circumstances and challenges facing those in the location from which he wrote. There may be several reasonable explanations for why Paul broached a particular subject that are not built on the assumption that he wrote from a particular location or that he wrote for a particular audience. In view of human nature and the common struggles experienced by Christians throughout the world, it is clear that Christians throughout the Greco-Roman would have benefited from Paul's instruction on a variety of topics. The city of Corinth, for example, was most certainly not the only location where sexual immorality, drunkenness, or idolatry were a

---

[13]Campbell, *Framing Paul*, 169.

concern! Because of the universal relevance of the content contained in the Pauline Epistles, it is often prudent to appeal to a writing's *Nebenadressat* only if its provenance may be reasonably determined on grounds other than the subjects that are treated.

IMPLICATIONS FOR THE STUDY OF THE PAULINE EPISTLES

Now that we have briefly discussed a few recent attempts to achieve a more historically informed understanding of the concept of an original audience, we may consider some of the possible implications of our findings. It has already been suggested that an awareness of a writing's possible *Nebenadressat* may offer insight into why certain subjects were addressed and why Paul's treatment of a number of topics may have been framed in a particular way. In addition to these general observations, we may also note that a more nuanced understanding of Paul's original audiences may yield useful insight related to the literary genre and authorship of these writings.

The "original audience" and the literary genre of the Pauline Epistles. In addition to insight related to various historical and hermeneutical matters, the awareness that Paul often wrote for the benefit of multiple audiences provides valuable insight pertaining to the literary genre of his writings. More than a century ago, Adolf Deissmann's influential *Light from the Ancient East* provided fresh observations about letter writing in the ancient world. Instead of treating terms such as *letter* and *epistle* interchangeably, Deissmann argued that many ancient writings, what came to be referred to as *epistles*, were of a different nature than the private everyday letters of antiquity. Letters, he contended, were much more common, typically shorter (most were fewer than three hundred words), and "intended only for the person or persons to whom it is addressed, and not at all for the public or any kind of publicity."[14] What might be described as *epistles*, on the other hand, tended to be more sophisticated, longer, and "intended for publicity." As such, "the more readers it obtain[ed], the better its purpose

---

[14]Adolf Deissmann, *Light from the Ancient East: The New Testament Illustrated by Recently Discovered Texts of the Greco-Roman World* (New York: George H. Doran Co., 1927), 228.

[was] fulfilled."[15] Deissmann concluded that while the writings of the Pauline corpus were typically much longer than an average letter, they were nonetheless written to a specific audience in order to address particular concerns. Paul's writings were "the outcome of a definite situation, which could not be repeated," he explained.[16] From his perspective, the assumption that specific instructions in Paul's letters were written with a larger audience in view overlooks the occasional nature of private letters and the circumstances that led to their composition.

The exception to Deissmann's classification of the Pauline Epistles as occasional letters are the Pastoral Epistles, three writings which he regarded as inauthentic works designed to be widely distributed and read by a more general audience.[17] Deissmann argued that the Pastorals should not be treated as Paul's personal instruction to trusted colleagues but instead as literary works produced after the apostle's lifetime that were designed to influence communities throughout the Christian world. Although Deissmann's work has exerted considerable influence over the years, a number of scholars have nuanced his basic theories or criticized them sharply. As Adam Copenhaver has recently argued, "What Deissmann contributes in creating a simple way to categorize the literature, he loses by overstating his case and flattening out the exceptions."[18] In basic agreement with Copenhaver, several contemporary scholars recognize that first-century letters cannot be neatly divided into just one of two basic genres. In light of the number of unique literary features of the surviving letters and the wide range of purposes they serve, it is clear that a more developed understanding of letters from the Greco-Roman world is needed.[19]

---

[15]Deissmann, *Light from the Ancient East*, 229.

[16]Adolf Deissmann, *Paul: A Study in Social and Religious History*, trans. W. E. Wilson (New York: Harper & Brothers, 1957), 12.

[17]Although Deissmann regarded the Pastorals as the only literary epistles attributed to Paul, he also recognized that Hebrews, James, Jude, and 1 Peter should also be recognized as public epistles rather than private letters.

[18]Adam Copenhaver, *Reconstructing the Historical Background of Paul's Rhetoric in the Letter to the Colossians*, LNTS 585 (London: T&T Clark, 2018), 43.

[19]With regard to their intended audience, Luke Timothy Johnson contends that the Pastoral Epistles, 1 Timothy and Titus in particular, "are not genuinely private letters; they are intended from the beginning to be read in public, both to support Paul's delegate in his work and to hold

Deissmann's conclusion that the majority of the Pauline writings lacked a more universal outlook is difficult to maintain. While considered inauthentic by some, it is notable that the epistle to the Colossians contains instruction for an interchange of letters with the nearby congregation in Laodicea (Col 4:16). In addition, 1 Thessalonians 5:27 calls for a public reading of the epistle, instruction that is in keeping with the recognition of its authoritative status. Noting the significance of these references, Tomas Bokedal observes, "The request to interchange letters indicates some public character of these writings, perhaps also an already established practice of reciting them beside the Jewish Scriptures as part of the worship service, or the initiation of such a practice among the provincial churches."[20]

In addition to instructions for the circulation of certain writings, the universal language of passages such as 1 Corinthians 1:2 has been cited as further evidence that Paul, or a later redactor, as some would argue, intended for his work to circulate among Christians outside of Corinth. Finally, Paul's description of the criticism he received from his opponents (2 Cor 10:10) and the early reference to a body of his epistles in 2 Peter 3:15-16 provide further support for the conclusion that he was widely known as the author of a collection of influential writings. Reflecting on the assertion of Paul's critics that "his letters are weighty and strong" (2 Cor 10:10), Gerd Theissen writes that "the Corinthians apparently measure his letters against a rhetorical ideal, and so treat them like literary letters."[21] Passages such as this suggest that Paul's intention, at least to some level and on some occasions, was for his writings to circulate between multiple communities and to be read in public gatherings. It is difficult to account for much of the instruction in these

---

the delegate to a standard of personal behavior that is exemplary." *The First and Second Letters to Timothy*, AB 35A (New York: Doubleday, 2001), 141. See also, Philip H. Towner, *The Letters to Timothy and Titus*, NICNT (Grand Rapids, MI: Eerdmans, 2006), 88-89; Benjamin Fiore, *The Function of Personal Example in the Socratic and Pastoral Epistles*, AnBib 105 (Rome: Pontifical Biblical Institute, 1986), 81-84; Michael Wolter, *Die Pastoralbriefe als Paulustradition*, FRLANT 146 (Göttingen: Vandenhoeck & Ruprecht, 1988), 164-80.

[20]Tomas Bokedal, *The Formation and Significance of the Christian Biblical Canon: A Study in Text, Ritual and Interpretation* (London: T&T Clark, 2014), 266.

[21]Gerd Theissen, *The New Testament: A Literary History* (Minneapolis, MN: Fortress, 2012), 72.

writings, their carefully designed literary structure, features, and length, and even their popularity throughout the Christian world without conceding that they were originally intended to be read by an audience that was much larger than those who were identified in the greetings of his writings.[22] As William Doty helpfully observes, "Far from being casual letters of the type found predominantly in the papyri, Paul's letters were intended for public use within the religious gatherings."[23]

Deissmann was by no means the only scholar to wrestle with features of the Pauline writings that provide insight related to their intended use. A bit more recently, Nils Dahl addressed what he described as the problem of particularity. According to Dahl, it is difficult to explain how the Pauline Epistles came to be recognized as relevant for all Christians given their specific instructions and occasional nature.[24] Why would Christians in Asia Minor, for example, view Paul's writings to those in Macedonia or Achaia as relevant to their particular situation if they were only written for those he specifically addressed? The simple answer to this question is that Paul's writings were quickly recognized as authoritative Scripture of universal relevance on the basis of their apostolic authority. Because Paul wrote with the authority of an apostle, his writings were widely recognized as authoritative instruction, despite the fact that they were addressed to specific congregations or individuals.

One of the interesting ways that the early church sought to address the tension between the particularity of the letters and their perceived universal relevance was by appealing to a tradition that Paul wrote to seven churches. Individual writings may have been originally written to specific readers, but the collection as a whole was for

---

[22]The conclusion that Paul's writings enjoyed widespread use in the years following his death was rejected by scholars such as John Knox, Edgar Goodspeed, and C. Leslie Mitton.

[23]William Doty, *Letters in Primitive Christianity* (Philadelphia: Fortress, 1973), 25.

[24]Nils A. Dahl, "The Particularity of the Pauline Epistles as a Problem in the Ancient Church," in *Eine Freundesgabe Herrn Professor Dr. Oscar Cullmann zu seinem 60. Geburtstag überreicht. Neotestamentica et Patristica*, NovTSup 6 (Leiden: Brill, 1962), 261-71. As Bruce Metzger notes, the problem of particularity "was tackled on two fronts: by an attempt at theological justification through number-symbolism, and by adjustment of the text in several of the epistles." *The Canon of the New Testament: Its Origin, Development, and Significance* (Oxford: Clarendon, 1997), 264.

the benefit of the universal church, they reasoned. The observation that this collection included letters to seven specific communities was regarded as an indication that he ultimately wrote to Christians everywhere. Similar to Irenaeus's famous comparison of the four Gospels to the four corners of the world,[25] early witnesses to the Pauline corpus such as the Muratorian Fragment refer to the seven churches to which Paul wrote, a number that was widely understood as representative of something that was complete or universal in nature.[26] As Dahl observes, the number was used symbolically "to prove the catholicity of the Pauline letters."[27]

It would seem that scholars in recent centuries have tended to emphasize one aspect of the epistles to the exclusion of the other. Deissmann may have overlooked the universal appeal of the Epistles he deemed genuine, but it might also be said that others have failed to recognize certain features, instructions, and exhortations contained in the Epistles that would have been of particular interest to those in specific communities. Fortunately, the difficulty of accounting for both the occasional and universal elements of the Pauline Epistles is mitigated by an awareness that Paul often wrote for the benefit of readers in multiple communities. Paul clearly wrote to address matters of particular relevance to those in specific communities, though the canonical writings also bear evidence that he often wrote for the benefit of those in a nearby location or for Christians in general.[28]

---

[25]Irenaeus, *Haer.* 3.11.8.

[26]The writer of the fragment states that "the blessed apostle Paul himself, following the example of his predecessor John, writes by name to only seven churches." Translation from Bruce Metzger, *The Canon of the New Testament*, 305-7. In addition to the Muratorian Fragment, witness to the seven-church tradition may be observed in the writings of Cyprian (*Test.* 1.20), Jerome (*Epist.* 53), and Victorinus of Pettau (*Commentary on the Apocalypse*). In addition, Amphilochius of Iconium creatively writes in his *Iambics for Seleucus* that Paul's epistles included "twice seven epistles." Finally, it is widely believed that there were seven original Marcionite Prologues. If this was indeed the case, it would provide further evidence for the early emergence and influence of the seven-church tradition.

[27]Dahl, "The Particularity of the Pauline Epistles," 262.

[28]As I have argued elsewhere, the writings that were preserved in the Pauline corpus appear to have been preserved not by chance but in large measure because of their perceived universal relevance. For additional insight, see my discussion of the "lost letters of Paul" in Laird, *The Pauline Corpus in Early Christianity*, 307-16; Benjamin P. Laird and Miguel Echevarria, *40 Questions about the Apostle Paul* (Grand Rapids, MI: Kregel, 2023), chap. 17.

Those who have served in some type of leadership position or raised children (a leadership position if there ever was one!) understand that on certain occasions it is beneficial to remind an entire group of particular expectations or of the importance of observing certain principles or truths. This is often the case even when it may have been a single individual who was responsible for prompting the instruction. A mother, for example, might remind all of her children of the importance of looking both ways when crossing a street after observing one child thoughtlessly chase a ball without looking for cars. Even though the mother's reminder may have been provoked by the actions of one child, she may choose to address all of her children together simply as a reminder of the importance of the practice. In a similar manner, there may have been occasions in which Paul addressed a number of subjects that were of special concern to those in a particular location—whether in a remote area or in his vicinity—while doing so with the intention and awareness that they would ultimately be read by Christians throughout the Mediterranean world. As Michael Kruger rightly explains, "While the New Testament documents had occasional dimensions to them, we should also note that they were still intended for wider distribution."[29] This is in keeping with Tertullian's assertion many centuries ago that "when the apostle [Paul] wrote to some he wrote to all."[30] In sum, the study of the content and background of the Pauline Epistles indicates that Paul often wrote with a primary, secondary, and even a universal audience in view. This particular insight allows interpreters to avoid the mistake of treating the Epistles strictly as private everyday letters of antiquity on the one hand or as literary documents disconnected from their historical context on the other.

The "original audience" and the authorship of the Pastoral Epistles. To this point we have emphasized that Paul's letters were often written for the benefit of multiple audiences. He seems to have written Romans,

---

[29]Michael J. Kruger, *The Question of Canon: Challenging the Status Quo in the New Testament Debate* (Downers Grove, IL: IVP Academic, 2013), 120. The fourth chapter of Kruger's volume makes a compelling case that the New Testament authors were aware of the authority of their writings.
[30]Tertullian, *Marc.* 5.17.1 (*ANF* 3).

for example, for the benefit of those living in both Rome (the stated recipients) and Corinth (the *Nebenadressat*), while treating a number of subjects of universal relevance. But what are we to make of writings that are addressed to specific individuals such as the Pastoral Epistles? How might the universal relevance of a writing written from one individual to another be recognized as universally relevant?

As noted above, the persuasion that the Pastorals are pseudonymous writings composed by an unknown writer led to Deissmann's conclusion that they were designed for a wide audience. Why would one bother, it might be asked, to write in the name of an apostle or well-known Christian leader for the benefit of a single individual? For Deissmann and others, the fact that these writings are addressed to individuals does not demand that they be understood as personal or private letters. According to a number of interpreters, "Timothy" and "Titus" were not the true original recipients of these writings; rather, these are names that were used simply to place the reader in the first-century world of Paul. According to this perspective, the writings should not be regarded as private correspondence to trusted companions but as well-developed instructions intended to be implemented throughout the Christian world.

One of the many well-known objections to the authenticity of the Pastoral Epistles is the nature of its content. Scholars have found it difficult to accept that Timothy and Titus would have been in need of basic instruction on matters of central importance such as the qualifications of elders and deacons, the dangers of false teaching, or the necessity of good works. As I. Howard Marshall explains, "The difficulty for Pauline authorship here is the nature and manner of the instruction given to colleagues of Paul who have worked with him for many years and should be in no need of what at times seems elementary instruction that should have been well known to them. There is also a formality and impersonal character which it is hard to envisage between people who have been close colleagues and companions."[31]

---

[31] I. Howard Marshall, *A Critical and Exegetical Commentary on the Pastoral Epistles*, ICC (London: T&T Clark, 1999), 74-75.

Marshall's observation is certainly perceptive. One finds it hard to imagine that Paul found it necessary to provide his trusted colleagues with basic instructions on several rudimentary subjects after spending significant time with them. A sensible explanation for the inclusion of this material is possible, however, with a more nuanced understanding of Paul's intended audience. If he often wrote for the benefit of a primary (e.g., Timothy and Titus), secondary (e.g., those in Ephesus, Crete, or in his nearby location), and a universal audience, the more formal character of the Epistles and its treatment of certain subjects would be much less difficult to explain.

Pseudonymity is certainly not the only explanation for the more formal style of the letters or for its treatment of various subjects. Assuming the authenticity of the writings, we may conclude that they were written in part to publicly endorse the mission and authority of Paul's representatives, to provide clarity regarding several matters crucial to their mission, and to simultaneously address a number of topics that were of relevance to those in Paul's vicinity and elsewhere. Some may ultimately determine that the Pastorals are inauthentic on the basis of a variety of other factors (e.g., their language, structure, style, theological content, chronological matters, or early textual witnesses to the Pauline corpus), but a dismissal of their authenticity on the sole basis of their literary genre alone would seem problematic in light of Paul's proclivity to compose his letters for the benefit of multiple audiences.

CONCLUSIONS

The first three chapters of this volume have explored ancient literary practices in the Greco-Roman world that provide insight related to the composition of the New Testament writings. Contrary to common assumptions, it was suggested in the first chapter that many of the New Testament authors likely worked directly with a number of individuals to compose and distribute their writings. The second chapter challenged the perception that there was a single original autograph produced of each writing, suggesting instead that multiple copies of the canonical writings were likely produced by the author's secretary or his companions at the end of the compositional process. It was further observed that the production of multiple copies may help explain some of the more complex textual issues in the New Testament. Finally, it was suggested in this chapter that each of the New Testament writings were intended for public use and that our concept of an "original audience" is in need of additional nuance and further reflection. It was seen, for example, that the apostle Paul frequently addressed certain subjects not merely for the benefit of those explicitly cited in the greeting of his writings but also for those in his nearby vicinity and elsewhere. This observation has clear implications for our understanding of the background of his letters. Just as one would not read the Gospel of Luke as though it is a private work designed for the sole benefit of Theophilus, so too should we avoid the notion that the Pauline Epistles were written for the sole benefit of the recipients directly cited in the text. In fact, the inclusion of these writings in the canon is a testament to their universal relevance.

Having now considered several literary practices that were common in the Greco-Roman world and what they may reveal about the manner in which the New Testament writings were composed and produced, our study will now transition to other important aspects of the study of the canon. After exploring several of the theological controversies and historical events that are often thought to have played an integral role in the establishment of the canon (chapter four), we will evaluate some of the more important witnesses to the early state and development of the canon (chapter five) and the circumstances that most likely led to the recognition of certain writings as canonical Scripture (chapter six). The volume will then conclude with an assessment of how the criterion of apostolicity may have impacted the formation of the New Testament (chapter seven) and a reflection on the apostolic authority of the canonical writings (chapter eight).

PART TWO

QUESTIONS RELATING to the FORMATION of the NEW TESTAMENT CANON

THEOLOGICAL CONTROVERSIES AND THE FORMATION OF THE NEW TESTAMENT CANON

DID THEOLOGICAL CONTROVERSIES PLAY A DECISIVE ROLE
IN THE FORMATION OF THE NEW TESTAMENT CANON?

*The crucible for the long process of canon formation was provided
by a complex interplay of historical circumstances, theological
controversies, traditions of interpretation, regional usages, judgments of ecclesiastical authorities, and even the technical aspects
of book manufacture and textual transmission. The scope of the
canon is therefore indebted to a wide range of contingent historical
factors and from a historical standpoint is largely fortuitous.*

HARRY Y. GAMBLE, *THE NEW TESTAMENT CANON*

OUR TREATMENT OF THE FORMATION of the New Testament canon will begin with a consideration of the possibility that theological disputes were directly related to the canon's formation. It is often assumed that it was necessary for the church to achieve a consensus on the scope of the canon before certain theological controversies could be adequately addressed. Without first achieving a consensus on the specific writings that are to be recognized as authoritative Scripture, it was simply not possible, some would suggest, for the church to achieve unity on key doctrinal matters such as the nature of Christ, the Trinity, and a host of other doctrines. As long as Christians were divided over which writings constitute sacred Scripture, theological conflict remained inescapable. The reason for this, it might be argued, is that several of the writings that achieved popularity in early Christianity articulated key doctrines in strikingly different ways. It would seem, for example, that those who recognized noncanonical works such as the *Gospel of Thomas* or the *Gospel of Peter* would have been much more likely to assume an understanding of the nature of Christ in significantly different ways than those who recognized only the four canonical Gospels. It is often observed, for instance, that the *Gospel of Peter* is more conducive to a docetic understanding of the nature of Christ.[1]

It is also possible, of course, to consider the relationship between the emergence of the canon and the theological controversies that took place in early Christianity from an alternative vantage point. Rather than viewing the general agreement about the core doctrines of the faith as a consequence of an established canon, one might argue that the formation of the canon was the natural byproduct of a theological consensus that was achieved at some point in early Christianity. Understood in this light, the works that were ultimately recognized as part of the canon are the works that were thought to be consistent with the beliefs that become dominant during a particular period of church history. Until a consensus related to the key doctrines of the faith had emerged, Christianity was simply too diverse, some might argue, for there to have been widespread recognition about the contours of the canon.

The perspective that early Christianity was characterized by widespread theological diversity has been championed most ardently in recent years by Bart Ehrman, one of a select number of scholars who has made a mark in the academy while also playing a significant role in shaping popular perceptions about the origin of the New Testament

---

[1] William R. Farmer and Denis M. Farkasfalvy, *The Formation of the New Testament Canon: An Ecumenical Approach* (Ramsey, NJ: Paulist, 1983), 30.

and the state of early Christianity. It has been observed that many of Ehrman's viewpoints parallel the work of the German historian and scholar Walter Bauer (1877–1960) who, among other things, was known for his influential volume on the nature and expansion of early Christianity and a notable Greek lexicon that remains widely used today.[2]

From the perspective of Bauer and Ehrman, the core beliefs and practices that are now commonly associated with Christianity did not always represent the viewpoints of a sizable number of Christians. To be sure, many of the theological beliefs that are often considered to be central to the Christian faith today were present in one form or another and affirmed by many early Christians. It is important to recognize, however, that there was a wide range of "Christianities" during the early centuries of the Christian era, many of which offered unique and conflicting perspectives on the nature of Christ and several other theological subjects. In many areas, "nonorthodox" viewpoints were actually predominant. The perspective that early Christianity was characterized by widespread theological diversity may be clearly observed in the following excerpt from one of Ehrman's earliest treatments of the subject:

> The wide diversity of early Christianity may be seen above all in the theological beliefs embraced by people who understood themselves to be followers of Jesus. In the second and third centuries there were, of course, Christians who believed in one God. But there were others who insisted that there were two. Some said there were thirty. Others claimed there were 365. . . . There were yet other Christians who said that Jesus never died. How could some of these views even be considered Christian? Or to put the question differently, how could people who considered themselves Christian hold such views? . . . Why didn't they just read the New Testament? It is because there was no New Testament. To be sure, the books that were eventually collected into the New Testament had been written by the second century. But they had not yet been gathered into a widely recognized and authoritative canon of

---

[2]One of Bauer's most influential works regarding the history of the early church is Walter Bauer, *Orthodoxy and Heresy in Earliest Christianity*, ed. Robert Kraft and Gerhard Krodel, trans. Paul Achtemeier (Philadelphia: Fortress, 1971).

Scripture. And there were other books written as well, with equally im-pressive pedigrees—other Gospels, Acts, Epistles, and Apocalypses claiming to be written by the earthly apostles of Jesus.[3]

As this passage illustrates, Ehrman regards the New Testament writings only as a partial witness to the beliefs and practices of early Christians. From his perspective, there is nothing inherently authori-tative about the canonical writings. In fact, he even suggests that many noncanonical works enjoyed "equally impressive pedigrees." The impli-cation of Ehrman's perspective is clear: the works of the New Testament do not bear any authority on their own and merely reflect the view-points of one particular segment of early Christianity that eventually came to dominate. If we really want to understand the character and nature of early Christianity, we must therefore look outside of the New Testament to the large body of noncanonical Christian literature that has survived. It is only by carefully examining the wider body of early Christian works, it might be suggested, that we can begin to appreciate the diverse nature of Christianity in the early centuries.[4] This is one of the reasons that there has been an increased amount of attention in recent years to noncanonical works.

If Christianity was as diverse as Ehrman and others have claimed, how was a consensus on key doctrinal matters ultimately achieved? Proponents of Ehrman's perspective might argue that the emergence of

---

[3]Bart D. Ehrman, *Lost Christianities: The Battles for Scripture and the Faiths We Never Knew* (New York: Oxford University Press, 2003), 2-3.

[4]For the alternative perspective that there were indeed core beliefs shared by many early Chris-tians, see Larry W. Hurtado, *Lord Jesus Christ: Devotion to Jesus in Earliest Christianity* (Grand Rapids, MI: Eerdmans, 2005). Other notable treatments of early Christology include the follow-ing: Martin Hengel, *Studies in Early Christology*, trans. Rollin Kearns (Edinburgh: T&T Clark, 1995); James D. G. Dunn, *Christology in the Making: A New Testament Inquiry into the Origins of the Doctrine of the Incarnation*, rev. ed (Grand Rapids, MI: Eerdmans, 1996); Dunn, *Did the First Christians Worship Jesus? The New Testament Evidence* (Louisville, KY: Westminster John Knox, 2010); C. F. D. Moule, *The Origin of Christology* (Cambridge: Cambridge University Press, 1977). Richard Bauckham, *Jesus and the God of Israel: God Crucified and Other Studies on the New Testa-ment's Christology of Divine Identity* (Grand Rapids, MI: Eerdmans, 2008); Oscar Cullmann, *The Christology of the New Testament*, trans. Shirley Guthrie and Charles Hall, rev. ed. (London: SCM, 1959); Michael F. Bird, *Jesus Among the Gods: Early Christology in the Greco-Roman World* (Waco, TX: Baylor University Press, 2022). For a number of primary texts relevant to the study of early Christology, see Gregory R. Lanier, *Corpus Christologicum: Texts and Translations for the Study of Jewish Messianism and Early Christology* (Peabody, MA: Hendrickson, 2021).

"orthodox" Christianity was the result of a concerted effort by the church's leadership to reach a consensus on doctrinal matters. The theological disputes that took place in the earlier centuries tended to be more localized and therefore less consequential, at least with respect to their influence on the broader movement. However, once Christianity became the dominant faith in the Roman world and the leadership of the church became more centralized, decisive measures were taken to arrive at a consensus on the core elements of the faith. In response to various theological disputes that threatened to divide Christendom, a number of major ecclesiastical councils were convened beginning in the fourth century. The theological viewpoints of the "winners" of these conflicts are thought to have eventually become associated with orthodoxy.[5] This was accomplished in large part, some would suggest, through the suppression of writings that stood at odds with the "orthodox" position and the promotion of the writings that were thought to support orthodox perspectives. As a consensus emerged surrounding the central doctrines of the faith, so too did a consensus form around the specific works that were recognized as sacred Scripture.

For Ehrman, the struggle to reach a theological consensus was not simply the result of competing hermeneutical approaches or exegetical disputes over key texts. It is certainly the case that early Christians did not always agree on how certain passages were to be read and applied. From his perspective, however, the theological diversity that characterized early Christianity is indicative of a lack of consensus about the scope of a canon. Even if a concept of a canon of sacred writings was present in the early centuries, there does not appear to have been a consensus about the particular writings that were to be recognized as authoritative Scripture. Widespread recognition of the specific writings that are a part of the Christian canon is thought to have been achieved only after the leadership of the church was able to effectively deal with

---

[5]For a critique of these viewpoints, see Michael J. Kruger and Andreas Köstenberger, *The Heresy of Orthodoxy: How Contemporary Culture's Fascination with Diversity Has Reshaped Our Understanding of Early Christianity* (Downers Grove, IL: InterVarsity Press, 2010); Paul Hartog, ed., *Orthodoxy and Heresy in Early Christian Contexts: Reconsidering the Bauer Thesis* (Eugene, OR: Pickwick, 2015).

a number of theological controversies that threatened to divide the church. Opinions differ with respect to the specific events and controversies that may have eventually precipitated the emergence of the canon. What is often assumed, however, is that the formation of the canon was largely a consequence of the major theological controversies that took place in early Christianity. Rather than a universally recognized canon that served as the foundation for early Christian doctrine, many remain convinced that those who were responsible for shaping early Christian teaching played a leading role in determining which writings were eventually recognized as part of the canon.

While it is beyond the scope of this chapter to offer a robust history of each major theological controversy that took place in early Christianity, it will be helpful to briefly consider two commonly held perspectives about the formation of the New Testament canon.[6] In addition to the possibility that initial attempts to establish a canon of Scripture were prompted by the threat of Marcion during the second century, we will consider the popular perception that the major christological controversies that took place during the fourth century provided the conditions necessary for the church to reach a widespread consensus on the extent of the canon.

The Influence of Marcion

A common perspective among contemporary scholars is that Marcion of Sinope (d. AD 155–65), a second-century figure widely condemned as a heretic, essentially forced the leadership of the church to begin the process of canonization.[7] Among other things, Marcion was notorious

---

[6]In addition to the major controversies and movements discussed below, some scholars point to the influence of other theological traditions such as the various Gnostic sects or Montanism.

[7]For a treatment of Marcion's life and legacy, see Judith Lieu, *Marcion and the Making of a Heretic: God and Scripture in the Second Century* (Cambridge: Cambridge University Press, 2015); Barbara Aland, "Marcion/Marcioniten," *TRE* 22 (1992): 89-101; Jason BeDuhn, *The First New Testament: Marcion's Scriptural Canon* (Salem, OR: Polebridge, 2013), 10-23; Ehrman, *Lost Christianities*, 103-12; E. C. Blackman, *Marcion and his Influence* (London: SPCK, 1948), 1-14; Heikki Räisänen, "Marcion," in *The Blackwell Companion to Paul*, ed. Stephen Westerholm (Chichester, UK: Wiley Blackwell, 2011), 301-15; Sebastian Moll, *The Arch-Heretic Marcion*, WUNT 250 (Tübingen: Mohr Siebeck, 2010); Moll, "Three Against Tertullian: The Second Tradition about Marcion's Life," *JTS* 59 (2008): 169-80; Markus Vinzent, "Marcion's Gospel and the Beginnings of Early Christianity," *ASE* 32 (2015): 55-87.

for espousing the viewpoint that the God of the ancient Hebrew people was a separate deity who was responsible for the creation of an evil world and that this God is not to be associated with Jesus or his Father. Jesus' purpose was to redeem the evil world from its fallen state, a purpose that placed him in direct opposition to the God revealed in the Hebrew Bible.[8] In keeping with these convictions, Marcion came to reject anything he regarded to be closely connected to Jewish beliefs and customs. Because of this, he was often charged with distorting the teachings of the apostles in an effort to expunge what he deemed to be the more objectionable facets of Christian belief and practice.

Needless to say, Marcion was not especially popular among many of the church's leaders. One famous story that is illustrative of the animosity of many toward him was passed down by Jerome. He recounts that Polycarp, the eminent bishop of Smyrna, was in Rome on one occasion to discuss matters pertaining to the observance of Passover. During this visit Polycarp happened by chance to encounter Marcion. "Do you know us?" Marcion asked when his delegation passed by Polycarp. Answering in the affirmative, Polycarp is said to have sharply retorted, "I know the firstborn of the devil!"[9] Regardless of whether this exchange took place in the precise fashion described in this account, the story is certainly reflective of the intense disdain that many had for this controversial figure during the second and third centuries.[10] Several writers such as Irenaeus and Tertullian expressed nothing but derision for Marcion and his teachings, the latter ôf whom even composed a massive five-book work in the early third century simply titled *Against Marcion* (*Adversus Marcionem*).

Historically, Marcion is perhaps best known for his unique teaching about the God of the Old Testament and for the communities that formed under his direction after he separated himself from the church

---

[8]Barbara Aland, "Sünde und Erlösung bei Marcion und die Konsequenz für die sogennante beiden Götter Marcions," in *Marcion und siene kirchengeschichtliche Wirkung*, ed. Gerhard May and Katharina Greschat, TU 150 (Berlin: de Gruyter, 2002), 147-58.

[9]Jerome, *Vir. ill.* 17 (*NPNF* 2.3).

[10]For a discussion on how Marcion's viewpoints were received by orthodox theologians, see Einar Thomassen, "Orthodoxy and Heresy in Second-Century Rome," *HTR* 97 (2004): 241-56.

in Rome. Over the last century, however, the possible role that he may have played in the formation of the New Testament canon has also garnered considerable attention. From the testimony that has survived in the writings of Tertullian and others, it is widely assumed that the communities that followed Marcion's teaching adopted his version of the Gospel of Luke—what some scholars refer to as the *Evangelikon*[11]— as well as an edited collection of ten of the Pauline letters sometimes referred to as the *Apostolikon*.[12] Scholars do not always agree about the degree to which Marcion may have edited these writings or why he apparently recognized only a small number of Christian writings as Scripture.[13] One common suggestion is that he only recognized the relatively small body of works that he deemed to be largely free of Jewish influence. Because Marcion is often thought to have been among the first to recognize a clearly defined corpus of Pauline writings, what might be determined regarding his work and influence is of significance for our understanding of the early formation of the New Testament. In our treatment of this consequential figure, we will briefly consider the probable content and features of Marcion's *Apostolikon*

---

[11]Not all scholars assume that the gospel account that circulated in Marcionite communities was an edited version of Luke's Gospel. See, for example, David Williams, "Reconsidering Marcion's Gospel," *JBL* 108 (1989): 477-96. According to Williams, it is inconclusive how Marcion may have developed his gospel, which sources he likely had access to, and even if he had even read the material that he is often accused of omitting.

[12]Several attempts have been made in recent scholarship to reconstruct the text of Marcion's canon of Scripture. See BeDuhn, *The First New Testament*; Dieter T. Roth, *The Text of Marcion's Gospel*, NTTSD 49 (Leiden: Brill, 2015); Matthias Klinghardt, *The Oldest Gospel and the Formation of the Canonical Gospels*, 2 vols. (Leuven: Peeters, 2021). Additional works treating Marcion's corpus of Scripture include Ulrich Schmid, *Marcion und sein Apostolos: Rekonstrucktion und historische Einordnung der Marcionitischen Paulusbriefausgabe*, ANTF 25 (Berlin: de Gruyer, 1995); Dieter T. Roth, "Marcion and the Early New Testament Text," in *The Early Text of the New Testament*, ed. Charles E. Hill and Michael J. Kruger (New York: Oxford University Press, 2012), 302-12; John James Clabeaux, *The Lost Edition of the Letters of Paul: A Reassessment of the Text of the Pauline Corpus Attested by Marcion*, CBQMS 21 (Washington, DC: Catholic Biblical Association of America, 1989); Markus Vinzent, "The Influence of Marcion on the Formation of the New Testament Canon," in *The New Testament Canon in Contemporary Research*, ed. Stanley E. Porter and Benjamin P. Laird, TENTS (Leiden: Brill, forthcoming).

[13]Earlier scholarship tended to assume that Marcion edited existing writings with a very heavy hand. This perspective has been challenged however by contemporary scholars who have suggested that some of the unique readings associated with Marcion may have originated from early witnesses to the Pauline writings that are no longer extant. See, for example, Clabeaux, *The Lost Edition of the Letters of Paul*; Schmid, *Marcion und sein Apostolos*; BeDuhn, *The First New Testament*.

and what role he may have played in the early history and development of the Pauline corpus in particular and the New Testament in general.

Marcion's scriptural collections. Although no textual witnesses to the *Evangelikon* or the *Apostolikon* have survived, several features of the scriptural collections that circulated in Marcionite communities are known through the writings of Marcion's opponents, most notably those of Tertullian.[14] In his *Against Marcion* (*Adversus Marcionem*), for example, Tertullian enumerated several of what he regarded as Marcion's theological errors and faulty interpretations, working carefully through his gospel as well as his collection of Paul's epistles, apparently in the order in which they appeared (see *Marc.* 5.2-21). It is interesting that Tertullian discusses Marcion's treatment of Paul's letters in a sequence that differs from what may be observed in many of the early Greek witnesses to the New Testament. If it was indeed the case that Tertullian's polemic followed the arrangement of the Epistles as they appeared in the *Apostolikon*, it may be possible that Marcion maintained a version of the Pauline corpus that included ten letters that were arranged in the following order: Galatians, 1–2 Corinthians, Romans, 1–2 Thessalonians, Laodiceans (his apparent title for the canonical writing known as Ephesians), Colossians, Philippians, and Philemon.[15] One of the most notable features of this arrangement is the placement of Galatians at the beginning of the corpus. There are several possible explanations for this. One possibility is that Marcion placed this work at the head of the collection simply because of his high estimation for its content. Because of its stern rebuke of those who wished to impose Jewish practices on Gentile converts, it might be assumed that Marcion was drawn to this writing and viewed it as a fitting introduction to the teaching of Paul.

---

[14]The two primary witnesses to the biblical text associated with Marcion are Tertullian's five-volume work *Against Marcion* (*Adversus Marcionem*) and Epiphanius's *Refutation of All Heresies* (*Panarion*). References to Marcion also appear in the extant writings of Adamantius, a lesser-known fourth-century writer.

[15]There are several questions related to the placement of Philemon. Tertullian's treatment of Marcion would suggest that Philemon was placed last in Marcion's New Testament. According to Epiphanius, however, Colossians appears to have been followed by Philemon with Philippians placed at the end of the corpus. Epiphanius, *Pan.* 42.9.4.

Also of interest is the fact that neither the Pastoral Epistles nor Hebrews appear to have been included in Marcion's *Apostolikon*. In Tertullian's extensive criticisms of Marcion, he does not refer to these writings, though he does accuse him of omitting several works. How might these apparent omissions be explained? One solution is that neither the Pastorals nor Hebrews were known to Marcion when he edited his collection around the middle of the second century. This would seem highly improbable, however, as there is strong evidence that these writings were well-known by the mid-second century. There is also very little in these writings that would seem to have been more objectionable to Marcion than what is contained in the other ten Pauline Epistles. In fact, it may have actually been the case that the emphasis placed in Hebrews on the superiority of Jesus over the institutions and practices associated with the old covenant would have resonated particularly well with him. The most plausible explanation therefore seems to be that Marcion did not make unilateral decisions regarding which writings to include in his *Apostolikon*, but that he simply adopted an existing edition of the Pauline corpus that contained only ten epistles.

The canonical significance of Marcion. Often regarded as the first known individual to circulate a collection of writings as Scripture, Marcion is widely believed to have essentially forced the leaders of the greater church to recognize a particular body of works as authoritative Scripture. As Helmut Koester argues, "The impetus for the formation of the canon, that is, for the singling out of a limited number of traditional writings of Christian authors as authoritative Holy Scripture, came from a radical theologian of the Pauline churches: Marcion."[16] The prospect of a well-known and controversial figure playing a leading role in the establishment of a body of sacred Scripture was simply not something that could be tolerated, many have concluded. As a result, several leaders of the church are thought to have swiftly recognized a larger body of writings than the collection that was circulating in the Marcionite communities. "Before Marcion there was

---

[16]Helmut Koester, *Introduction to the New Testament. Volume Two: History and Literature of Early Christianity* (Philadelphia: Fortress, 1982), 8.

no New Testament," writes Jason BeDuhn. "With him it took its first shape, and after him it gradually developed into the form we now know. . . . So it was that Marcion collected, for the first time in history, a set of authoritative writings intended to be afforded a status above that of other Christian literature."[17]

Although a number of scholars over the last century have shared the viewpoint expressed by BeDuhn, not all would agree with this conclusion. In fact, a growing number of contemporary scholars are of the persuasion that Marcion's legacy, at least as it relates to the formation of the Christian canon, was much more limited than is sometimes suggested. According to John Barton, when Marcion selected books to incorporate into his collection of sacred writings, one of his purposes was to restrict certain works that were already recognized as sacred Scripture in a number of Christian communities. He also makes the important observation that early readers do not appear to have used the canonical writings either more or less frequently after the lifetime of Marcion than they did before.[18] It may have been the case, therefore, that Marcion simply recognized a number of writings from a larger body of works that had already been widely regarded as authoritative Scripture and that he was not as innovative as is often alleged. As Barton concludes, it was his "doctrine that was novel, not the literary forms in which it was expressed."[19]

Although the evidence that Marcion played a significant role in shaping or establishing the canon may not be as strong as is often alleged, he remains an important witness to the state of the canon in the second century. In particular, the textual and canonical features of the *Apostolikon* provide valuable insights related to the early history of the Pauline corpus. Produced roughly a half century prior to $\mathfrak{P}^{46}$, one of the earliest and most important Greek manuscripts, Marcion's *Apostolikon* provides an important witness to a particular edition of the

---

[17]BeDuhn, *The First New Testament*, 6.
[18]John Barton, "Marcion Revisited," in *The Canon Debate*, ed. Lee Martin McDonald and James A. Sanders (Peabody, MA: Hendrickson, 2002), 342-43. See also, Barton, *Holy Writings, Sacred Text: The Canon in Early Christianity* (Louisville, KY: Westminster John Knox, 1997), 35-62.
[19]Barton, "*Marcion Revisited*," 354.

Pauline Epistles that was apparently more limited in scope and contained a unique arrangement of the canonical material.

CONSTANTINE AND THE THEOLOGICAL CONTROVERSIES OF THE FOURTH CENTURY

In addition to the perspective that Marcion played a significant role in prompting the formation of the New Testament canon, it has also been assumed that the events that transpired following the rise of Emperor Constantine and the so-called peace of the church (c. AD 313) played a decisive role in the formation of the canon. One common perspective is that Constantine and/or various fourth-century church councils were largely responsible for establishing the extent of the canon and for shaping it into the form that is known today. In what follows, we will briefly evaluate these viewpoints.

Constantine and the New Testament canon. It is difficult to overstate the influence of the Emperor Constantine on the course of church history. Throughout much of the first three centuries of the Christian era, the Roman Empire actively sought to suppress the expansion of the faith. The effort to curtail the advancement of Christianity ebbed and flowed and was applied in some locations more intensely than in others. There were, however, several periods in which large numbers of Christians endured significant hardships as a result of the specific measures enacted by Roman authorities. Some of the more intense periods of persecution took place during the reigns of Nero and Domitian in the first century; Trajan, Hadrian, and Marcus Aurelius during the second century; Decius, Valerian, and Diocletian during the third century; and Galerius during the early fourth century. The effort to thwart the expansion of Christianity largely came to an end during the rule of Constantine the Great, the first emperor to identify as a Christian, though many Christians experienced persecution for a brief time during the rule of Julian the Apostate in the mid-fourth century and on other occasions.

Upon the death of his father, Constantius I, Constantine began to reign as one of four rulers who together comprised the *tetrarchy*, a system of Roman rule established just over a decade prior by Diocletian. Under this system, two emperors (the *augusti*) ruled Roman territory—one in the East and the other in the West—with junior partners (the *caesares*) serving alongside each. The assumption was that each Caesar would eventually become the supreme ruler if they outlived the emperor and everything unfolded as planned (which seems to have been a rarity!). This system was well intentioned and arguably sound in theory but was incapable of surviving the ambitions of four powerful figures. Constantine was declared the Caesar of the western regions of the empire in AD 306, though his army recognized him sole ruler of the West, not just as Caesar. During the ensuing years, he defeated several of his rivals, including Licinius and Maxentius, prominent figures who previously served alongside him as part of the tetrarchy. In the autumn of 312, Constantine famously defeated Maxentius at the Battle of the Milvian Bridge just outside of Rome. This victory was followed by several others, eventually leading to the defeat of each of his rivals. By 324, Constantine had become the first figure in many years to serve alone as the unquestioned ruler of the empire.

At the time Constantine came to power, Christians had compelling reasons to distrust the Roman authorities and to question their motivations and intentions. Previous emperors such as Diocletian and Galerius actively sought to suppress the growth of the church, treating Christianity as a threat to the unity, peace, and prosperity of the empire. In contrast to his predecessors, Constantine quickly took measures to ensure that Christians would no longer be the target of persecution or harassment from Roman authorities, while enacting a number of policies designed to benefit the church. Early in his reign, for example, he approved of the so-called Edict of Milan, an agreement made with his then coemperor Licinius in 313. This "edict," as it has been labeled, was built on a recent measure of Galerius and ensured that individuals would no longer be targeted for persecution simply for engaging in Christian worship. Throughout the remainder of his reign, Constantine continued to treat Christians favorably. In addition to openly identifying himself as a Christian, he is said to have funded the construction of several churches, placed a large number of the clergy on the imperial payroll, convened a large ecumenical council in Nicaea, and enacted several policies which he considered advantageous to the expansion and well-being of Christianity.

For many Christians living at the time, Constantine was nothing short of a miraculous gift from God. After years of oppression and harassment from the Roman authorities, there was popular sentiment that they now had an ally at the highest level of government who would not just tolerate their faith but play an active role in accommodating and even advancing it. This conviction is expressed most clearly and colorfully by the bishop and church historian Eusebius in his *Life of Constantine* (*Vita Constantini*). For Eusebius, Constantine was the direct conduit of God's blessing to humankind and the providential means by which the church would continue to expand and thrive. The work of Eusebius includes what are purported to be firsthand accounts of Constantine's reflections about the Christian faith and his perceptions about the role to which he had been providentially appointed. In one passage, for example, Constantine is supposed to have stated, "He examined my service and approved it as fit for his own purpose."[20] Whether defeating God's enemies on the battlefield, eradicating deadly disease, or eliminating evil from society, Constantine firmly believed that he was appointed by God for a divine purpose. Such convictions did not belong to Constantine alone, however. At the end of his work, Eusebius makes the extravagant claim that

> He alone of all the Roman emperors has honoured God the All-sovereign with exceeding godly piety; he alone has publicly proclaimed to all the word of Christ; he alone has honoured his Church as no other since time began; he alone has destroyed all polytheistic error, and exposed every kind of idolatry; and surely he alone has deserved in life itself and after death such things as none could say has ever been achieved by any other among either Greeks or barbarians, or even

---

[20]*Vit. Const.* 2.28. All translations of this work derive from *Eusebius, Life of Constantine: Translated with Introduction and Commentary*, trans. Averil Cameron and Stuart Hall (Oxford: Clarendon, 1999).

among the ancient Romans, for his like has never been recorded from the beginning of time until our day.[21]

In view of the unique posture of Constantine toward Christianity and the significant ways in which his policies changed the status of Christians in the Roman world, it comes as little surprise that he has been the focus of considerable attention throughout church history. Few figures from the fourth century, or from any time in the Roman era for that matter, are discussed so frequently. Despite this significant attention and interest, a number of questions remain about the nature of Constantine's faith, the impact of his policies on the history of the church, and his possible influence on the formation of the New Testament canon.[22]

With regard to the canon, it is often supposed that Constantine's decrees and measures played a role, either directly or indirectly, in orchestrating the events which effectively established the New Testament canon. Many assume that the first ecumenical council that convened in Nicaea in 325 played a pivotal role in determining which writings were to be included in the Christian canon. Others have suggested that Constantine played a more indirect role in shaping the canon through his commission for the production of fifty Bibles or through his effort to suppress movements regarded as unorthodox. Echoing the persuasion of many scholars, Burton Mack contends, "The event that triggered the creation of the Christian Bible was the conversion of Constantine and the sudden reversal of imperial status experienced by the Christian churches."[23] Given the common assumption that Constantine made a significant impact on the development of the canon, it will be helpful to briefly consider the possible significance of the fifty copies of the Bible commissioned by Constantine and the role that various councils such as Nicaea may have played in the origin of the canon.

---

[21]*Vit. Const.* 4.75.

[22]Readers may wish to consult the thorough study of H. A. Drake who argues that Constantine recognized a potential means of unifying his empire in Christianity. *Constantine and the Bishops: The Politics of Intolerance* (Baltimore, MD: Johns Hopkins University Press, 2000).

[23]Burton Mack, *Who Wrote the New Testament? The Making of the Christian Myth* (New York: Harper One, 1996), 287.

Constantine's fifty Bibles. Our knowledge of Constantine's order to produce fifty copies of the Scriptures—no meager gift by fourth-century standards—comes to us exclusively through the testimony of Eusebius, who, as cited above, believed that the hand of the Lord guided Constantine's reign. Eusebius preserved an important letter he received from Constantine, which we will cite in full:

> Victor Constantinus, Maximus Augustus, to Eusebius.
>
> In the City which bears our name by the sustaining providence of the Saviour God a great mass of people has attached itself to the most holy Church, so that with everything there enjoying great growth it is particularly fitting that more churches should be established. Be ready therefore to act urgently on the decision which we have reached. It appeared proper to indicate to your Intelligence that you should order fifty volumes with ornamental leather bindings, easily legible and convenient for portable use, to be copied by skilled calligraphists well trained in the art, copies that is of the Divine Scriptures, the provision and use of which you well know to be necessary for reading in church. Written instructions have been sent by our Clemency to the man who is in charge of the diocese that he see to the supply of all the materials needed to produce them. The preparation of the written volumes with utmost speed shall be the task of your Diligence. You are entitled by the authority of this our letter to the use of two public vehicles for transportation. The fine copies may thus most readily be transported to us for inspection; one of the deacons of your own congregation will presumably carry out this task, and when he reaches us he will experience our generosity.
>
> God preserve you, dear brother.[24]

Several details in this account are of interest. We first observe that the commissioned Bibles were to be distributed throughout the churches in the city of Constantinople, the city "which bears our name,"

---

[24]*Vit. Const.* 4.36. A report of the completion of the Bibles is provided in the following section (4.37). The precise date of the commission is unclear. Scholars have suggested a commissioning as early as 322 to as late as 337, the year of Constantine's death.

and that Eusebius was charged with overseeing the effort, a task he was most certainly willing to embrace given his fondness of the Scriptures and his interest in their reception (see *Hist. eccl.* 3.3.5-7 and 3.25.1-7). Finally, Constantine's instruction may give the impression that he was more concerned about the aesthetic quality of the Bibles than he was about the specific content that was to be included. This may not have been the case, but it is an impression given in the letter.

Contrary to what might be assumed, the order to produce fifty Bibles for the churches of Constantinople is unlikely to have been a straightforward process involving little more than the recruitment of scribes and the acquisition of the necessary materials.[25] As part of his task of overseeing such a large production, it might be assumed that Eusebius would have been responsible for determining the specific writings to include in each copy. The fact that he was commissioned to produce multiple volumes containing "the Divine Scriptures" would suggest that he was entrusted to produce copies of a specific collection, yet it is not entirely clear which specific writings Eusebius would have been expected to produce, if there even was a particular expectation about the content of the volumes. Because the canonical status of some writings was not universally recognized during the early fourth century, it might be thought that some type of decision was necessary about the content of the copies and that this decision had a profound effect on how the church came to understand the scope of the canon. The letter itself does not refer to the content, however, and Eusebius, perhaps surprisingly, refrains from elaborating on the writings that were included in the Bibles. This leaves us to speculate about what was included in each volume and whether Eusebius's decision may have played a role in solidifying perceptions about the parameters of the canon.

Although a list of the writings included in these Bibles has not survived, David Dungan, author of one of the most extensive treatments of

---

[25]For a discussion of the logistics that was likely involved in the production of these copies, see T. C. Skeat, "The Codex Sinaiticus, The Codex Vaticanus and Constantine," *JTS* 50 (1999): 583-625. Skeat also considers the provenance and dating of Codex Sinaiticus and Codex Vaticanus and whether they may have been among the fifty copies produced by Eusebius.

the possible influence of Constantine on the formation of the New Testament canon, finds it significant that the canonical lists that began to appear in the following decades (e.g., Athanasius's Festal Letter of 367 and the list associated with the Council of Carthage in 397) each cite the specific twenty-seven writings that are now recognized as canonical.[26] Similarly, F. F. Bruce suggests that the question of which writings were included by Eusebius "is not seriously in doubt" and that it likely "contained all the books which Eusebius lists as universally acknowledged (including Hebrews, of course, but also including Revelation) and the five Catholic Epistles which he lists as disputed by some—in short, the same twenty-seven books as appear in our copies of the New Testament today."[27] Everett Ferguson follows Bruce, but suggests that the Bibles produced by Eusebius are unlikely to have included Revelation.[28]

Constantine's instruction to produce a large number of Bibles for the churches in a single city may at first appear to be fairly insignificant. It might be understood as a kind gesture that illustrates his concern for the well-being and expansion of the church but was ultimately of little consequence for the establishment of the canon. Others have taken the opposing viewpoint that this was a pivotal event that inexorably forced a decision regarding the specific content that was to be included in the Christian canon. As Lee Martin McDonald writes, "If Constantine's fifty copies included the current twenty-seven books of the NT, this in itself would have had a powerful impact on the eventual acceptance of a twenty-seven book NT canon."[29] Dungan also suggests that the commissioning of the fifty Bibles likely played a decisive role in putting to rest the question of which writings were to be regarded as canonical. Because of the influence of Constantine over both the church and the state, few, Dungan argues, would have dared question the canonical

---

[26]David Dungan, *Constantine's Bible: Politics and the Making of the New Testament* (Minneapolis, MN: Fortress, 2006), 122.

[27]F. F. Bruce, *The Canon of Scripture* (Downers Grove: InterVarsity Press, 1988), 204.

[28]Everett Ferguson, "Factors Leading to the Selection and Closure of the New Testament," in *The Canon Debate* (Peabody, MA: Hendrickson, 2002), 318-19.

[29]Lee Martin McDonald, *The Biblical Canon: Its Origin, Transmission, and Authority* (Grand Rapids, MI: Baker Academic, 2006), 320.

status of any of the writings included in these Bibles or made an out-spoken case for the canonical status of a writing that was omitted. Re-gardless of Constantine's intentions, it might be thought that the presence of these Bibles in the city of Constantinople would have had the effect of silencing those with alternative viewpoints related to the canonical status of certain writings. Dungan summarizes his under-standing the impact of this event as follows:

> After's Constantine's Bible had been produced, and in the tense atmo-sphere that followed the Council of Nicaea, what bishop would dare use a Bible in his cathedral that differed in content from one used by the bishops in Constantinople? He would likely be informed upon and in-vestigated. He could lose his office or worse! . . . After Constantine or-dered his Bible and Eusebius proudly filled the order, the evidence shows that the debate over 'true' and authentic Scripture simply withered up and practically disappeared. The number of scholars after Eusebius who had anything to say about which writings to use in worship were few and far-between—and they just repeated Eusebius' findings. Compared to the earlier centuries' tumultuous debates, this remarkable conformity cannot have been a coincidence.[30]

Dungan does not offer the only perspective of the significance of this event, of course. Another viewpoint is that Constantine did not state the specific content that was to be included in the copies or instruct Eusebius to make this determination simply because there was already a strong consensus on this matter. Rather than Eusebius assuming a pivotal role in determining which writings to include in a particular edition of the Bible that set a precedent for future copies, it might be argued that he simply included the works that were already recognized by those in Constantinople or by the majority of those in the eastern regions of the empire.

Yet another possibility is that the copies produced in Constantinople only included a portion of the Bible and consequently failed to settle

---

[30]David Dungan, *Constantine's Bible*, 122.

the question of the scope of the canon. Most tend to think that the commissioned copies would have included the entire Bible or at least the entire New Testament. It should be recalled, however, that manuscripts containing the entire Bible or even the entire New Testament remained uncommon during the fourth century. It is a possibility, therefore, that the copies in Constantinople included only a portion of the Scriptures. In the interest of saving time, it might be suspected that each Bible contained only the four Gospels, the most commonly read portion of the New Testament canon. As Harry Gamble suggests, "Since the scope of the Christian Bible was still variable in the early fourth century . . . and since even in later periods manuscripts of the entire Greek Bible were unusual, it is perhaps more likely that these were volumes of the four Gospels only."[31] If this was the case, the production of Bibles would have been of little consequence to the formation of canon as the fourfold Gospel had long been recognized by this time. Unlike today, it would not have been unusual for a church to possess a Bible that "only" included the Gospels given that few manuscripts from this time included the entire biblical canon.

While there are reasonable arguments for each position, the simple reality is that it is impossible to determine whether "the Divine Scriptures" Constantine referred to included the entire Bible, the whole of the New Testament, or only a smaller collection of Scripture such as the Gospels. Given the urgency of Constantine's request and the fact that few Greek manuscripts from this period included the entire New Testament, let alone the entire Bible, a compelling argument could be made that the Bibles did not include all sixty-six writings found in modern Protestant Bibles and that they contained only the four Gospels, the most commonly read writings in early Christianity.

The argument made by Dungan and others that the production of the fifty Bibles was a decisive event may initially seem reasonable. Who would be so audacious or naive, we might ask, as to dare question the judgment of Eusebius, the famous historian who produced the volumes

---

[31]Harry Y. Gamble, *Books and Readers in the Early Church* (New Haven, CT: Yale University Press, 1995), 159.

at the behest of none other than the emperor? In response, it might be noted that diverse viewpoints on a hosts of matters continued long after Constantine's lifetime. Even an event as monumental as the Council of Nicaea did not render a fatal blow to aberrant movements such as Arianism. Although the movement clearly experienced a setback after Nicaea, its influence continued for many years thereafter. The young presbyter Athanasius, who later became bishop of Alexandria and a leading proponent of Nicene Christology, was later forced into exile by his Arian opponents. Constantine himself was even baptized on his deathbed by Eusebius of Nicomedia, a leading proponent of the Arian cause! We later find that several of the Gothic invaders who assumed control of large sections of the western empire adopted forms of Arian Christology. Nicaea was clearly a victory for those who championed the eternality and the full divinity of the Son, but it was not the decisive victory that is sometimes assumed.

If the consensus made by those in Nicaea did not result in a final end to the controversy over the nature of Christ, why should it be assumed that the mere production of fifty Bibles in a single city settled the question of canonicity? If anything, this event would have been much less influential than the judgments made by the ecumenical council that convened in Nicaea. It is likely that only a small number of church leaders in the fourth century had even been to Constantinople, much less felt pressure to endorse the specific collection of writings that appeared in the copies of the Bible found in churches throughout the city. The inclusion of Constantine's letter by Eusebius seems to be designed to show how quickly the church was growing in Constantinople and to showcase Constantine's generosity to the churches. If the production of the fifty Bibles did in fact play a role in the development of the New Testament canon, it was certainly not emphasized by Eusebius.

THE ECCLESIASTICAL COUNCILS OF THE FOURTH AND FIFTH CENTURIES

At this point it might be asked what role the various councils that convened during the fourth and fifth centuries may have played in the formation of the New Testament canon. Even if the production of the fifty Bibles was not as instrumental as is sometimes alleged, what are we to make of the legacy of these consequential events? Is it not reasonable to suppose that something as significant as the extent of the Christian canon would have likely been taken up at one or more of the councils that took place during this time? Many would answer this question in the affirmative. McDonald suggests that there were seven canonical works that remained disputed during the time of Eusebius and Constantine. As he contends, "Later on in the fourth and fifth centuries, church councils met to deliberate the matter of which literature would serve the church as its Scriptures."[32] Similarly, Gamble writes that "so far as canonization is understood strictly as the determination of a fixed and closed list of authoritative Scriptures, official ecclesiastical decisions rendered by bishops or councils must be given their due." He also explains that "the judgments of ecclesiastical authorities . . . had the effect of concluding discussion about the authority of individual writings and of finalizing the scope of the canon."[33] In light of the consequential role that the ecclesiastical councils of the fourth and fifth centuries are often thought to have played in the establishment of the New Testament canon, it will be helpful to briefly survey what is known about these gatherings and the role that they may have served in the process of canonization.[34]

The First Council of Nicaea (AD 325). Nicaea was by no means the first gathering of Christian leaders to discuss matters of theological or ecclesiastical importance. In fact, Acts 15 records a gathering of the apostles and other prominent leaders in Jerusalem during the middle of the first century which sought to reach a consensus on the relationship

---

[32]McDonald, *The Biblical Canon*, 314.

[33]Gamble, *The New Testament Canon*, 66-67.

[34]Readers may wish to consult the following surveys of the ecclesiastical councils that took place in early Christianity: Leo Donald Davis, *The First Seven Ecumenical Councils (325–787): Their History and Theology* (Collegeville, MN: Liturgical, 1990); Norman P. Tanner, *The Councils of the Church: A Short History* (New York: Crossroad, 2001); Joseph F. Kelly, *The Ecumenical Councils of the Catholic Church: A History* (Collegeville, MN: Liturgical, 2009); Charles Joseph Hefele, *A History of the Christian Councils From the Original Documents*, 5 vols., trans. and ed. William Clark (London: T&T Clark, 1871–1896).

of Gentile converts to the Mosaic law. Over the next several centuries, a number of additional assemblies of church leaders were organized in order to address a variety of pressing concerns. Nicaea was unique, however, in that it was the first major gathering convened by a Roman emperor. It was also noteworthy simply because of the sheer number of participants. Early estimates of the number of bishops in attendance differ but tend to fall in the general range of 250 to 325. The actual number in attendance would have been much larger than this, however, as many of the bishops would have likely been accompanied by several assistants (e.g., presbyters and deacons). Although precise numbers are difficult to determine, Nicaea would have clearly been the largest gathering of church leaders in a single location to this point in church history. The vast majority of the bishops were from the East, though it would be a mistake to consider the event a mere regional gathering of church leaders as there were bishops in attendance from all throughout the Roman world. We can imagine that the council would have been one of the most memorable events ever experienced by those in attendance.

As is well-known, the council was convened by Constantine largely in response to the Arian controversy that had originated in Alexandria and spread throughout the empire. Was Jesus the eternally divine Son of God and equal to God the Father in nature and majesty, or was he to be regarded as a created being of lesser status? It is not difficult to understand why many are inclined to agree with the perspective that this council was decisive in establishing the limits of the canon. As leaders of the church considered whether Jesus was eternal and coequal with the Father, it is often thought that the question of the canon would have inevitably become a pressing concern. As discussed above, some might argue that a consensus on foundational theological matters could have only been achieved if there was a consensus on the scope of the canon. In line with this thinking, it might be concluded that the writings that came to be widely recognized as authoritative Scripture during the fourth century are simply the writings that were closely aligned with the theological perspective of the "winners" of the major theological debates that were waged during this time.

This perspective on the christological debates of the fourth century and its implications for the development of the canon is suggested throughout popular works such as Dan Brown's *The Da Vinci Code*. "More than eighty gospels were considered for the New Testament," a major character in the novel suggests, "and yet only a relative few were chosen for inclusion—Matthew, Mark, Luke, and John among them."[35] A few pages later, it is suggested that the establishment of "Christ's divinity was critical to the further unification of the Roman empire and to the new Vatican power base. By officially endorsing Jesus as the Son of God, Constantine turned Jesus into a deity who existed beyond the scope of the human world, an entity whose power was unchallengeable. . . . Christ as Messiah was critical to the functioning of Church and state."[36] The implication of Brown's novel, of course, is that there were significant disagreements regarding the nature and work of Christ as well as the extent of the canon at the time of the gathering at Nicaea. As long as there was dispute about one of these major subjects, dispute regarding the other was inevitable. The Council of Nicaea, therefore, is often thought to have dealt decisively with both subjects.

Despite the common assumption that the Council of Nicaea played a significant role in the formation of the New Testament, there is simply no historical evidence to suggest that the council made any binding declarations related to the content of the canon or that perceptions regarding the status of certain writings were influenced in one way or another by this event. As noted above, the council was primarily concerned with the controversy that originated in Alexandria over the Christology of Arius, not with the scope of the canon. Even those who affirm that theological concerns played a significant role in the development of the canon have found it difficult to conclude that Nicaea was a consequential event in the canon's formation. As Bart Ehrman correctly observes, "The historical reality is that the emperor Constantine had nothing to do with the formation of the canon of Scripture: he did not choose which books to include or exclude, and he did not order the

---

[35]Dan Brown, *The Da Vinci Code* (New York: Doubleday, 2003), 251.
[36]Brown, *The Da Vinci Code*, 253.

destruction of the Gospels that were left out of the canon. The formation of the New Testament was instead a long and drawn-out process that began centuries before Constantine and did not conclude until long after he was dead."[37]

Despite the fact that many scholars are unconvinced that Nicaea played a pivotal role in the development of the canon, this assumption remains common on a popular level. It is not clear precisely when the perceived link between Nicaea and the establishment of the canon originated. One of the earliest known claims to Nicaea's role in establishing the canon derives from a ninth-century Greek writing referred to as the *Synodicon Vetus*.[38] This work provides a survey of several of the councils and synods that took place from the early church through the end of the ninth century. Although the writing provides a valuable source of historical information for several events that have not been preserved elsewhere, some of the traditions it includes are clearly fanciful and of questionable historical credibility. With regard to Nicaea, for example, it is recorded in chapter 35 that those who attended the council prayed that God would separate the authoritative Gospels from a large body of writings. Numerous writings were placed on the floor near the alter of a church, some canonical and some apocryphal, and, miraculously, the four canonical Gospels separated themselves from the others and appeared together on top of the altar! This account is obviously to be dismissed as little more than a legendary story that originated at some point long after the council convened. Prior to this account, there is simply a lack of historical evidence that Nicaea took up the subject of canon. No mention of the status of the canonical writings is mentioned in any of the early descriptions of Nicaea, nor is the subject of canon addressed in any of the decrees of the council.

Synod of Laodicea (c. AD 363). This particular synod appears to have involved a smaller gathering of participants at some point during

---

[37]Bart D. Ehrman, *Truth and Fiction in* The Da Vinci Code (New York: Oxford University Press, 2004), 74.

[38]For additional background regarding this event, see Ronald Huggins, "Did Constantine Decide the New Testament Canon?" *MJT* 8 (2010): 102-14; John Duffy and John Parker, *The Synodicon Vetus*, Corpus Fontium Historiae Byzantine XV (Washington, DC: Dumbarton Oaks, 1979), 29.

the middle of the fourth century. Our knowledge of the historical background relating to this event is limited. Even the date of the event is disputed with estimates ranging from as early as the 340s to as late as 381, the date of the first ecumenical council in Constantinople. The most common theory is that the synod was convened fairly soon after the death of Emperor Julian "the apostate" in 363. Julian is perhaps best known for his effort to revive the ancient worship of the Roman gods, a decision which fueled his effort to suppress the Christian faith during a time in which it was experiencing significant growth. His abrupt death at the Battle of Samarra had far-reaching implications for both the state of the empire and the church. In an attempt to navigate several significant challenges facing the church in the aftermath of Julian's reign, a small group of leaders from Asia Minor met to achieve a consensus on a number of disputed subjects. Much of the discussion seems to have been centered around aspects of Christian worship and matters related to the affairs of the local church such as the proper treatment of church members and the qualifications and responsibilities of those serving in certain ecclesiastical positions.

The synod, or council, as it is sometimes described, was not a grand event similar to that of Nicaea. It was not convened by an emperor, nor did it draw bishops from the greater Roman world. Rather, it was a relatively small event in which a gathering of around thirty bishops from Phrygia and other locations in Asia Minor are thought to have taken part. The most important historical source pertaining to the council that has survived is a set of fifty-nine canons—that is, guidelines and instructions in the form of decrees that were affirmed on by those in attendance. With regard to the formation of the New Testament, Canon 59 stipulates that it is only the writings contained in the Old and New Testaments that are to be read in the assembly of the church. This decree is followed in some witnesses by the more well-known Canon 60, which many historians regard as a later addition designed to provide clarity regarding the specific content of the Old and New Testaments. This possible addition lists each of the individual writings contained in both the Old and New Testament by name, thus offering clarity regarding the specific writings that may be used in public worship. The canon cites the four Gospels, Acts, the seven Catholic Epistles, and the fourteen epistles of Paul (Hebrews included). Only Revelation is omitted from the list.

With regard to the development of the New Testament canon, the Synod of Laodicea appears to have been neither innovative nor influential. Even if those who gathered in Laodicea did in fact make an attempt to reach a resolution regarding the extent of the canon, it is unlikely that they would have garnered much influence outside of the immediate area. In fact, it is possible to regard the brief reference to the New Testament in Canon 59 as an indication that there was already a broad recognition of the canonical works by this time. Another possibility, however, is that the decree was not designed to settle which writings were part of the New Testament canon, but simply to provide clarity regarding the manner in which noncanonical works were to be treated. Was it possible to read works outside of the canon of Scripture to the assembled gathering of the church? Were they to play a role in the establishment of Christian doctrine? Should they be consulted for instruction regarding public worship? The determination of those who convened in Laodicea, of course, was that it is only the canonical writings that are to be read when the church gathers. Even if Canon 60 is regarded as an early interpolation, there is nothing that appears particularly noteworthy about the works it cites. The only detail that stands out in this list of New Testament writings is the omission of Revelation, a writing that was not universally recognized at this time.

The Synod of Rome (c. AD 382). This little-known gathering of bishops took place in the city of Rome during the reign of Pope Damascus I in the year 382. The synod was largely concerned about the relationship of the See of Rome to the eastern churches. Damascus and many bishops in the West were opposed to the emperor's appointment of Nectarius as the archbishop of Constantinople following the death of the highly esteemed Gregory of Nazianzus. It was a common perception that Nectarius was woefully inexperienced and unqualified to serve in such a prestigious and influential position. There were also significant disputes regarding the relationship of the church of Constantinople to other eastern churches such as Antioch and Alexandria. The major council that met in Constantinople during the previous year had elevated the status of Constantinople over the other churches and had questioned the influence of Rome when it came to matters that were of particular concern to the eastern churches.

Some have suggested that the synod that convened in Rome the following year was the likely origin of a particular list of canonical writings known as the "Damasian list." As the title suggests, the list is often attributed to Damascus who, among other things, played a significant role in the transmission of the Latin Bible. His secretary was none other than Jerome, whom he commissioned to produce the Vulgate. With regard to the New Testament, the list cites, in the following order, the four Gospels, the fourteen epistles of Paul with Hebrews placed at the end of the list, Revelation, Acts, and the seven Catholic Epistles. Of particular interest in the list of the Catholic Epistles is the distinction made between "John the Apostle," who is identified as the author of one of the three Johannine Epistles, and another individual referred to as "John the Presbyter," who is said to have composed the other two epistles.

While traditionally attributed to Pope Damascus, the precise origin of this list is disputed. Some have suggested that it is unlikely to have emerged until the fifth century given that the earliest witness to this list appears in the *Decretum Gelasianum*, a work associated with Pope Gelasius I, who did not reign until the final decade of the fifth century. Despite the difficulties of establishing the precise origin of this list, it remains possible that it originated during the tenure of Damascus and that it was later adopted by subsequent writers. Even if this was the case, however, there is little reason to conclude that this particular synod was instrumental in determining the precise content of the New Testament canon.

The Synod of Hippo (AD 393) and the Council of Carthage (AD 397). Several synods took place in the late-fourth and early-fifth centuries in Hippo, a city on the coast of modern Algeria where for many years the famed theologian and bishop Augustine lived and ministered. The first synod, which met in 393, is regarded by some as the first major ecclesiastical gathering to approve a specific list of New Testament writings. Those who hold this perspective often conclude that prior gatherings did not address the subject of canon or that the lists associated with them are either spurious or of later origin.

Historical witnesses relating to the synod in Hippo are limited. On the basis of what is known of other events that took place in the years that followed, however, it would appear that many of the decisions made on this occasion were subsequently approved by those who took part in the Council of Carthage just four years later. One of the most important historical witnesses to these councils is a Latin and Greek text compiled by Christofle Justel (also spelled "Justellus") in 1615 that is referred to as *Codex Canonum Ecclesiae Africanae*. The text includes historical information related to the various councils that convened in northern Africa during the fourth and fifth centuries. Perhaps most importantly, the source provides a record of the New Testament writings that were identified in Hippo in 393 and affirmed by those who took part in the Council of Carthage in 397. It reveals that the twenty-seven writings that are now widely regarded as canonical were recognized on both occasions. With respect to the council that took place in Carthage in 397, Canon 24 makes clear reference to the twenty-seven canonical writings. The text refers to four Gospels, each of the Pauline Epistles, and the writings that are part of the Catholic Epistles. One detail that stands out is the separation of the Pauline Epistles from Hebrews. The corpus is numbered at thirteen with Hebrews listed separately. This reflects the common recognition of the canonical status of Hebrews during this time as well as the awareness of several questions related to its compositional history. By this time, the canonical status of Hebrews was widely recognized, though questions remained about its precise relationship to the apostle Paul. It is interesting that just a few decades later, the council that met in Carthage in 419 simply affirmed the fourteen epistles of Paul without separating Hebrews from the collection. Although Hippo is of interest because it numbered twenty-seven canonical writings, it is arguably unwarranted to conclude that it played a decisive role in forming the canon or determining its specific content. It would seem more appropriate to view the event simply as further evidence that a general consensus regarding the scope of the canon had been achieved by this time.

THE RELEVANCE OF THE ECCLESIASTICAL COUNCILS FOR THE DEVELOPMENT OF THE NEW TESTAMENT CANON

For many scholars, the theological debates that took place in early Christianity cannot be separated from the subject of the canon's origin. As Bart Ehrman contends, "The battle for converts was, in some ways, the battle over texts, and the proto-orthodox party won the former battle by winning the latter. One of the results was the canonization of the twenty-seven books that we now call the New Testament."[39] But what was the specific battlefield on which the "battle over texts" was waged? Was there a particular event that decisively established which writings were to be regarded as canonical, or was there a protracted and lengthy battle in which the general theological climate of the fourth and fifth centuries eventually led to a greater appreciation of some writings and a less favorable estimation of others? In short, how likely is it that the New Testament canon was formed in response to, or as a consequence of, the theological disputes of this time?

We may first address these questions by noting that the mere presence of theological controversy in early Christianity does not in itself imply that the canon was in a largely unsettled state. As the study of early Christian literature makes clear, there was no single or uniform method of biblical interpretation at this time, nor was there universal agreement as to the precise role that the Scriptures were to serve in the establishment of Christian doctrine.[40] Some interpreters were heavily influenced by one school of interpretation or another (e.g., the famous Antiochene or Alexandrian schools of thought), while a number of philosophical and

---

[39]Ehrman, *Lost Christianities*, 180.
[40]For a basic introduction to the various ways that Scripture was interpreted in the early centuries of the Christian era, see Gerald Bray, *How the Church Fathers Read the Bible: A Short Introduction* (Bellingham, WA: Lexham, 2022).

theological traditions often influenced which doctrines were emphasized and how they were understood. As Sara Parvis explains, Christian
theologians during this time often "discuss[ed] the technical meaning of
the words [of Scripture] both with reference to Greek linguistic and
philosophical usage, and with reference to Scripture. But their discussions ultimately take place also within the parameters of what is a
thinkable thought in their culture, and what will safeguard their own
soteriological concerns."[41] Parvis draws attention to several unsuspecting
canonical texts that were often used in support of a particular theological
perspective. She notes, for example, the various ways that Proverbs
8:22-25 and Romans 1:4 were understood and how they were thought to
contribute to our understanding of the incarnation of Christ. Noting the
prominent role that Scripture played in the christological debates in late
antiquity, Stephen Need explains that "like Arius, Athanasius used biblical texts to support his case" and that "although the Arians also used
biblical texts to support their case (and sometimes the same texts, e.g.,
Proverbs 8), the more radical Athanasius sometimes seems to fail to see
their more obvious meaning."[42]

In addition to Proverbs 8:22-25 and Romans 1:4, passages such as
John 1:1-18; 14:28; Colossians 1:15; and Hebrews 1:5-6 were occasionally
used to emphasize different aspects of Jesus' mission or even to defend
alternative positions on his nature. Those associated with the Marcionite and Arian movements, for example, appear to have used Colossians 1:15 and Hebrews 1:5-6 in support of their conviction that Jesus is
a created being who is subordinate to the Father.[43] The majority of the
church disputed these conclusions, of course, insisting instead that
these passages are compatible, and even supportive, of the viewpoint

---

[41]Sara Parvis, "Christology in the Early Arian Controversy: The Exegetical War," in *Christology and Scripture: Interdisciplinary Perspectives*, ed. Angus Paddison and Andrew Lincoln, LNTS 348 (London: T&T Clark, 2007), 122.

[42]Stephen Need, *Truly Divine and Truly Human: The Story of Christ and the Seven Ecumenical Councils* (Peabody, MA: Hendrickson, 2008), 46-47.

[43]See *Marc.* 5.19 for Tertullian's critique of Marcion's understanding of the word *firstborn* (πρωτότοκος; *prōtotokos*), a theologically rich term that appears in important christological passages such as Col 1:15, 18 and Heb 1:6. See also Epiphanius's criticism of Arius's christology in *Pan.* 69.

that Jesus is the divine Son of God, that he is uncreated, and that he shares the same divine attributes as the Father. In sum, theological debates often centered around how certain texts were to be interpreted and understood, not simply which texts were to be given priority.

We may also observe from early witnesses to the canon that a core body of writings were widely recognized as Scripture long before the Arian controversy emerged and certainly before the various councils and synods convened during the latter half of the fourth century. It is simply untenable therefore to conclude that the writings that exhibit a more discernible "orthodox" understanding of the nature of Christ began to be recognized only after they were embraced by the "winners" of the theological conflicts that took place in the fourth century and thereafter. It is evident from the earliest witnesses to the canon, limited though they may be, that no writing was widely recognized as authoritative Scripture prior to the fourth century, only to be summarily rejected at some point during the fourth century as a result of the decree of a particular synod or council. Conversely, there does not appear to be compelling evidence that a particular writing was widely rejected or unknown prior to the fourth century, only to receive widespread canonical recognition after leaders of the church sought to address a particular theological matter during the fourth century or a later period. Put simply, the evidence does not seem to favor the viewpoint that the theological disputes of the fourth century or the various ecclesiastical events during this time played a direct or consequential role in formation of the canon. Mark Edwards's judicious reflections helpfully summarize this point:

> To say that we owe our canon to the rulings of a synod, however august
> in reputation, suggests to modern ears that, but for the intrigues of a
> handful of ecclesiastical courtiers, our New Testament might have had
> an entirely different list of contents. This is to overestimate the authority
> of councils even in matters of doctrine and discipline, for it was not
> Nicaea, or even Constantinople, that established the orthodox doctrine
> of the Trinity, and those who think Pelagianism a heresy cannot cite an
> ecumenical decree to that effect. . . . In short, a council cannot create

consensus where there is none. The most that it can do is to give a sharper definition to an incipient consensus, leaving the points that it has not yet determined to be canvassed by individual theologians in the light of its decrees.[44]

In light of the factors discussed above, it is perhaps best to view the various pronouncements associated with the fourth- and fifth-century councils as reflective of a growing consensus related to the scope of the canon rather than as official decrees or decisions that directly impacted its formation.

CONCLUSIONS

This chapter has addressed the possibility that certain theological controversies played a major role in prompting the formation of the New Testament canon. In contrast to the perspective that the canon was created largely in response to concerns about the teaching of Marcion in the second century or that the scope of the canon was determined by a particular ecclesiastical council in the fourth century, it has been suggested that these factors are unlikely to have played a significant role in the canon's development or recognition. There is simply little evidence that early Christians embraced or rejected certain writings as a result of Marcion's influence. In addition, it is becoming more commonly recognized that Marcion was likely familiar with a collection of Paul's writings that he simply adopted for use in his communities. With regard to the events that took place during the fourth century, we have found that there is a lack of evidence that a particular council was responsible for establishing the extent of the canon. The extant canonical lists that were produced during this time are best understood as evidence for a growing consensus on the scope of the canon rather than as pronouncements that played a consequential role in its formation.

---

[44]Mark Edwards, "What Influence Did Church Councils and Theological Disputes Play in the Formation of the New Testament Canon?" in *The New Testament Canon in Contemporary Research*, ed. Stanley E. Porter and Benjamin P. Laird, TENTS (Leiden: Brill, forthcoming).

THE PRIMARY
WITNESSES TO THE
EARLY STATE OF THE
NEW TESTAMENT CANON

WHAT ARE THE MOST IMPORTANT WITNESSES
TO THE EARLY STATE OF THE NEW TESTAMENT CANON?

*The formation of the New Testament Canon is a story told not
only by the early church fathers who used and cited these
books, but also by the earliest physical remnants of Christianity, the manuscripts themselves.*

MICHAEL J. KRUGER, *CANON REVISITED*

WE OBSERVED IN THE PREVIOUS CHAPTER that there is a lack
of compelling evidence that the formation of the New Testament was
prompted by a particular theological crisis or that it was decisively
settled by a particular ecclesiastical body. But if we are to reject the
notion that the canon was determined at a particular time in church
history in response to a particular theological crisis or that a particular
religious body played a leading role in its formation, how are we to account for its creation? Surely something must have prompted early
Christians to collect and recognize the authority of a specific body of
writings. The canon obviously did not emerge by chance or fall out of
the sky in its completed form. How might we explain, then, how a

diverse body of twenty-seven writings of different genres composed by multiple authors who wrote in different places and at different times came to be recognized as a single, discrete collection of sacred Scripture?

In order to answer this important question, it is essential that we first identify and analyze the most important witnesses to the early state of the canon. By so doing, we will gain a better sense of which writings were generally recognized during the early centuries of the Christian era and whether the formation of the canon likely took place on a particular occasion or if it was a more gradual process. No single witness is capable of answering all questions about the early history of the canon, but by examining a wide range of early witnesses, we will be much better positioned to make general observations about its early formation and development.

In what follows, we will briefly survey several of the most important early witnesses to the canon. Those familiar with the study of canon may find that there are several early witnesses that have been omitted from our discussion. Rather than identifying and treating every early witness to one or more of the New Testament writings, our aim here is to identity the most significant early witnesses to the canon and to consider what they reveal about the general state of the canon in the centuries immediately following the birth of the church. We will begin our survey with a brief treatment of early witnesses that enumerate the specific works that belong to the canon before transitioning to some of the most consequential Greek manuscripts that provide insight relating to the scope of the canon in early Christianity.

EARLY CANONICAL LISTS

One of the most important types of witnesses to the early state of the New Testament are what might loosely be described as a canonical lists.[1] Several ancient witnesses contain a list of all or a portion of the

---

[1]The most thorough modern treatment of the early canonical lists is Edmon Gallagher and John Meade, *The Biblical Canon Lists from Early Christianity: Texts and Analysis* (New York: Oxford University Press, 2017). See also F. F. Bruce, *The Canon of Scripture* (Downers Grove, IL: InterVarsity Press, 1988), 115-230.

canonical writings or provide some type of reference to the canon's major components. These lists appear in a variety of sources, some being more detailed and structured than others. In some cases they appear in biblical manuscripts in which scribes have provided a list of the number of lines (*stichoi*) contained in each writing, while on other occasions they appear in the decrees of ecclesiastical councils or in the writings of the church fathers. These lists appear to have served a variety of purposes. In biblical manuscripts they often functioned as something like a bill that was due the scribe (scribes were often paid for the number of lines they produced). In the lists associated with the ecclesiastical councils, the objective was often to distinguish the specific works that were to be read in public gatherings and considered authoritative Scripture from those that provided edifying reading but lacked authority or from the writings that were to be rejected altogether.

Although it is doubtful that the surviving canonical lists played an influential part in shaping which writings early Christians treated as Scripture, they offer a snapshot of how certain individuals, communities, and ecclesiastical bodies understood the extent of the canon at particular times. By comparing the various canonical lists, we gain a better sense of which writings were commonly regarded as canonical, which writings appear to have been disputed or not as well-known, and the general period in which a consensus related to the scope of the canon appears to have been achieved. Because a number of councils and synods were discussed in the previous chapter, we will limit our attention in this section to the lists contained in early Christian writings.

The Muratorian Fragment. Our treatment of the early witnesses to the state of the canon begins with the important and much discussed Muratorian Fragment, a seventh- or eighth-century manuscript discovered by Ludovico Antonio Muratori during the eighteenth century in the Ambrosian Library of Milan, Italy. A rather obscure manuscript written several centuries after the birth of the church may not initially seem all that significant. This particular manuscript is not as old as many other witnesses, and the text is widely recognized as a sloppy Latin translation of a Greek original with a number of inaccurate historical references. Despite these shortcomings, the fragment contains a notable eighty-five-line description of the content of the New Testament canon which many scholars understand to be quite primitive and therefore of great importance.[2]

The fragment is of special significance because it references each major unit of the New Testament canon including the Gospels, Acts, the Pauline Epistles, a selection of the Catholic Epistles, Revelation, as well as a small number of noncanonical works. The surviving portion of the list begins with a description of Luke as the third Gospel and John as the fourth, a clear indication that the author was familiar with the fourfold Gospel and that the four writings were widely recognized as a discrete collection. With regard to the Pauline Epistles, the author of the fragment makes clear reference to the thirteen canonical writings attributed to Paul but omits Hebrews, a writing that circulated exclusively as part of the Pauline letter collection. Finally, the fragment refers to the epistle of Jude, two epistles of John—that is, if the language is understood correctly—as well as Revelation. The canonical writings that were excluded from the list, therefore, are Hebrews, James, the two Petrine Epistles, and one of John's epistles (2 or 3 John?). This amounts to twenty-two total writings.

The precise period in which the list is likely to have originated is a matter of scholarly debate. Traditionally thought to have emerged during the late second century, scholars such as Albert Sundberg and Geoffrey Hahneman have concluded that the list is unlikely to have

---

[2]For an overview of research relating to the Muratorian Fragment and a discussion of the various theories of its origin, see Joseph Verheyden, "The Canon Muratori: A Matter of Dispute," in *Biblical Canons*, ed. J.-M. Auwers and H. J. de Jonge (Leuven: Leuven University Press, 2003), 487-556; Eckhard Schnabel, "The Muratorian Fragment: The State of Research," *JETS* 57 (2014): 231-64; Gallagher and Meade, *The Biblical Canon Lists*, 175-83. Although written over a century ago, Theodor Zahn and Samuel Tregelles's works are among the most scholarly treatments of the fragment. Theodor Zahn, *Geschichte des Neutestamentlichen Kanons*, 2 vols. (Erlangen: Deichert, 1890), 2:1-143; Samuel P. Tregelles, *Canon Muratorianus: The Earliest Catalogue of the Books of the New Testament* (Oxford: Clarendon, 1867). The most thorough recent publication on the fragment is Clare K. Rothschild, *The Muratorian Fragment: Text, Translation, Commentary*, STAC 132 (Tübingen: Mohr Siebeck, 2022). For a study of the dating of the list, see John Lingelbach, "The Date of the Muratorian Fragment: An Inference to the Best Explanation" (PhD. diss., Liberty University, 2019).

originated before the fourth century.[3] The list of writings enumerated in the fragment is simply too developed to have been created during the second century, it has been argued, and is more reflective of the state of the canon during later centuries when the canon was more established. Some who favor a later date have also suggested that the list is of Eastern origin, an opinion that runs counter to the more common assumption that the list originated in the West.

Despite the growing number of scholars who argue for a later date, many remain convinced that the evidence favors a second-century date of origin.[4] A clue in the text that may point in this direction is the description of the *Shepherd of Hermas* as a work written "in our times, in the city of Rome, while bishop Pius, his brother, was occupying the [episcopal] chair."[5] A statement such as this would arguably seem a bit out of place during the fourth century or later.[6] This might be compared to a modern reference to the American Civil War as an event that took place "in our times." It would also seem that arguments in favor of a later date of origin run counter to what the early textual witnesses and the extant writings of early Christian writers may reveal about the state of the canon in the early centuries of the Christian era. It is certainly the case that well-defined lists of canonical writings are uncommon prior to fourth century. When all the available witnesses are

---

[3] Albert Sundberg, "Canon Muratori: A Fourth-Century List," *HTR* 66 (1973): 1-41; Sundberg, "The Biblical Canon and the Christian Doctrine of Inspiration," *Int* 29 (1975): 352-71; Geoffrey M. Hahneman, "More on Redating the Muratorian Fragment," ed. E. A. Livingstone, StPatr 19 (Louvain: Peeters, 1989), 359-65; Hahneman, *The Muratorian Fragment and the Development of the Canon* (Oxford: Clarendon, 1992); Hahneman, "The Muratorian Fragment and the Origins of the New Testament Canon," in *The Canon Debate*, ed. Lee Martin McDonald and James A. Sanders (Peabody, MA: Hendrickson, 2002), 405-15.

[4] See Everett Ferguson, "Canon Muratori: Date and Provenance," StPatr 17 (1982), 677-83; Charles E. Hill, "The Debate over the Muratorian Fragment and the Development of the Canon," *WTJ* 57 (1995): 437-52; Verheyden, "The Canon Muratori: A Matter of Dispute," 487-556; Bruce Metzger, *The Canon of the New Testament: Its Origin, Development, and Significance* (Oxford: Clarendon, 1987), 193-94.

[5] Translation from Metzger, *The Canon of the New Testament*, 305-7.

[6] The statement regarding Pius is considered by many to be anachronistic or at least sloppy, leading to the allegation that the fragment is a later forgery attempting to appear as a second-century canonical list. This viewpoint is considered in Clare K. Rothschild, "The Muratorian Fragment as Roman Fake," *NovT* 60 (2018): 55-82. For a rebuttal, see Christophe Guignard, "The Muratorian Fragment as a Late Antique Fake? An Answer to C. K. Rothschild," *RevScRel* 93 (2019): 73-90.

considered, however, the evidence appears to suggest that a core body of the canonical writings was widely recognized by the second century and that the works that were omitted from the Muratorian Fragment tended to be the works that were disputed during the earliest period of the canon's history. While proponents of a later date often emphasize that the specific list contained in the fragment is too developed to have derived during the second century, it is helpful to consider the dating of the fragment from the opposite perspective. Rather than limit our concern to whether the list of writings is too developed for the second century, we should also consider the possibility that it is too primitive to have originated during the fourth. When the wider body of witnesses to the early state of the canon are evaluated, a compelling case could be made that the content contained in the Muratorian Fragment would have actually been somewhat underdeveloped by fourth-century standards. The various witnesses from the latter half of the fourth century seem to indicate that all twenty-seven of the canonical writings were generally recognized by this time and that the canon was largely settled.

Origen's **Homily on Joshua**. The extant writings of the famed theologian Origen of Alexandria (c. AD 184–253) provide valuable insights related to the reception of the canonical writings during the early third century.[7] Perhaps the most important witness for our present interests is found in a very unlikely place, a homily on a passage from the Old Testament book of Joshua (*Homiliae in Josuam* 7.1). The background of this writing is difficult to establish given that the original Greek version has not survived. All that has been preserved is a Latin translation completed by Rufinus, a fourth-century theologian who translated several of Origen's works and other well-known writings such as Eusebius's *Ecclesiastical History*. It has been suggested that Rufinus often resorted to paraphrase and that he even took the liberty on some

---

[7]For a survey of patristic citations to the canonical writings, see Andrew Gregory and Christopher Tuckett, eds. *The Reception of the New Testament in the Apostolic Fathers* (New York: Oxford University Press, 2005). This source builds upon Oxford Society of Historical Theology, *The New Testament in the Apostolic Fathers* (Oxford: Clarendon, 1905).

occasions to incorporate his own viewpoints into his translations. Most would agree that this was the case, at least in some instances, yet a plausible case could be made that the list contained in Rufinus's translation of Origen's treatment of Joshua accurately reflects Origen's understanding of the extent of the canon.[8]

Assuming that it has been reliably translated and preserved, Origen's list is remarkably developed and offers a valuable witness to the state of the canon at a time in which some scholars assume it was still in a primitive state. Rarely reluctant to draw parallels between aspects of Israel's history to later people, events, or subjects that relate to the Christian faith, Origen equated the trumpets used by the Israelites during the fall of Jericho to the Christian Scriptures, later "trumpets" that likewise oppose human thinking and idolatrous worship. Origen refers to each of the four Gospels by name, along with the two epistles of Peter,[9] James, Jude, the epistles of John,[10] Acts, and the fourteen epistles of Paul (Hebrews included).[11] Revelation does not appear in some of the witnesses to this writing, though Origen's other works make clear that he accepted the work as authoritative Scripture.

It is interesting to compare Origen's treatment of the canonical writings to what appears in the Muratorian Fragment. Both Origen and the fragment clearly recognize the four Gospels, Acts, the Pauline Epistles (Hebrews is omitted in the fragment), a portion of the Catholic Epistles, and Revelation. Assuming the traditional date of the Muratorian Fragment, this source, coupled with the testimony of Origen, would suggest that the basic contours of the canon were more or less

---

[8]For further background on these issues, see Michael J. Kruger, "Origen's List of New Testament Books in *Homiliae in Josuam* 7.1: A Fresh Look," in *Mark, Manuscripts, and Monotheism*, ed. Chris Keith and Dieter T. Roth, LNTS 528 (London: T&T Clark, 2015), 99-117; Edmon Gallagher, "Origen via Rufinus on the New Testament Canon," *NTS* 62 (2016): 461-76.

[9]While two epistles are referenced in this list, Eusebius records that Origen was aware of the questions surrounding the authenticity of 2 Peter (*Hist. eccl.* 6.25.8).

[10]It is not entirely clear how many epistles Origen attributed to John. Because he does not specifically state that there were three epistles or refer to them by name, we cannot be certain that he recognized each writing.

[11]Hebrews is not listed by name, but there should be no dispute regarding Origen's recognition of this work. Whenever early Christian writers referred to fourteen epistles of Paul, the presence of Hebrews was assumed.

settled by the late second and early third century. Aside from questions relating to the status of Hebrews and some of the Catholic Epistles, there appears to have been a general recognition of the remaining works of the canon that came to be regarded as canonical Scripture.

Eusebius's **Ecclesiastical History.** Eusebius's work on the life and reign of Constantine was briefly discussed in the previous chapter. His most well-known and important contribution, however, was his *Ecclesiastical History*, an invaluable record of the first three hundred years of the Christian movement (c. AD 325).[12] On two occasions in this writing, Eusebius surveys the reception of the canonical writings. He refers to fourteen epistles of Paul but explains that the reception of Hebrews was disputed by those in Rome (*Hist. eccl.* 3.3.5) because of its questionable authorship. Shortly thereafter, the text includes one of the most detailed summaries of the scope of the New Testament that has survived from early Christianity. The canonical list recorded in *Ecclesiastical History* 3.25 is well-known for its division of early Christian literature into separate categories: writings that were accepted by the church and were undisputed (*homologoumena*), writings that were often accepted as Scripture but remained disputed (*antilegomena*), writings that may provide beneficial instruction or encouragement but cannot make a legitimate claim as Scripture (*notha*), and, finally, writings that may are heretical and are to be rejected by the church. Some scholars reject the distinction between the *antilegomena* and *notha*, but these four categories are generally recognized.

Eusebius's treatment provides clear evidence of the recognition of the circulation of major canonical subcollections. The Gospels, for example, are referred to as a fourfold unit and are not even referred to individually by name. He describes them on one occasion, for example, as "the holy quaternion of the Gospels."[13] In addition to the four Gospels, Eusebius refers to Acts, the Pauline Epistles, one epistle of John, one of

---

[12] For a recent study of the legacy and contribution of Eusebius, see Michael Hollerich, *Making Christian History: Eusebius of Caesarea and His Readers*, CLA 11 (Berkeley: University of California Press, 2021).

[13] Eusebius, *Hist. eccl.* 3.25.1 (*NPNF* 2.1). The Greek reads τὴν ἁγίαν τῶν εὐαγγελίων τετρακτύν (*tēn hagian tōn euangeliōn tetraktun*).

Peter, and Revelation as undisputed Scripture. His treatment of Revelation raises a number of questions. Curiously, Eusebius indicates that he would later provide arguments for its recognition. Even more odd is that he places Revelation both under the category of *homologoumena*, a placement which he seems to suggest is somewhat tenuous ("if it seems right"), and under his list of works described as *notha*.

In addition to Revelation, Eusebius's survey of the canonical writings indicates that questions related to the background of several of the writings that comprise the Catholic Epistles collection continued into the early fourth century. Eusebius clearly regarded 1 Peter and 1 John as authentic works but acknowledges that there were questions related to James, 2 Peter, 2–3 John, and Jude. He does not seem entirely confident in the authenticity of these writings, especially James and 2–3 John. On the other hand, he is one of the first known authors to refer explicitly to the subcollection as the Catholic Epistles, a description he used earlier in his history (*Hist. eccl.* 2.23.25). Despite questions related to their authenticity, he makes clear that each of the Catholic Epistles were well-known to Christian readers. In Eusebius, we therefore find evidence that the scope of the New Testament canon during the early fourth century was fairly well established, though the authority of a small number of works continued to be questioned.

***Cyril of Jerusalem's* Catechetical Lectures**. Early in his career, the fourth-century theologian and bishop Cyril of Jerusalem offered several lectures to new converts (*catechumens*) in Jerusalem that were designed to provide instruction pertaining to a number of foundational doctrines and subjects.[14] Of significance to our study is the fourth of the twenty-four lectures that have been preserved. This particular lecture includes a list of the works in the Old and New Testament and offers insight related to the background of several writings. Cyril makes clear reference to the four canonical Gospels, the only four Gospels he recognized as authoritative Scripture and part of an established collection (*Lec.* 4.36). Other gospels were also in circulation, he reveals, but they falsely

---

[14]For a discussion of the possible date of these writings, see Alexis James Doval, "The Date of Cyril of Jerusalem's Catecheses," *JTS* 48 (1997): 129-32.

proport to have been written by the apostles and may even be detrimental to those who lack discernment.[15] Following his reference to Acts, Cyril refers to the Catholic Epistles, citing James, Peter, John, and Jude as the authors, and explicitly asserts that there are seven writings in the collection. He then refers to the Pauline Epistles, declaring that there are fourteen, thus recognizing the canonical status of Hebrews. What stands out in Cyril's treatment is the omission of Revelation and the placement of the Catholic Epistles before the Pauline Epistles, an arrangement that was common in Greek manuscripts.

The Cheltenham List. The Cheltenham List is an ancient stichometric list—that is, a list citing the number of total lines contained in specific sections or writings. Its title derives from the city in England where it was discovered in 1885. Alternatively, it is referred to as the Mommsen Catalogue after Theodor Mommsen, the scholar who discovered the list in a Latin manuscript belonging to the collection of a library in Cheltenham. On the basis of the internal evidence, the list cited in this manuscript is thought to have originated around AD 360–365 in northern Africa. The list refers to the four Gospels and cites them by name in the traditional order. This is followed by a reference to the thirteen epistles attributed to Paul, Acts, Revelation, and several of the Catholic Epistles. Omitted from the list are Hebrews, James, and Jude, while the status of 2 Peter and 2–3 John is not altogether clear given the challenges related to the interpretation of the stichometric data.

Athanasius's Thirty-Ninth Festal Letter. Widely esteemed as a champion of orthodox Christology, Athanasius served as a deacon under the bishop Alexander at the time of the first ecumenical council in Nicaea (AD 325). Soon thereafter, he was installed as the bishop of Alexandria, a position he held for several decades. His tenure as bishop was anything but uneventful. For years, Athanasius continued to engage in theological dialogue with proponents of Arian Christology and to navigate the ever-changing relationship between the church and the Roman authorities.

---

[15]Cyril uses the Greek adjective βλαβερός (*blaberos*) to describe these works, a word that appears in the New Testament in 1 Tim 6:9.

Athanasius's annual festal letter dated to 367 is often identified as the first writing to explicitly cite each of the twenty-seven writings of the New Testament by name. Some have even suggested that he may have been largely responsible for the development of the New Testament. It should be recognized, however, that few witnesses prior to the fourth century have survived. This proclamation of Athanasius may certainly be the first extant source to individually cite each of the twenty-seven New Testament writings by name, but it is doubtful that he was the first in history to recognize the canonical status of the twenty-seven writings or that he was directly responsible for the canonical recognition of any of the writings in the list. As discussed above, it is even possible that Origen held a similar, if not identical, view of the scope of the canon roughly a century earlier. The textual witnesses that predate Athanasius also indicate that the canonical writings enjoyed widespread circulation before this list was composed.

In this work, Athanasius calls attention to the fact that some had recognized certain writings as Scripture that had the potential to deceive individuals and draw them away from the faith. Echoing the language contained in the prologue of Luke's Gospel, Athanasius states that he had carefully evaluated which writings had a rightful place in the canon. He cites by name the four Gospels, Acts, the Catholic Epistles, which he numbers at seven while citing each of the four authors (James, Peter, John, and Jude), the fourteen epistles of Paul (Hebrews included), and Revelation. The language used by Athanasius suggests that his delineation of the contents of the canon was not innovative and that he was simply passing along what he understood to have been widely recognized. In addition to referring by name to the canonical writings, he distinguished between the true works of Scripture that were of divine origin and those that are apocryphal or simply edifying.

Epiphanius's **Panarion**. Epiphanius served as the bishop of Salamis, one of the larger cities of Cyprus, during the final quarter of the fourth century. Known as a zealous champion of orthodox doctrine, Epiphanius's most famous work was his *Panarion*, a title variously translated as "medicine chest" or "bread basket."[16] In this writing, Epiphanius identifies and discusses some eighty teachings and movements which he regarded as heretical and contrary to the faith, some that were no longer active or dominant and some that remained influential. The work is generally thought to have been completed around twenty to twenty-five years before the close of the fourth century.

In his extensive treatment of the Anomoeans (*Pan.* 76.22.5), Epiphanius emphasizes the necessity of those who have been truly born of the Holy Spirit and are disciples of the apostles and prophets to examine the Scriptures from beginning to end. In addition to the writings of the Old Testament, Epiphanius makes reference to the four Gospels, fourteen epistles of Paul, Acts, the Catholic Epistles, and Revelation. Of interest is the unique arrangement of the material belonging to the major canonical subcollections. He cites the Pauline Epistles before the Catholic Epistles and places Acts near the end of his list prior to Revelation. His description would suggest that the Catholic Epistles were widely recognized by this point. He refers to the authors of this collection as James, Peter, John, and Jude, an order that appears to have become commonplace by this time.

***Gregory of Nazianzus's* Carmina**. Gregory of Nazianzus, a bishop of Constantinople, was a leading figure in the trinitarian debates of the fourth century who represented the orthodox position at the major ecumenical council that convened in his own city in AD 381. Among his many pieces set to song (*Carmina*) is a poetic piece that enumerates the works contained in both the Old and New Testament.[17] The poem is introduced with the title *Concerning the Genuine Books of Divinely Inspired Scripture*. In this concise and straightforward enumeration of the canonical writings, Gregory refers to the four Gospels, Acts, the fourteen epistles of Paul, and the seven Catholic Epistles. Similar to the list of Cyril discussed above, Revelation is noticeably omitted by Gregory. Many scholars have concluded on the basis of this omission that Gregory rejected its canonical status. This is certainly possible,

---

[16]The work also began to be referred to by the title *Against Heresies* many centuries later.

[17]Gregory of Nazianzus, *Carmen de veris scripturae libris* 12.31.

though it may have simply been the case that he personally regarded the work as Scripture but did not include it in his list because it was not as widely recognized where he ministered in the East.

Amphilochius of Iconium's Iambics for Seleucus. The poetic work known as *Iambics for Seleucus* is one of the most unique articulations from the fourth century of the makeup of the New Testament canon, though questions remain about its background and composition. Originally thought to have been written by the more well-known theologian Gregory of Nazianzus, it is now widely believed to have derived from his lesser-known cousin Amphilochius, who served as bishop for a time in the city of Iconium. Those who attribute the work to Amphilochius typically assume that it was composed at some point after he was installed as bishop (c. AD 374), perhaps as a teaching tool for his nephew Seleucus. Estimates typically range from AD 380–395.

The work instructs readers to recognize only the four canonical Gospels, Acts, the fourteen epistles of Paul, the Catholic Epistles, and Revelation. With regard to the Pauline Epistles, the work states that the number is "twice seven." There was a well-known tradition in early Christianity that Paul wrote to seven churches that may be observed as early as the Muratorian Fragment. For some, this early tradition precluded the possibility that Hebrews may have been composed by Paul. Paul could not have composed this writing, some argued, because this would increase the total number of communities or churches that received Paul's letters to eight. Amphilochius's work is interesting in that it affirms the Pauline authorship of Hebrews while also making appeal to the seven-church tradition. Rather than rejecting Hebrews because of its supposed inconsistency with established tradition, Amphilochius states that Paul wrote "twice seven" epistles. This is as if to say that the recognition of Hebrews as Pauline results in a collection of the Pauline Epistles that is doubly perfect! With regard to the Catholic Epistles, Amphilochius asserts that seven writings are to be recognized, but acknowledges that some had questioned the authenticity of two epistles of John (presumably 2–3 John), one epistle of Peter (presumably 2 Peter), and Jude. Finally, he observes that Revelation is accepted by some but regarded as spurious by others. This would indicate that questions related to the canonical status of some of the Catholic Epistles and Revelation continued well into the fourth century.

Jerome's **Letter to Paulinus (Epistle 53).** Dated to AD 394, Jerome's lengthy letter to a little-known bishop of Nola named Paulinus (*Epist.* 53) provides an overview of the scope of the entire biblical canon. Near the end of the letter (section 8), Jerome identifies each of the writings in the Hebrew canon and makes several comments related to their background, general content, and significance. He then transitions in the following section (section 9) to a discussion of the works that comprise the New Testament. Jerome refers to the four Gospels in the traditional order, describing them as "the Lord's team of four."[18] He then mentions Paul's epistles "to seven churches," a description that demonstrates his recognition of the seven-church tradition alluded to above. After making reference to the seven churches addressed by Paul, Jerome refers to Hebrews and the Pauline writings addressed to individuals. The epistles addressed to Timothy, Titus, and Philemon are listed as though they were among the recognized writings of Paul, even though they were not among the writings that were dispatched to the seven churches. Hebrews is treated a bit differently, however. Jerome refers to it as "the eighth epistle," a description that is in keeping with his assertion that it "is not generally counted in with the others." He offers further explanation of his understanding of the background of Hebrews in a subsequent letter addressed to an individual named Dardanus (*Epist.* 129) and in his better-known work *Lives of Illustrious Men* (*Vir. ill.* 5). In these later writings, Jerome explains that Hebrews was received by many Christians throughout the Roman world but that some in the West remained hesitant to recognize its status as authoritative Scripture. He seems to have personally held the viewpoint that the work should be recognized as Scripture on the basis of its long-standing use in Christian worship, though he appears to be unsettled about the subject of its authorship. He was thus one of a few individuals

---

[18]All translations in this section derive from *NPNF* 2.6.

at this time who appears to have recognized the authority of Hebrews despite having personal reservations about its authorship.

Following his treatment of the Gospels and the Pauline Epistles, Jerome refers to Acts and the Catholic Epistles. In addition to identifying James, Peter, John, and Jude as the authors of the Catholic Epistles, he describes this collection as "seven epistles at once spiritual and to the point, short and long, short that is in words but lengthy in substance." His review of the New Testament canon fittingly concludes with a reference to Revelation. In sum, Jerome's detailed letter to Nola provides additional evidence for the recognition of the twenty-seven volume New Testament canon around the end of the fourth century.

Augustine's **On Christian Doctrine**. Augustine's famous work *On Christian Doctrine* provides further evidence for the widespread recognition of a twenty-seven-volume canon by the end of the fourth century. The first three books of this writing (of a total of four) were published in AD 397, around the same time as the notable ecumenical council held in Carthage. In the second book of this work (*Doctr. chr.* 2.8), Augustine enumerates the content of both the Old and New Testaments. With regard to the scope of the New Testament, Augustine cites the four Gospels by name, which he then follows with a reference to the fourteen Pauline Epistles (Hebrews is placed at the end), the seven Catholic Epistles, Acts, and Revelation. While Augustine cites the four traditional authors of the Catholic Epistles, he does so in the unusual order of Peter, John, Jude, and James. Also of interest is the placement of Acts between the Catholic Epistles and Revelation, a placement that may also be observed in Epiphanius's *Panarion*.

Rufinus of Aquileia's **Exposition of the Creed**. Our treatment of the earliest and most important canonical lists concludes with a brief word about the work of Rufinus of Aquileia, also known as Tyrannius Rufinus, who was a monastic scholar and close associate of Jerome. As noted earlier, Rufinus is known primarily for his Latin translations of the Greek works of prominent writers such as Origen and Eusebius. After facing conflict with Jerome over the nature of his translations, he relocated to the West, where he continued to face controversy. Of interest to our present study is his commentary on the Apostles' Creed. Written around the year AD 400, section 37 of this work lists the writings of the New Testament canon in the following order: the four Gospels, Acts, the fourteen Pauline Epistles, the Catholic Epistles, and Revelation. With regard to the Catholic Epistles, Rufinus identifies two epistles of Peter, one of James, one of Jude, and three of John. Nothing unusual stands out in Rufinus's list of the canonical writings, but it does provide additional evidence that the twenty-seven canonical writings were widely recognized at the end of the fourth century. The fact that these works were well established by this time may be observed in Rufinus's remark that they had been recognized by "the fathers." This would suggest that he did not regard the canon as a recent innovation or development. Finally, Rufinus explains in the following section (section 38) that some works, such as the *Shepherd of Hermas*, continued to be read though they do not serve as the basis of Christian doctrine.

NEW TESTAMENT GREEK MANUSCRIPTS

Having surveyed a number of canonical lists from the second, third, and fourth centuries, we may now consider some of the more important textual witnesses. While typically studied for what they reveal regarding the transmission of the New Testament text, an often-overlooked value of the early Greek manuscripts is what they reveal about the state of the New Testament canon during the early centuries of the Christian era. Because early Christians commonly included multiple writings in a single manuscript, the manuscripts that have survived often provide valuable insight about which works were regarded as Scripture, the state of the canonical subcollections during various periods, and how the canonical writings were typically arranged.

Before exploring what the individual Greek manuscripts may reveal about the early state of the canon, it will be helpful to make a few general observations regarding these witnesses. We may first note that the majority of extant Greek manuscripts produced throughout church history were produced in codex form. This appears to have been the case even during the earliest periods of transmission. The codex was particularly conducive to the transmission of literary collections because of the fact that it could hold more material than a typical roll (scroll). Works that were routinely placed together in a single codex often became closely associated with each other, and in many cases became recognized as a discrete literary collection. It is also of interest that, so far as can be determined, only a small number of Greek manuscripts appear to have contained a single canonical writing in their original state. We might suspect that Acts and Revelation often circulated independently since they do not belong to one of the larger canonical subcollections. Yet even Acts appears to have often circulated alongside the Catholic Epistles. Although the fourfold Gospel appears to have emerged remarkably early, we find evidence that the Gospels occasionally circulated independently. One example of this is $\mathfrak{P}^{66}$, a manuscript containing the Gospel of John that has been dated to as early as the second century and as late as the fourth century. Aside from a few exceptions, the majority of manuscripts that contain a single writing were not produced until the eleventh century or later. In most cases, manuscripts with a single writing include one of the four Gospels.

In addition to the fact that only a small portion of the extant biblical manuscripts appear to have originally included a single writing, it is also helpful to recognize that only a small number of manuscripts are likely to have contained the entire New Testament canon. Of the large body of Greek manuscripts that have been cataloged to date, only about sixty may be determined with reasonable certainty to have originally included all twenty-seven writings of the New Testament, and only about ten of these are thought to have contained the entire Bible.[19] Needless to say, volumes that contained a large body of writings appear to have been exceedingly rare prior to the availability of the printing press. This all leads to an obvious question: If the majority of manuscripts did not

---

[19]For an overview of various estimates relating to the number of manuscripts containing the entire New Testament, see Daryl D. Schmidt, "The Greek New Testament as a Codex," in *The Canon Debate*, 469-84. Schmidt observes that estimates have typically ranged from the upper fifties to the low sixties. According to Eldon Epp, there are approximately 150 additional manuscripts which include the entire New Testament with the exception of Revelation. Eldon J. Epp, "Issues in the Interrelation of New Testament Textual Criticism and Canon," in *The Canon Debate*, 487.

contain the whole of the New Testament, what did they include? In most cases, Greek manuscripts included material from one of four canonical subcollections: (1) the fourfold Gospel; (2) the Pauline Epistles (Romans–Hebrews); (3) the Catholic Epistles (James–Jude), a collection which often circulated with Acts to form a larger collection known as the *Praxapostolos*; or (4) Revelation.

In what follows, we will briefly survey some of the most important early textual witnesses to the state of the New Testament canon. Although a large number of Greek manuscripts provide insight related to the early state of the canon, there are four early codices that are of special significance: Codex Vaticanus (B 03), Codex Sinaiticus (א 01), Codex Alexandrinus (A 02), and Codex Ephraemi Rescriptus (C 04). Each of these codices contain the writings of multiple subcollections and were produced during the fourth or fifth centuries. Because they contain a large number of the canonical writings, each of these manuscripts serves as a witness to the general state of the New Testament canon at this time. In the following chapter we will consider additional witnesses that provides insight relating to each subcollection.

Codex Vaticanus (B 03)—Commonly dated by scholars to the early fourth century, this codex is likely to have originally included the entire New Testament canon. Like Alexandrinus, the canonical writings appear in the order of Gospels, Acts, Catholic Epistles, Pauline Epistles. Missing from the codex in its present state are the final chapters of Hebrews, the Pastoral Epistles, Philemon, and Revelation. The possibility that Revelation was excluded cannot be dismissed, though it is probable that the missing writings were originally present in the codex before it was damaged many centuries ago. The writings of the Catholic Epistles follow the standard order known to modern English readers, while in the Pauline Epistles, Hebrews is placed between 2 Thessalonians and 1 Timothy, a location that appears to have been common in manuscripts produced at this time.

Codex Sinaiticus (א 01)—Typically dated to the fourth century, this famous manuscript contains all twenty-seven of the canonical writings and places the subcollections in the order of Gospels, Pauline Epistles,

Acts, Catholic Epistles, Revelation. Like Vaticanus, Sinaiticus places Hebrews between the Thessalonian epistles and the Pastorals. The material contained in the Catholic Epistles follows the traditional order (i.e., the writings of James, Peter, John, and Jude) though these writings are placed after the Pauline Epistles, a placement that does not appear to have been common at the time. What is most unusual about the arrangement of the material is the placement of Acts between the Pauline and Catholic Epistles. In the majority of witnesses from this time, Acts is placed immediately after the Gospels. Also of interest is that Sinaiticus contains two noncanonical writings, the *Epistle of Barnabas* and the *Shephard of Hermas*, neither of which were linked to one of the canonical subcollections or frequently appeared in biblical manuscripts. While the two writings continued to be read by a number of Christian readers during the fourth century, it is clear that they were not widely regarded as authoritative Scripture at this time.

Codex Alexandrinus (A 02)—This manuscript has been known to scholars for many centuries and is typically thought to have been produced during the first half of the fifth century. The codex originally included the entirety of the New Testament, though several pages have since been lost or damaged. The writings are arranged in the order of Gospels, Acts, Catholic Epistles, Pauline Epistles, Revelation. The Catholic Epistles are arranged in what came to be regarded as the standard order, while Hebrews is placed between 2 Thessalonians and 1 Timothy. Like Sinaiticus, Alexandrinus includes a few additional noncanonical Christian works—in this case, the epistles of *1* and *2 Clement*.[20]

Codex Ephraemi Rescriptus (C 04)—This lesser-known codex is an important palimpsest—that is, a manuscript in which the original material was scrubbed off in order to be repurposed. Unlike papyrus, parchment manuscripts could be scrubbed clean and reused. In this case,

---

[20]It is unnecessary to assume that the mere inclusion of writings such as *1* and *2 Clement* in Alexandrinus or the *Epistle of Barnabas* and the *Shephard of Hermas* in Sinaiticus indicates that they were regarded as canonical Scripture. They appear to have been included in these codices simply for the sake of convenience. It was not all that uncommon for individuals to include an eclectic body of writings in a single volume. The fact that these writings were placed after the canonical writings in each codex is consistent with this viewpoint.

the original manuscript included almost the entirety of the New Testament before it was scrubbed clean several centuries later in order to record the works of the fourth-century church father Ephrem of Edessa. Although the manuscript is incredibly difficult to read in its current condition, Constantin von Tischendorf, a scholar known primarily for his discovery of Codex Sinaiticus, was able to establish the original text of the biblical material during the 1840s, an important achievement that made a significant contribution to the study of the early state of the New Testament text. The writings of 2 Thessalonians and 2 John are not present in the extant state of the codex, though a plausible case could be made that they would have been part of the original manuscript. The codex arranges the material in the order of Gospels, Acts, Catholic Epistles, Pauline Epistles, Revelation. The Catholic Epistles are arranged in the customary order. In the Pauline corpus, Hebrews is placed between 2 Thessalonians and the Pastoral Epistles.

When these notable codices are compared, it becomes evident that a fairly standard arrangement of the material within each of the major canonical collections appears to have been widely recognized by the fourth century, though there does seem to be some variability with regard to the arrangement of the various subcollections. As might be expected, the Gospels are always placed at the beginning of larger codices and Revelation is always placed at the end. In the remaining material, however, there was not always uniformity. In some manuscripts, such as Sinaiticus, the Pauline Epistles are placed prior to the Catholic Epistles. In three of the four codices discussed above, however, the Catholic Epistles are placed between Acts and the Pauline Epistles.[21]

CONCLUSIONS

The canonical lists and Greek manuscripts discussed throughout this chapter indicate that a core body of writings was likely recognized as

---

[21] As a result of this common practice, the editors of the recently published critical edition of the Greek New Testament produced by the staff at Tyndale House in Cambridge, England, elected to place the Catholic Epistles between Acts and the Pauline Epistles. It is also anticipated that the forthcoming twenty-ninth edition of the Nestle-Aland Greek New Testament (*Novum Testamentum Graece*) will follow this arrangement.

Scripture well before the major ecclesiastical councils convened during the fourth century. Although there was not complete agreement on the canonical status of works such as Hebrews, several of the Catholic Epistles, and Revelation, there appears to have been a widespread recognition of the core elements of the canon during the second, third, and early fourth centuries. The evidence would suggest that there was an even greater consensus on the scope of the canon by the second half of the fourth century. We may further observe that the surviving evidence contradicts the notion that there were writings that were widely recognized as sacred Scripture during the early centuries of the Christian era that were ultimately rejected as canonical Scripture.

THE CANONICAL
SUBCOLLECTIONS AND
THE FORMATION OF THE
NEW TESTAMENT CANON

WHAT WAS THE LIKELY PROCESS THAT LED TO THE
FORMATION OF THE NEW TESTAMENT CANON?

The New Testament is not so much a collection of individual writings but rather the inclusion of some two to four codices or part-volumes (typically Gospels, the Pauline letters, the Praxapostolos and Revelation) under the rubric "New Testament." The earliest part-collections most probably emerged prior to the formation of the larger corpus of writings titled "the New Testament." Scholars are still challenged by the question when this happened.

TOMAS BOKEDAL, *THE FORMATION AND SIGNIFICANCE*
OF THE CHRISTIAN BIBLICAL CANON

NOW THAT WE HAVE ADDRESSED several matters related to the composition of the New Testament writings and surveyed a number of the primary witnesses to the early state of the canon, we may attempt to formulate in greater detail the likely process that led to the canon's formation. Rather than a decisive event in which a particular council determined which writings were to be recognized as authoritative Scripture, the early witnesses to the canon seem to suggest that the process of canonization began very early but that it was not until the latter half of the fourth century or thereabouts that a widespread consensus related to the precise content of the canon was achieved. By this time there appears to have been a general recognition of the twenty-seven canonical writings that Christians continue to recognize today.

A key observation that can be made from the study of the early witnesses to the canon is that the majority of the canonical writings commonly circulated as part of a particular canonical subcollection, or, to use the more formal term, a subcorpus (plural: subcorpora). In most cases, Greek manuscripts contained either the four Gospels, Acts, the Pauline Epistles, the Catholic Epistles, or Revelation. Rather than twenty-seven individual writings circulating independently until a decisive event prompted the creation of the canon, the earliest textual witnesses reveal that the vast majority of the writings first circulated as part of a particular canonical subcollection. As briefly noted in the previous chapter, only about sixty of the vast number of extant Greek manuscripts that have been preserved and cataloged may be determined with relative certainty to have originally included the entire New Testament. Even more surprising is that only around ten of these manuscripts appear to have contained the entire Bible—that is, all sixty-six writings contained in the Old and New Testaments.[1]

The fact that few biblical manuscripts prior to the development of the printing press are likely to have contained the entire New Testament corpus, let alone the entire Bible, may come as a surprise to modern readers who know only of a Bible that includes the standard sixty-six writings arranged in a particular order. Because modern readers are familiar only with a standard volume of recognized writings, it is only natural for questions to be raised about who or what prompted the canon's creation. The twenty-seven writings that comprise the New Testament canon obviously did not just appear one day as part of a

---

[1]For a complete list, see Daryl D. Schmidt, "The Greek New Testament as a Codex," in *The Canon Debate*, ed. Lee Martin McDonald and James A. Sanders (Peabody, MA: Hendrickson, 2002), 479-84. While Schmidt only cites Codex Sinaiticus and Codex Alexandrinus as early witnesses to the complete New Testament, it is plausible that Codex Vaticanus and Codex Ephraemi Rescriptus included the entirety of the New Testament in their original state.

single collection, so a consequential decision must have been made at a particular time and place, it is often assumed. This assumption often leads to curiosity about the particular events or personalities that may have played an influential role in the canon's formation.

But is the assumption that the New Testament is the creation of a particular religious body or an influential figure in church history an inescapable conclusion? The evidence would actually suggest that this is not the case. Rather than assume that the creation of the canon must have resulted from the influence of a particular individual such as Marcion or Constantine or that it was the result of a decisive decision made by a particular ecclesiastical council, early witnesses to the canonical writings indicate that a core body of writings were recognized very early as Scripture and that the development and recognition of a twenty-seven-volume New Testament was a lengthy but natural process. As a number of early witnesses are analyzed, it becomes evident that the process of canonization was inseparable from the development and recognition of the various canonical subcollections.

Among other things, the formation of the canon may be observed in a number of early textual witnesses. The circulation of discrete canonical subcollections such as the fourfold Gospel and the Pauline Epistles continued for many centuries, though it was apparently not long before scribes began to occasionally produce larger codices that included material from two or more subcollections. As an example, one manuscript might include the four Gospels and the Pauline Epistles, while another might include the Gospels, Acts, and the Catholic Epistles.[2] This combination of subcollections inevitably led to the concept of a larger body of canonical works. What we refer to today as the New Testament (Καινὴ Διαθήκη; *Kainē Diathēkē*), therefore, is best understood not as a collection of twenty-seven individual writings that were chosen from a vast body of Christian works on a particular occasion, but as a collection of collections, a combination of smaller canonical

---

[2]Eldon Epp's study provides useful information regarding the number of manuscripts that contain only certain portions of the New Testament. Eldon J. Epp, "Issues in the Interrelation of New Testament Textual Criticism and Canon," in *The Canon Debate*, 485-515.

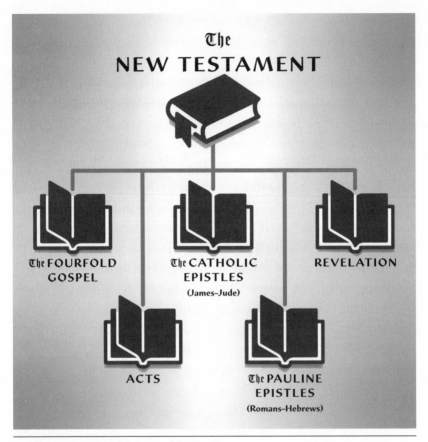

Figure 6. Canonical subcollections of the New Testament

units that eventually came to be closely associated with one another.[3] In light of this development, the formation of the canon appears to have been a rather natural process that had more to do with literary practices, book technology, and the demand for apostolic literature than it did with executive decisions and pronouncements from powerful individuals and religious bodies. It is also helpful to understand that each of the canonical collections has a unique history and background. Some of the collections appear to have developed very early and in a more straightforward fashion than others. By the second half of the

---

[3]For background related to this emergence of the title *New Testament*, see Wolfram Kinzig, "Καινὴ διαθήκη: The Title of the New Testament in the Second and Third Centuries," *JTS* 45 (1994): 519-44.

fourth century, however, each of the collections appear to have been more or less established and to have been widely recognized as authoritative Scripture.

In what follows, we will provide a concise overview of what may be determined regarding the development of each of the major canonical subcollections. Building on the major witnesses to the canon discussed in the previous chapter, we will draw on a wide range of evidence that provides information about the state of each collection at various stages in church history. In many cases we will examine witnesses that are even earlier than those discussed in the previous chapter that provide evidence for the early state of a specific subcollection. Our objective here is not to offer an exhaustive treatment of each of the witnesses to the canon or a full account of the reception of certain works, but rather to consider what may be determined regarding the origin and development of the canonical subcollections and what their early circulation may reveal about the formation of the larger canon.[4]

THE FOURFOLD GOSPEL

The four canonical Gospels have served as the primary witness to the life and work of Jesus for nearly two thousand years. One of the first canonical collections to circulate in Christian communities throughout the Greco-Roman world, the fourfold Gospel was unsurpassed in terms of popularity, influence, and the extent of its circulation.[5] Various explanations

---

[4]For further background on the canonical development of the subcollections of the New Testament, see W. Edward Glenny and Darian R. Lockett, eds., *Canon Formation: Tracing the Role of Sub-Collections in the Biblical Canon* (London: T&T Clark, 2023); Stanley E. Porter and Benjamin P. Laird, eds., *The New Testament Canon in Contemporary Research*, TENTS (Leiden: Brill, forthcoming).

[5]The following studies provide further treatment of the early canonical history of the Gospels or reflections on the nature of their fourfold witness and its function in the canon: Charles E. Hill, *Who Chose the Gospels? Probing the Great Gospel Conspiracy* (New York: Oxford University Press, 2010); Peter J. Williams, *Can We Trust the Gospels?* (Wheaton, IL: Crossway, 2018); Martin Hengel, *The Four Gospels and the One Gospel of Jesus Christ* (Norcross, GA: Trinity Press International, 2000); Jordan D. May, "The Four Pillars: The Fourfold Gospel before the Time of Irenaeus," *TJ* 30 (2009): 67-79; Graham Stanton, "The Fourfold Gospel," *NTS* 43 (1997): 317-46; Francis Watson, *Gospel Writing: A Canonical Perspective* (Grand Rapids, MI: Eerdmans, 2013); Jens Schröter, *From Jesus to the New Testament: Early Christian Theology and the Origin of the New Testament Canon*, trans. Wayne Coppins, BMSEC (Waco, TX: Baylor University Press, 2013).

have been offered as to what may have led to the early recognition of this specific collection. Considering the popularity of Jesus and the fact that many accounts were written about his life and ministry (cf. Luke 1:1-4), we might have expected the early Christians to have recognized more than four Gospels. On the other hand, there were some such as Marcion and Tatian who appear to have only favored the recognition of a single gospel, a position that has the advantage of eliminating any perceived complications that might arise when attempting to reconcile multiple accounts about the life, teaching, and ministry of Jesus. Falling between these two positions, the church came to recognize four specific Gospels as authoritative Scripture. This would indicate that early Christians were selective in which Gospels they recognized but also that they valued a plurality of authoritative witnesses to the life and teaching of Christ.

There were likely many reasons the four canonical Gospels were embraced as authoritative Scripture from and early period and why they were read more frequently than any of the other written accounts about the life and teaching of Jesus. Most importantly, each of the canonical Gospels were perceived to have been written either by Jesus' disciples (Matthew and John) or by those who were personally acquainted with Paul or members of the Twelve (Mark and Luke). Their practical value also appears to have played a role in their favorable reception. As Ronald Piper helpfully explains, the four Gospels offer a rich account of Jesus' teachings without losing sight of the historical context in which his life and ministry took place:

> Unlike 'gospels' that were mainly sayings material (e.g., the *Gospel of Thomas*) or dialogues and sayings (the *Dialogue of the Saviour*) without narrative, the four gospels offer the reader or hearer Jesus' teaching in the context of Jesus' ministry. Furthermore, unlike narrative 'gospels' that focus upon distinctive but often curious parts of the life of Jesus (e.g., the *Infancy Gospel of Thomas*), the four gospels offer a focus upon Jesus' ministry and passion, bringing the two together.[6]

---

[6]Ronald Piper, "The One, the Four and the Many," in *The Written Gospel*, ed. Markus Bockmuehl and Donald Hagner (Cambridge: Cambridge University Press, 2005), 272-73.

In contrast to the canonical Gospels, each of the known non-canonical gospels appear to have been written after the time of the apostles and were thus disconnected from direct apostolic witness.[7]

Early textual witnesses to the fourfold Gospel. As discussed above, it is clear from the earliest witnesses to the canon that the four Gospels quickly emerged as a discrete collection of canonical Scripture, a re-markable development in light of the large body of early Christian lit-erature that is known to have circulated. We find strong evidence for the early reception of the four Gospels in a variety of early witnesses including biblical manuscripts and the works of early Christian writers. With regard to early biblical manuscripts, it has already been observed that the four Gospels were present in each of the major codices from the fourth and fifth century and that these codices present the Gospels in a consistent order. When several earlier textual witnesses are examined, we find further evidence for the early circulation of the four Gospels. Almost half of the extant Greek papyri containing a portion of the New Testament, that is, nearly seventy of around 140 total wit-nesses, preserve the text of one or more of the canonical Gospels. Of these papyri, John appears most frequently with slightly fewer wit-nesses containing the text of Matthew. This would suggest that Matthew and John were the two most popular Gospels in early Christianity.

Because many of the extant papyri are fragmentary, it is often dif-ficult to assess if they originally contained only a single Gospel or the entire fourfold Gospel. In some cases, we possess only a short passage of a single writing and cannot determine what material would have originally been included in the manuscript. On other occasions we have a better sense of the material that would have been originally in-cluded, either because of the amount of material that remains extant or because of the pagination that has been preserved. It would seem that a number of early papyri contained only one Gospel, though they are

---

[7]For additional discussion regarding the major characteristics of the canonical Gospels and some of the important differences between these writings and noncanonical gospels, see Simon Gath-ercole, *The Gospel and the Gospels: Christian Proclamation and Early Jesus Books* (Grand Rapids, MI: Eerdmans, 2022); Darrell L. Bock, *The Missing Gospels: Unearthing the Truth behind Alterna-tive Christianities* (Nashville: Thomas Nelson, 2006).

difficult to identify. If codices consistently contained all four of the Gospels, we might expect to find roughly the same number of textual witnesses to each of the four writings. The fact that Matthew and John appear in the extant manuscripts much more frequently than Mark and Luke is thus a strong indication that codices containing a single Gospel did in fact circulate and that the Gospels of Matthew and John were the most popular. This would by no means suggest, however, that the fourfold Gospel was a later development. To the contrary, there is every indication that codices containing each of the four canonical Gospels began to circulate together as a canonical subcollection remarkably early.

Perhaps the most significant early papyri containing multiple Gospels are $\mathfrak{P}^{45}$ and $\mathfrak{P}^{75}$. $\mathfrak{P}^{45}$, an important early textual witness to the New Testament that is part of the Chester Beatty collection, is typically dated to the third century. In addition to a portion of Acts, the papyrus contains material from the four Gospels and arranges the writings in the traditional order. Also of importance is $\mathfrak{P}^{75}$, a manuscript that is part of the Bodmer collection. Typically dated to the late second or early third century, the extant portion of $\mathfrak{P}^{75}$ contains portions of Luke and John.[8] It would seem likely that the original manuscript also contained Matthew and Mark, as manuscripts containing the Gospels tended to contain either one Gospel or all four. Other important early textual witnesses to the fourfold Gospel outside of the papyri and the major codices discussed in the previous chapter include Codex Bezae (D 05) and Codex Washingtonianus (W 032), notable codices that are thought to have been produced during the fourth or fifth century, and Codex Guelferbytanus B (Q 026) and Codex Borgianus (T 029), both of which contain portions of Luke and John and are thought to have been composed during the fifth century. Bezae and Washingtonianus are particularly noteworthy in that they contain all four Gospels and place them in the less common order of Matthew, John, Luke, Mark.

---

[8]Because the text of this manuscript is similar to that of Codex Vaticanus, it has been suggested that the papyrus originated in the fourth century. See Brent Nongbri, "Reconsidering the Place of Papyrus Bodmer XIV-VI ($\mathfrak{P}^{75}$) in the Textual Criticism of the New Testament," *JBL* 135 (2016): 405-37.

Witness to the fourfold Gospel in early Christian writings. In addition to what might be ascertained about the early emergence of the fourfold Gospel from extant textual witnesses, we may also observe that a number of early Christian writers were familiar with the four canonical Gospels. Several early writers such as Ignatius, Polycarp, Justin Martyr, Clement of Alexandria, and Didymus the Blind, just to name a few, make allusion or reference to the text of one or more of the four Gospels, thereby indicating that they were familiar with these writings and that they regarded them as authoritative Scripture. One of our most important and earliest references to the four Gospels comes from Irenaeus, who was quite emphatic that it is only the four canonical Gospels that are to be recognized as Scripture. As he famously exclaimed in his work *Against Heresies*:

> It is not possible that the Gospels can be either more or fewer in number than they are. For, since there are four zones of the world in which we live, and four principal winds, while the Church is scattered throughout all the world, and the "pillar and ground" of the Church is the Gospel and the spirit of life; it is fitting that she should have four pillars, breathing out immortality on every side, and vivifying men afresh. From which fact, it is evident that the Word, the Artificer of all, He that sitteth upon the cherubim, and contains all things, He who was manifested to men, has given us the Gospel under four aspects, but bound together by one Spirit.[9]

Often overlooked is Irenaeus's reference to the four Gospels at the beginning of this same book of *Against Heresies* (*Haer.* 3.1.1). While the lengthier assertion quoted above is well-known for its colorful and assertive description of the Gospels, the earlier reference also provides an important reference to the four Gospel writers. Irenaeus refers to each writer by name and observes that they passed along their testimony in written form only after they had proclaimed the good news of Jesus Christ in public settings and after they were empowered by the

---

[9]Irenaeus, *Haer.* 3.11.8 (*ANF* 1).

Spirit and came to possess "perfect knowledge." It is their writings alone, he asserts, that serve as "the ground and pillar of our faith."[10]

An additional reference to the fourfold Gospel may be found in the writings of Tertullian. In his polemical work *Against Marcion*, Tertullian asserts that "of the apostles, therefore, John and Matthew first instill faith into us; whilst of apostolic men, Luke and Mark renew it afterwards."[11] Finally, Origen observes in his *Homily on Luke* that there were multiple gospels written about the life of Christ but that it is only the four canonical Gospels that are to be recognized as authoritative Scripture. Unlike those who determined on their own accord to compose an account of the life of Christ, the four Gospel writers wrote under the direction of the Spirit, Origen explains. "Matthew, Mark, John, and Luke," he writes, "did not 'try' to write; they wrote their Gospels when they were filled with the Holy Spirit." As a result, "the Church has four Gospels" while "heretics have very many."[12]

On the basis of the early textual witnesses to the four canonical Gospels and the numerous appeals to these writings in the works of the church fathers, it is plausible that each of the four canonical Gospels were recognized as authoritative Scripture soon after their composition and that the fourfold Gospel collection had emerged at some point during first half of the second century. While we do not have definitive evidence that the fourfold Gospel had begun to circulate prior to the mid-second century, the witnesses that may be dated to the second half of the second century and early third century would suggest that the collection was established and widely known by this time, a likely indication that the collection emerged sometime earlier.

---

[10]Irenaeus, *Haer.* 3.1.1 (*ANF* 1). While some scholars have drawn alternative conclusions about the background of Irenaeus's reference to the four Gospels in *Haer.* 3.1.1, Denis Farkasfalvy has argued that Irenaeus was appealing in this section to an official statement that originated in Rome during the mid-second century. "Irenaeus's First Reference to the Four Gospels and the Formation of the Fourfold Gospel Canon," *PRSt* 43 (2016): 415-27. For additional reflections on the probable state of the fourfold Gospel prior to Irenaeus, see May, "The Four Pillars."

[11]Tertullian, *Marc.* 4.2 (*ANF* 3).

[12]Origen, *Hom. Luc.* 1.1-3, *Fathers of the Church: A New Translation*, vol. 94 (Washington, DC: Catholic University of America Press), 2009.

Conclusions regarding the formation of the fourfold Gospel. The early and widespread reception of the four canonical Gospels becomes all the more remarkable when their reception is compared to that of the noncanonical gospels. The noncanonical gospels are not particularly well attested in early Christian writings and rarely appear in Greek manuscripts. In fact, many of these works have been preserved in only a few extant witnesses. The text of the *Gospel of Judas*, for example, was unknown for many centuries until the Coptic manuscript Codex Tchacos was discovered in the 1970s. Similarly, the full text of the Gnostic *Gospel of Thomas* was unknown until the mid-1940s when ancient manuscripts were discovered at Nag Hammadi.

In addition to the limited textual witnesses to the noncanonical gospels, it is commonly observed that no early codices have survived which combine the four canonical Gospels with noncanonical gospels. One will not find, for example, a single fourth-century codex containing the four canonical Gospels placed alongside noncanonical gospels such as the *Gospel of Peter* or the *Gospel of Philip*. As noted above, early biblical manuscripts tended to contain either a single canonical Gospel, or the entire fourfold Gospel. This would indicate that the four Gospels were quickly and widely recognized as a single literary collection. Other Christian gospels were in circulation, but they never obtained the same degree of notoriety or influence as the canonical Gospels.

It is difficult to discuss early Christian literary collections without briefly commenting on writing technology during the early centuries of the Christian era. We may observe that the emergence of the fourfold Gospel as a discrete collection appears to have developed around the same time that the codex was initially becoming the preferred medium for the preservation of Christian Scripture.[13] Long before the codex

---

[13]For a treatment of the emergence of the codex and its relevance for canon studies, see Tomas Bokedal, *The Formation and Significance of the Christian Biblical Canon: A Study in Text, Ritual and Interpretation* (London: T&T Clark, 2014), 125-55; Colin H. Roberts and T. C. Skeat, *The Birth of the Codex* (Oxford: Oxford University Press, 1983); Harry Y. Gamble, *Books and Readers in the Early Church* (New Haven, CT: Yale University Press, 1995), 42-81; Larry W. Hurtado, *The Earliest Christian Artifacts: Manuscripts and Christian Origins* (Grand Rapids, MI: Eerdmans,

became the most commonly used format for the production of liter-ature in the greater Roman world, Christians appear to have been using it with regularity. In fact, it has been estimated that roughly 70 percent of Christian manuscripts from the second century were codices, com-pared to only about 5–6 percent of the total number of works that have survived from this period.[14]

Although it remains somewhat unclear as to the reason the codex became popular among early Christian readers, it is evident that one of its major advantages was its capacity to store a large amount of ma-terial. Unlike a standard roll, the codex was capable of including larger collections of texts such as the four Gospels or the entirety of the Pauline letter corpus. The ability of the codex to include the text of multiple writings in a single manuscript had the indelible effect of es-tablishing a close literary and conceptual relationship between a number of writings that were written at different times and in many cases were written by different authors. As an important consequence, it provided a practical means of establishing definitive boundaries of the various subcollections that came to serve as the core elements of the greater New Testament canon. Reflecting on the influence of the codex, Roger Kraft observes that "once it was possible to produce and view (or visualize) 'the Bible' under one set of physical covers, the concept of 'canon' became concretized in a new way that shapes our thinking to the present day and makes it very difficult for us to re-capture the perspectives of earlier times."[15]

The use of the codex would have certainly played a significant role in the early reception of the Gospels. Unlike single rolls that would have apparently included only the text of a single Gospel, codices could conveniently include all four. Although we have only limited infor-mation regarding the early reception of the Gospels, it would seem

---

2006), 43-94; Roger S. Bagnall, *Early Christian Books in Egypt* (Princeton, NJ: Princeton Univer-sity Press, 2009), 70-90; Eric G. Turner, *The Typology of the Early Codex* (Eugene, OR: Wipf & Stock, 1977); William A. Johnson, "The Ancient Book," in *The Oxford Handbook of Papyrology*, ed. Roger S. Bagnall (New York: Oxford University Press, 2009), 256-81.

[14]Hurtado, *Earliest Christian Artifacts*, 47-48.

[15]Robert A. Kraft, "The Codex and Canon Consciousness," in *The Canon Debate*, 229-33.

evident that the four canonical Gospels were quickly set apart and that they enjoyed an influence and reception that far surpassed that of the many other written accounts of the life and ministry of Jesus. We may infer that the fourfold Gospel likely began to circulate in codex form at some time during the first half of the second century and that these collections enjoyed widespread circulation by the mid-second century. Unlike some of the writings associated with the Pauline Epistles and Catholic Epistles, there does not appear to have been significant controversy regarding the specific content of the collection. The collection does not seem to have expanded over the years from say, two Gospels, to three, and then ultimately to four. Nor does there appear to have been a gradual reduction of the collection from five or six writings, for example, to only four.

The Pauline Corpus

It is evident that the Pauline Epistles were familiar to a large body of readers in early Christianity and that they were quickly treated as authoritative Scripture by a number of prominent Christian writers.[16] In contrast to the opinion of a number of early-twentieth-century scholars such as Edgar Goodspeed, John Knox, and C. Leslie Mitton who suggested that Paul's writings were largely neglected until the final years of the first century, the evidence would suggest that the Pauline Epistles were frequently used in early Christian worship and that they were regarded as authoritative Scripture from a remarkably early time.

One of the first matters to consider when attempting to ascertain the impetus for the formation of the Pauline letter collection is whether the corpus is more likely to have derived from copies of writings that were circulating throughout the Roman world or from the copies that were in the possession of one or more individuals in the Pauline circle who were responsible for editing the original collection. Regarding the first

---

[16]For a more thorough discussion of the Pauline corpus, see Benjamin P. Laird, *The Pauline Corpus in Early Christianity: Its Formation, Publication, and Circulation* (Peabody, MA: Hendrickson, 2022); Stanley E. Porter, ed., *The Pauline Canon*, PAST 1 (Leiden: Brill, 2001); David Trobisch, *Paul's Letter Collection: Tracing the Origins* (Minneapolis, MN: Fortress, 1994); C. Leslie Mitton, *The Formation of the Pauline Corpus of Letters* (Eugene, OR: Wipf & Stock, 2009).

possibility, there have been two basic proposals. Some might assume that a particular individual, perhaps one familiar with Paul's missionary activities, traveled throughout the Roman world in search of the letters Paul had written throughout his missionary career. According to this perspective, he or she may have come into possession of a number of the Pauline writings and eventually placed them in a single collection after retracing Paul's journeys and securing a copy of the writings known to those in Christian communities throughout the Roman world. After traveling through Macedonia, for example, the individual may have discovered and secured copies of Philippians and the two epistles to the Thessalonians. A similar viewpoint is that the communities that received one or more letters from Paul began to exchange what was in their possession with those in other areas who possessed writings of their own. Understood in this light, it might be imagined, for example, that those in Philippi or Thessalonica may have exchanged letters with those in Corinth. As the mutual exchange of writings continued, the body of writings attributed to Paul continued to expand and become more widely known.

There are several variations of this basic theory, of course. Some have suggested that a certain individual or community was responsible for assembling the available works into a single collection. Perhaps a particular group—what might be described as a Pauline school—collected the existing material and supplemented it with several writings that were composed at some point after Paul's death. These later pseudonymous works are often thought to have been written in order to preserve and enhance the apostle's legacy or to address contemporary subjects with apostolic authority. Evoking Paul's authority would have been a convenient though controversial way for writers to ensure that their work would gain attention and be recognized as authoritative Scripture. Writings included in the Pauline corpus that are often identified by modern scholars as pseudonymous include Ephesians, Colossians, 2 Thessalonians, and the three Pastoral Epistles. Universal agreement over the authorship of these writings has not been achieved, however, and a number of scholars continue to defend their authenticity.

Another major theory that has grown in popularity in recent years is what is often described as the personal involvement theory. According to this perspective, Paul or a member of his apostolic circle simply took the copies of the writings that were already in his possession and prepared them for their initial publication. This could have taken place near the end of Paul's lifetime, in which case Paul himself may have taken part in preparing the writings for public circulation. Alternatively, one or a small number of Paul's trusted associates may have prepared these writings for their initial publication at some point after his martyrdom. The process may have involved not only the collection of his writings but the selection and arrangement of material, the creation of titles, and other related tasks.

One of the factors that seems to support the personal involvement theory is that Paul is known to have worked directly with a secretary (also known as an amanuensis) when composing his letters (see, for example, Tertius's greeting in Rom 16:22), a practice that was likewise observed by other ancient authors such as Cicero and Seneca. As discussed earlier in the volume, one of the common tasks of secretaries in the ancient world was to produce an extra copy of the documents they produced for their clients. Having a copy of one's work ensured that the content would be preserved, even if the manuscript sent to the recipient was later lost or destroyed. It also provided the author the opportunity to consult material that was previously dispatched. Given the likelihood that Paul and/or his close companions maintained copies of his writings, it would seem plausible that one or more of the earliest collections of his works derived from these copies.

While personal involvement is arguably the most persuasive explanation for the origin of the corpus, several questions remain about how the collection may have developed and taken shape. What may we conclude about the state of the corpus in the years following its initial formation? Which writings are likely to have been included or excluded in the initial collection? Also, is it possible that the collection expanded in the years following its initial publication? In order to answer these types of fundamental questions, it will be helpful to return to the

earliest witnesses to the corpus. We have already noted that Codex
Sinaiticus and Codex Alexandrinus included all fourteen of the works
associated with Paul, a collection that included the Pastoral Epistles as
well as Hebrews. Portions of Vaticanus, it will be recalled, have not
survived. Philemon and the Pastorals are missing from the end of the
extant manuscript, though there is a high probability that these writings
were originally included. We find a similar situation with Codex
Ephraemi Rescriptus. In its present form, this manuscript does not include 2 Thessalonians, though it is difficult to imagine that it was not
part of the manuscript in its original state.

On the basis of the major codices and other witnesses from this time
(e.g., the various canonical lists), we may safely conclude that collections of the Pauline Epistles typically included fourteen epistles by the
fourth century. But might it be possible to make even more definitive
conclusions regarding the state of corpus in previous centuries on the
basis of earlier textual witnesses and other pieces of evidence such as
the extant writings of early Christians? In what follows, we will briefly
summarize what these types of witnesses may reveal about the early
state and development of the corpus.

Early textual witnesses to the Pauline corpus. As the following
survey reveals, early textual witnesses to the Pauline corpus are not
limited to the four major codices discussed above.[17]

$\mathfrak{P}^{13}$ (third or fourth century)—This small fragment contains a small
portion of the text of Hebrews. Of note is the extant pagination suggesting that the original manuscript contained a collection of Paul's
letters and that Hebrews was placed near the beginning of the corpus,
possibly after Romans.

$\mathfrak{P}^{30}$ (third century)—The extant manuscript contains portions of
1 and 2 Thessalonians. It would seem probable that the text originally

---

[17]The list of early manuscripts included in this section is not exhaustive. A number of early papyri
containing a portion of the Pauline corpus have been omitted because they do not provide useful
information relating to the early collection of Paul's writings, that is, information useful in assessing how many writings may have been included in the collection or how the material was
arranged. The dates provided for the following witnesses are mere approximations of the likely
date of composition.

contained multiple writings given the lack of evidence that the two Thessalonian epistles commonly circulated together apart from other writings of the corpus.

$\mathfrak{P}^{46}$ (late second or early third century)—Arguably the most important textual witness to the Pauline corpus, the surviving portion of this manuscript contains each of the writings associated with the collection with the exception of 2 Thessalonians, the Pastoral Epistles, and Philemon. Like $\mathfrak{P}^{13}$, the papyrus places Hebrews near the beginning of the corpus, in this case between Romans and 1 Corinthians. It is apparent that the manuscript originally included one or more of these missing writings as the final pages have not survived, though scholars continue to debate which writings were likely included. Some have suggested that the manuscript would have included Philemon but not the Pastorals since there would not have been sufficient space to include these writings in the leaves that did not survive. This is certainly a possibility, though we might observe that there are no other known Greek manuscripts from this time that appear to have included Hebrews but not the Pastorals.[18]

$\mathfrak{P}^{92}$ (third or fourth century)—In its extant state, this manuscript contains only small portions of Ephesians and 2 Thessalonians. It is probable, however, that the original manuscript included a fairly sizable collection of the Pauline Epistles.

$\mathfrak{P}^{126}$ (early fourth century)—Like $\mathfrak{P}^{13}$, this papyrus contains only small fragments of Hebrews. The surviving pagination also suggests that the manuscript originally included a number of epistles and that Hebrews was placed closer to the beginning of the corpus, perhaps after 2 Corinthians or Galatians.

Codex Freerianus (I 016; fifth century)—The extant manuscript contains portions of each writing in the Pauline corpus with the exception of Romans, an epistle that would have almost certainly been included

---

[18]It has been observed that the amount of material on each page steadily increases throughout the manuscript, a possible indication that the scribe was seeking to include several writings in the limited space that remained in the codex. This argument is articulated in Jeremy Duff, "$\mathfrak{P}^{46}$ and the Pastorals: A Misleading Consensus?" *NTS* 44 (1998): 578-90.

in the manuscript's original state. Hebrews is placed after 2 Thessalonians rather than at the end of the corpus.

Codex Vaticanus Graecus (048; fifth century)—Both Galatians and 2 Thessalonians are no longer extant, though they would have surely been included in the original codex. Like several other manuscripts from this time, the codex arranges the material in what has come to be regarded as the standard order.

Codex Coislinianus (H 015; fifth or sixth century)—In its present state, this manuscript includes each of the Pauline Epistles with the exception of Romans, Ephesians, and Philemon. It is highly probable, however, that these writings were included in the original manuscript. Coislinianus arranges the epistles in the same manner found in modern English translations with Hebrews placed at the end of the corpus.

Codex Claromontanus (D 06; sixth century)—This notable manuscript contains all fourteen letters of the Pauline corpus. Like Coislinianus, the letters are arranged in the standard order found in modern English translations.

Witness to the Pauline corpus in early Christian literature. In addition to the textual witnesses listed above, the writings of several early Christian writers attest to the early recognition of a large body of writings attributed to Paul. A full survey of these early sources will not be possible in this chapter, though it will be helpful to briefly discuss several of the more notable early witnesses to the Pauline letters and to consider what the extant writings of early Christian writers may reveal about the state of the corpus in the early phases of its development.

The majority of contemporary biblical scholars have decidedly rejected the Pauline authorship of Hebrews, and many continue to find it difficult to recognize the authenticity of Ephesians, Colossians, 2 Thessalonians, and the Pastoral Epistles. Because of this, it is often assumed that the original collection of the Pauline Epistles was much smaller than the fourteen-volume collections that came to be widely recognized no later than the fourth century. Many assume that a smaller body of authentic works was gradually expanded in the decades following Paul's death with a number of pseudonymous writings. A major difficulty of this assumption is that each of the six disputed writings consistently appear in ancient canonical lists, early Greek manuscripts, and witnesses to the versions of the New Testament (e.g., Latin and Coptic), and are often referenced or alluded to in the works of early Christian writers. In fact, there is little historical evidence that Christian communities once rejected these epistles or that they were not incorporated into the Pauline letter corpus until long after the collection first began to circulate. Aside from the apparent omission of the Pastorals in Marcion's canon and a few other possible witnesses, such as $\mathfrak{P}^{46}$, each of these writings are well attested in patristic and early Christian literature. To cite but a few examples, a compelling case could be made that the Pastorals are quoted from or alluded to in *1 Clement* (*1 Clem.* 1:3; 2:7), the writings of Ignatius (*Eph.* 14.1; 20.1; *Magn.* 8.1), Polycarp (Pol. *Phil.* 4.1), and in later writings from authors such as Athenagoras (*Suppl.* 37.2-3), Theophilus (*Autol.* 3.14), Irenaeus (*Haer.* 1 preface; *Haer.* 3.3.3; 3.3.4; 3.14.1), and Clement of Alexandria (*Protr.* 1; 9; 11 and a large number of references in *Miscellanies*).[19]

To this point we have observed that the testimony of early Christian writers provides compelling evidence that each of the thirteen canonical writings attributed to Paul were quickly recognized as authoritative Scripture and that they commonly circulated as part of the Pauline corpus. But what are we to conclude about Hebrews? Does the evidence also suggest that it was widely regarded as a genuine Pauline epistle? Contrary to common assumptions, the recognition of the apostolic authority of Hebrews does not appear to

---

[19]For additional treatment of the reception of the Pauline Epistles in patristic literature, see the following sources: Laird, *The Pauline Corpus in Early Christianity*, 113-89; Andreas Lindemann, *Paulus im ältesten Christentum: Das Bild des Apostels und die Rezeption der paulinischen Theologie in der frühchristlichen Literatur bis Marcion* (Tübingen: Mohr Siebeck, 1979); Ernst Dassmann, *Der Stachel im Fleisch: Paulus in der frühchristlichen Literatur bis Irenäus* (Münster: Aschendorff, 1979); Kenneth Liljeström, ed., *The Early Reception of Paul*, PFES 99 (Helsinki: Finish Exegetical Society, 2011); Michael F. Bird and Joseph R. Dodson, eds., *Paul and the Second Century*, LNTS 412 (London: T&T Clark, 2011); Jens Schröter, Simon Butticaz, and Andreas Dettwiler, eds., *Receptions of Paul in Early Christianity: The Person of Paul and His Writings through the Eyes of his Early Interpreters*, BZNW 234 (Berlin: de Gruyter, 2018); Jennifer R. Strawbridge *The Pauline Effect: The Use of the Pauline Epistles by Early Christian Writers*, SBR 5 (Berlin: de Gruyter, 2015).

have been a late development and was not limited to those in the East. Writing near the close of the first century, the author of *1 Clement*, for example, quotes extensively from Hebrews. It also appears that many additional writers such as Clement of Alexandria, Origen, Eusebius, Adamantius, Epiphanius, Athanasius, Gregory of Nyssa, Gregory of Nazianzus, Didymus, Cyril, Amphilochius, and Chrysostom regarded Hebrews as a Pauline writing and recognized its authoritative status. This viewpoint was by no means universal, of course. Early figures such as Gaius of Rome and Victorinus of Pettau were among those who are said to have objected to the Pauline authorship of Hebrews.[20] There were also a small number of individuals who appear to have regarded Hebrews as authoritative Scripture even though they did not affirm its Pauline authorship (e.g., Tertullian and possibly Jerome).[21]

We may finally note the possible significance of the reference to Paul's writings in 2 Peter 3:15-16. The passage is notable in that it refers to "all his letters," language that seems to imply that a collection, whatever its particular size at this point, was not only established but fairly well known. While the passage does not offer details about the extent of the collection, it is of interest in that it provides one of the earliest discernible references to a collection of the Pauline Epistles. Just how early of a reference we have in this passage depends of course on the subject of the authorship of the epistle. If 2 Peter is authentic, the passage would provide a remarkably early reference to a collection of Paul's writings that was known to Peter's readers during the final years of his lifetime. Even if the authenticity of this work is not affirmed, however, a plausible case could still be made that 2 Peter was written during the first century. Some of the parallels between the text of

---

[20]As noted above, the Muratorian Fragment, an early witness assumed to be of Western origin, omits Hebrews, another indication that it was not universally recognized.

[21]For further discussion of the reception of Hebrews during the patristic period, see Steven R. Harmon, "Hebrews in Patristic Perspective," *RevExp* 102 (2005): 215-33; Rowan A. Greer, *The Captain of Our Salvation: A Study in the Patristic Exegesis of Hebrews*, BGBE 15 (Tübingen: Mohr Siebeck, 1973); David Young, *The Concept of Canon in the Reception of the Epistle to the Hebrews*, LNTS 658 (London: T&T Clark, 2021).

1 Clement and 2 Peter, for example, may suggest that 2 Peter was known by the mid-90s of the first century.

Conclusions regarding the formation of the Pauline corpus. When the evidence relating to the early state of the Pauline corpus is evaluated, it becomes apparent that three major archetypal editions of the corpus emerged soon after each of the writings were composed and that they circulated simultaneously for several centuries. Some early editions of the corpus appear to have included ten epistles (the Pastorals and Hebrews excluded), some thirteen (the Pastorals included but Hebrews excluded), and some all fourteen writings (both the Pastorals and Hebrews included). Precisely when and how the initial collection emerged remains disputed, as does the question of how this initial collection may have been related to subsequent corpora of Paul's writings that included a larger number of writings. Based on the evidence that has survived, a plausible solution is that the initial collection was based on the duplicate copies in the possession of either Paul or one or more of his associates and that it included only ten epistles. Subsequent editions containing either thirteen or fourteen epistles appear to have emerged soon thereafter.

Contrary to common thought, it is unnecessary to assume that expanded editions of the corpus could not have circulated until several decades or even centuries after the death of Paul. A compelling case could be made that each of the three major editions of the corpus emerged remarkably early and that they circulated simultaneously for some time before larger editions containing all fourteen epistles began to predominate. It was not uncommon for ancient writers to release an initial collection of their works before producing an expanded edition with additional material at a later time. In the case of the Pauline writings, it is possible to affirm the early circulation of editions containing ten or thirteen epistles while also recognizing the authenticity of works such as the Pastoral Epistles. As it so happens, a case could be made that the ten epistles that were likely included in the initial collection of Paul's writings were composed before the Pastorals and Hebrews. It is an intriguing possibility, therefore, that a smaller collection of ten writings was released in the final decade of Paul's lifetime (e.g., during his first Roman imprisonment) and that the Pastorals and Hebrews were incorporated into the collection soon after they were composed.[22]

ACTS AND THE CATHOLIC EPISTLES

The early state and development of the collection of the Catholic Epistles (CE) is decidedly more difficult to trace than that of the fourfold Gospel or the Pauline Epistles.[23] There are far fewer extant textual witnesses to these writings and they are quoted or alluded to much less frequently by early Christian writers. In fact, several notable second- and third-century Christian writers do not appear to have been familiar with each of the seven writings of this subcollection or at least do not appear to have made significant use of them. In addition to the limited attestation to these writings prior to the fourth century, the study of the canonical history of the CE is made even more difficult by the fact that the collection contains writings composed by multiple authors. This factor alone renders the study of the canonical development of the CE to be especially difficult.

In addition to evaluating the authorship of these writings and the circumstances surrounding their composition, scholars are also faced with the challenge of discerning when the collection may have first begun to circulate and the precise writings it likely contained. Did the works attributed to Peter and John first circulate in smaller units before they began to circulate as part of a larger canonical collection? Might it be possible, for example, that a "Petrine corpus" or a "Johannine corpus" circulated independently for some time before the

---

[22]For further discussion of this theory, see Lewis Foster, "The Earliest Collection of Paul's Epistles," *BETS* 10 (1967): 44-55.

[23]For additional treatment of the canonical formation of the Catholic Epistles, see David Nienhuis and Robert W. Wall, *Reading the Epistles of James, Peter, John & Jude as Scripture: The Shaping & Shape of a Canonical Collection* (Grand Rapids, MI: Eerdmans, 2013); Nienhuis, *Not by Paul Alone: The Formation of the Catholic Epistle Collection and the Christian Canon* (Waco, TX: Baylor University Press, 2007); Karl-Wilhelm Niebuhr and Robert W. Wall, eds., *The Catholic Epistles and Apostolic Tradition: A New Perspective on James to Jude* (Waco, TX: Baylor University Press, 2009); Darian R. Lockett, *Letters from the Pillar Apostles: The Formation of the Catholic Epistles as a Canonical Collection* (Eugene, OR: Pickwick, 2017); Carey C. Newman, "Jude 22, Apostolic Theology, and the Canonical Role of the Catholic Epistles," *PRSt* 41 (2014): 367-78.

seven-epistle collection of the CE was formed? If so, is it reasonable to conclude that the formation of the CE was in many ways a microcosm of the formation of the larger New Testament canon—that is, that it emerged as something like a collection of collections as scribes eventually brought together smaller literary units into a single codex (i.e., the epistles of James, Peter, John, and Jude)? These are just a few of the many difficult historical questions that scholars have attempted to address over the years that relate to the development of this canonical collection.

A common persuasion of contemporary scholars is that several of these writings are pseudonymous and were therefore composed much later than traditionally assumed and that anything resembling a canonical collection was a later development. Others, however, affirm the authenticity of all seven writings and contend that the canonical relationship between the writings was likely formed much earlier. Still others find themselves somewhere between these two ends of the spectrum, recognizing the authenticity of some writings but not others. Regardless of one's viewpoint of the authenticity of each of the writings, determining how an eclectic collection of writings that were composed by a number of authors in different locations and at different times came to be regarded as a discrete canonical collection is a daunting task. Before attempting to draw any conclusions, it will be helpful to provide a brief overview of some of the most important textual witnesses to the early state of the CE as well as the relevant testimony from early Christian writers.

Early textual witnesses to the Catholic Epistles. In addition to the major codices treated in the previous chapter, the following textual witnesses are among the earliest and most important witnesses to the state of the CE in early Christianity.

$\mathfrak{P}^{23}$ (second or third century)—The extant portion of this manuscript contains only seven verses of the first chapter of James. The surviving pagination suggests that James was the first writing placed in the codex. Unfortunately, it is not possible to determine what, if anything, would have originally followed this epistle.

$\mathfrak{P}^{72}$ (third or fourth century)—This papyrus contains the text of Jude and 1–2 Peter. It has been suggested on the basis of the manuscript's pagination and scribal hand that these three writings originally existed as part of a smaller unit and that they were incorporated into this manuscript along with a variety of noncanonical writings. If it were indeed the case that the manuscript drew from a source that included only three of the CE, it may serve as evidence that there were smaller collections of epistles in circulation in the early centuries of the Christian era.

$\mathfrak{P}^{100}$ (third or fourth century)—This manuscript is similar to $\mathfrak{P}^{23}$ in that it is limited to portions of James. The extant pagination suggests that the epistle was originally placed at the beginning of the codex.

Uncial 048 (fifth century)—Also known as Codex Vaticanus Graecus, this manuscript contains portions of each of the CE with the exception of Jude. Like many of the major codices, the CE are placed between Acts and the Pauline Epistles.

Uncial 0166 (fifth century)—Fragmentary witness that contains a small portion of Acts along with James. Because the text of Acts is placed on one side of the lone page that has survived and the text of James on the other, it is clear that Acts and the CE were placed alongside one another in the original codex.

Uncial 0173 (fifth century)—Manuscript that contains a small portion of the first chapter of James. On the basis of the extant pagination, it is possible that the original codex included a small number of epistles prior to James (e.g., 1–3 John or 1–2 Peter).

$\mathfrak{P}^{54}$ (fifth or sixth century)—Papyrus that contains fragments of James. The extant pagination may suggest that the epistles of John or Peter were originally placed at the beginning of the manuscript.

Uncial 093 (sixth century)—Fragmentary manuscript of only two leaves that include a small portion of Acts and 1 Peter, thus a possible witness to the *Praxapostolos*, the canonical collection that includes Acts and the CE.

$\mathfrak{P}^{74}$ (seventh century)—While not particularly early, this manuscript is of importance as it contains the entire CE collection along with Acts. Aside from the larger codices that include most or all of the New Testament, this papyrus is one of the most significant textual witnesses to the *Praxapostolos*.

Witness to the Catholic Epistles in early Christian writings. One of the most important witnesses to the CE is Eusebius's *Ecclesiastical History*. It is clear from his account that he was aware of each of the CE and that this collection had become well-known by the time he composed his seminal work during the early fourth century. Eusebius demonstrates an awareness of questions related to the authenticity of James, 2 Peter, 2 and 3 John, and Jude, though he refers to these writings as Scripture and the collection as a whole with the term καθολικός (*katholikos*).[24] Unfortunately, evidence relating to the formation of the CE from Christian writers before Eusebius is sparse and somewhat inconclusive. A number of early writers allude to or quote from one or more of the epistles and treat them as Scripture. However, these sources provide only limited insight relating to the early state of the collection. It is certainly possible that an author's reference to multiple epistles is indicative of an awareness of an established collection of these writings, though it is also possible that they become familiar with these writings through their circulation in smaller units.

To cite but a few examples, Polycarp's *Epistle to the Philippians* makes several references to 1 Peter and 1 John. There is even a possible allusion to the text of 3 John (see Pol. *Phil.* 10:1). We also find that Origen appears to have been familiar with a substantial number of writings from this collection. His commentary on the text of Joshua, a text discussed in the previous chapter, indicates that he was familiar with each of the CE with the possible exception of one or more of the Johannine Epistles.[25] Writers such as Irenaeus, Clement of Alexandria, and Tertullian also appear to have been familiar with multiple writings contained in the CE. While the extant works of these early writers seem to indicate

---

[24]See *Hist. eccl.* 2.23.25. For a survey of the various references to one or more of the writings in the subcollection of the CE, see Lockett, *Letters from the Pillar Apostles*, 62-71; Nienhuis, *Not by Paul Alone*, 29-97.

[25]Origen's familiarity with the CE may be observed in his extant writings, though it is not always clear what he understood about the historical background of each work.

that each of the writings that are a part of the CE were received as authoritative Scripture by many readers long before Eusebius, they provide only limited insight regarding the state of the corpus during the second and third centuries. It may be that the individual writings of this collection were generally known during this time but that the collection as a whole was still in a state of development or that it was not circulating extensively in certain areas.

The canonical relationship between Acts and the Catholic Epistles. An interesting observation that can be made from the extant textual witnesses is that that the CE shared a close canonical relationship with Acts. Some early manuscripts contain only Acts,[26] some only the CE,[27] while some place Acts and the CE together.[28] Not all Greek manuscripts place the Catholic Epistles immediately following Acts, though this appears to have been a fairly common practice. As a result of this canonical relationship, Acts and the Catholic Epistles have often been treated as something like a joint canonical collection that has traditionally been referred to as the *Praxapostolos*.

Modern readers may question why English translations consistently place the CE after the Pauline Epistles if this was not the most common arrangement in the Greek tradition. The simple answer is that many of the earliest printed English Bibles followed the arrangement of the material that may be observed in various manuscripts of the Latin Vulgate. While Latin manuscripts arranged the canonical material in a variety of ways over the years,[29] several editions of the Vulgate

---

[26]Because Acts was typically placed before all other writings except for the Gospels, it is often difficult to ascertain which writings, if any, followed Acts in several Greek manuscripts. Several early textual witnesses include portions of Acts, but it is unclear whether the Catholic Epistles would have also been included in the original manuscript. This is the case with papyri such as $\mathfrak{P}^8$, $\mathfrak{P}^{29}$, $\mathfrak{P}^{33}/\mathfrak{P}^{58}$ (the two papyri are now thought to have originated as one manuscript), $\mathfrak{P}^{38}$, $\mathfrak{P}^{41}$, $\mathfrak{P}^{48}$, and $\mathfrak{P}^{50}$, as well as Codex Laudianus (E 08) and possibly Codex Mutinensis (H 014) and Codex Angelicus (L 020).

[27]Examples of Greek manuscripts that may have included only the CE include $\mathfrak{P}^{23}$, $\mathfrak{P}^{54}$, $\mathfrak{P}^{72}$, $\mathfrak{P}^{100}$, and Uncial 0173.

[28]In addition to the four major codices discussed above, possible examples include $\mathfrak{P}^{74}$, Uncial 048, Uncial 0166, and Uncial 093.

[29]H. A. G. Houghton, *The Latin New Testament: A Guide to its Early History, Texts, and Manuscripts* (New York: Oxford University Press, 2018), 195.

produced around the sixteenth century followed the order of Gospels, Acts, Pauline Epistles, Catholic Epistles, Revelation. This may be observed, for example, in Erasmus's groundbreaking work, *Novum Instrumentum omne*. First published in 1516, Erasmus's Latin-Greek diglot placed his updated text of the Vulgate side-by-side with his newly created critical edition of the Greek text. Because his main objective was to update the Vulgate, he followed what had become a common arrangement of the New Testament writings in the Latin tradition. The influence of Erasmus's critical edition of the Greek text proved decisive, and subsequent English versions tended to follow this arrangement regardless of whether they were translated from the Latin or the Greek.

When the New Testament canon is viewed as a whole, the placement of the Catholic Epistles between Acts and the Pauline Epistles might seem natural. Three of the four individuals traditionally recognized as the authors of the Catholic Epistles—James, Peter, and John—are major figures in the first half of Acts, with Paul becoming the primary figure in the second half of Luke's narrative. Acts could thus be viewed as an introduction to the authors of the epistles that follow. One of the possible disadvantages of the placement of the CE near the end of the New Testament canon is that it may give the impression to some readers that the collection contains "leftover" or miscellaneous material that is of less importance or practical value than the other writings of the canon. The CE have never been read as frequently as the Gospels or the Pauline Epistles, and probably never will, but the placement of these writings near the end of the New Testament has arguably done little to emphasize their importance.

Conclusions regarding the formation of the Catholic Epistles. Having briefly surveyed a number of extant textual witnesses and early Christian writings, we may conclude that the CE were widely recognized as a discrete canonical collection no later than the middle of the fourth century. Aside from a few exceptions, it would appear that each of the seven epistles were frequently placed alongside each other in Greek codices by this time in the standard order of James, 1-2 Peter,

1-3 John, Jude and that they were well known to Christian readers. While we have a fairly clear picture of the state of the CE collection during the latter half of the fourth century, it is more difficult to ascertain the state of the collection prior to this time. These writings were clearly associated with each other in some form and to some degree prior to the mid-fourth century, though it would seem that this edition did not always appear in the standard form known to contemporary readers. In some cases, fewer than seven epistles may have been included, and the writings do not appear to have been consistently placed in the same order. As previously observed, the Muratorian Canon, a list traditionally thought to have originated during the late second century, refers only to Jude and two of the epistles of John. We may also observe that Origen's reference to the writings of James, Peter, Jude, and John in the first half of the third century may also suggest that he was familiar with a corpus that included all seven epistles. During the early fourth century, Eusebius affirms 1 John and 1 Peter, and acknowledges questions about the authenticity of the other five epistles. At some point in the fourth century, apparently a bit later than Eusebius, the Cheltenham List affirmed each of the Petrine and Johannine Epistles. James and Jude are referred to in this list, but the author notes that their authenticity was questioned. Witness to the collection may also be observed in the extant works of later writers such as Athanasius, Cyril of Jerusalem, Epiphanius, Gregory of Nazianzus, Amphilochius, and Augustine.[30]

Based on the evidence that has survived, it would appear that the individual writings that came to be associated with the CE were generally regarded as Scripture prior to the mid-fourth century and that they occasionally circulated together, though not always as part of a full seven-epistle corpus. Thus, the formation of the CE appears to have been a rather slow process that ultimately culminated with the widespread canonical acceptance of all seven epistles. Some writers during the second and third centuries appear to have been familiar with some

---

[30]For a survey of what these writers reveal regarding the state of the CE, see Nienhuis, *Not by Paul Alone*, 75-79.

writings, but not others. With each passing decade, however, each of the seven writings appear to have become familiar to a larger body of readers and to have been more widely recognized for their antiquity and apostolic authority. Precisely where and when all seven writings that are part of the CE first began to circulate as a canonical collection remains difficult to determine, though we might infer that this likely took place at some point before the middle of the fourth century but that it was not immediately embraced throughout the Mediterranean world. In the end, it is perhaps best to conclude that various editions of the CE that contained different material and features are likely to have emerged around the second century, that a seven-letter edition had begun to circulate sometime around the third century, and that this larger edition with the seven writings placed in a standard order became widely recognized by the fourth century.

REVELATION

Our survey of the early subcollections of the New Testament will conclude with a brief overview of the canonical reception of Revelation.[31] Depending on how one designates Acts, the book of Revelation would serve as either the fourth or fifth canonical subcollection, if we might use the term *collection* rather loosely in reference to a canonical unit. The Apocalypse appears to have been received as Scripture very early in a number of Christian communities, though questions relating to its authorship and date of composition were occasionally raised throughout the patristic period. With regard to the textual evidence, the writing appears in the codices of Sinaiticus, Alexandrinus, and Ephraemi

---

[31]For additional treatment of the early canonical reception of Revelation, see Paula Fredriksen, "Apocalypse and Redemption in Early Christianity: From John of Patmos to Augustine of Hippo," *VC* 45 (1991): 151-83; Charles E. Hill, "The Book of Revelation in Early Christianity," in *The Oxford Handbook of the Book of Revelation*, ed. Craig R. Koester (New York: Oxford University Press, 2020), 396-411; Tobias Nicklas, "The Book of Revelation in the New Testament Canon," in *The Oxford Handbook of the Book of Revelation*, 361-72; Christopher Rowland, "The Reception of the Book of Revelation: An Overview," in *The Book of Revelation and its Interpreters*, ed. Ian Boxall and Richard Tresley (London: Rowman and Littlefield, 2016), 1-25; Michael J. Kruger, "The Reception of the Book of Revelation in the Early Church," in *Book of Seven Seals: The Peculiarity of Revelation, Its Manuscripts, Attestation, and Transmission*, ed. Thomas Kraus and Michael Sommer, WUNT 363 (Tübingen: Mohr Siebeck, 2016), 159-74.

Rescriptus. It does not appear in the extant form of Vaticanus, but a plausible case could be made that it would have been included in the missing portion of the manuscript. The text of Revelation is also preserved in early papyri such as $\mathfrak{P}^{18}$, $\mathfrak{P}^{24}$, $\mathfrak{P}^{47}$, $\mathfrak{P}^{85}$, $\mathfrak{P}^{98}$, and $\mathfrak{P}^{115}$, and in several early uncials such as 0163, 0169, 0207, and 0308.

In addition to the placement of Revelation in several early biblical manuscripts, the testimony of early writers and church leaders such as Justin Martyr, Irenaeus, Clement of Alexandria, Hippolytus, Tertullian, Origen, Jerome, and Augustine may also be cited as evidence for the early recognition of Revelation as authoritative Scripture, as does its inclusion in the Muratorian Canon.[32] Revelation does not appear to have been as popular or read as widely as the four Gospels or several of the other canonical writings, but it was clearly recognized as Scripture by many early Christian readers. We may also observe from the early patristic witnesses that the apostle John was widely regarded as the author of the writing but that this consensus slowly began to erode. Eusebius discusses some of the objections to Johannine authorship and the theory that it was written by a figure such as Cerinthus.[33] He explains that some were reluctant to embrace Revelation as Scripture because of questions related to its authorship and the perception that the text was in many ways unintelligible and indiscernible. Rather than offering clarity regarding key events that will take place at the end of the age, some were of the persuasion that it offered an obscure and unclear picture of the events it described, something that was regarded as contrary to a genuine apostolic work. These types of concerns appear to have become more common by the second half of the fourth century, especially in the East. Revelation was apparently not recognized by the Council of Laodicea (if, indeed, Canon 60 provides reliable information), or by figures in the East such as Cyril of Jerusalem (*Lec.* 4.36) or Gregory of Nazianzus (*Carmen de*

---

[32]Reference or allusions to Revelation may be observed in the works of Justin (*Dial.* 81.4), Irenaeus (several occurrences in *Against Heresies*), Clement of Alexandria (*Paed.* 1.6; 2.11 and *Strom.* 6.13, 16), and Hippolytus of Rome (*Haer.* 7.24).

[33]See, for example, Eusebius's treatment regarding the opinion of Dionysius in *Hist. eccl.* 7.24-25.

veris scripturae libris 12.31). It was also excluded from early editions of the Peshitta, the common Syriac translation of the New Testament used during the fifth century.

One of the more difficult challenges associated with the study of Revelation's canonical history is accounting for the odd manner in which Eusebius treats this writing in *Hist. eccl.* 3.25.1-7. As previously noted, Eusebius refers to Revelation in his treatment of the recognized works (*homologoumena*) and in his treatment of the spurious writings (*notha*). He clearly recognizes the long-standing recognition of Revelation as Scripture but is also aware of uncertainty related to its background and canonical status. How might his inclusion of Revelation in two very different categories of texts be explained? It has recently been suggested that this may have been the result of the tension Eusebius experienced between established methods of categorizing bibliographical material and his own awareness of the background of the writing.[34] For Eusebius, it was appropriate to recognize Revelation for its orthodoxy and widespread use in Christian worship, while also acknowledging that questions had been raised about its authorship and other matters.

Revelation is unique in that it is the one writing in the New Testament that may have actually received less canonical recognition during the third and fourth centuries than in previous periods. In the early centuries, its Johannine authorship appears to have been widely recognized, especially in the West. In his *Dialogue with Trypho*, for example, Justin observes that Revelation was composed by John, one of the apostles of Christ (*Dial.* 81.4). Beginning in the third century, however, some in the East such as Dionysius, a well-known bishop of Alexandria, began to question its Johannine authorship.[35] In addition to concerns about the background of this writing, some appear to have become uncomfortable with aspects of its content. These types of

---

[34]David Young, "The Revelation of John in Eusebius' Catalogue of Scriptures," *WesTJ* 55 (2020): 134-47. For additional discussion of the categories articulated by Eusebius, see Everett R. Kalin, "The New Testament Canon of Eusebius," in *The Canon Debate*, 386-404.

[35]Eusebius provides a brief description of the viewpoints of Dionysius in his work *On the Promises*. See *Hist. eccl.* 7.25.1-27.

concerns appear to have remained fairly common in the East for some time before eventually subsiding. During the late fourth century, the text was affirmed by various councils and appears in various canonical lists. In later centuries, the recognition of the canonical status of Revelation became even more widely recognized.

Conclusions

The evidence examined in this chapter leads to several important conclusions about the formation of the New Testament canon.

The canonical subcollections as the foundation of the canon. As the evidence presented in this chapter has suggested, the formation of the New Testament canon might best be described as a collection of collections. Rather than a twenty-seven-volume collection that slowly took shape over many years as one writing was added at a time, or on a specific occasion in which a consequential decision was made about what should be regarded as Christian Scripture, the evidence would suggest that the canon's formation was the result of a natural process in which smaller subcollections of apostolic writings emerged and eventually became closely associated with one another. Each of the canonical subcollections has its own history that must be explored, and it is only through the study of these smaller collections that one can understand the story of how the greater collection, the New Testament, was formed.

Debate and controversy regarding the canonical status of individual writings were often related to questions about their rightful place within a particular subcollection. Disagreement regarding the status of Hebrews, for example, was not so much over whether it should be admitted into the New Testament, but whether it had a rightful place within the Pauline letter corpus. Rather than fourteen individual writings that just happened to be associated with Paul working their way into the canon independently over a lengthy period of time, it was simply the case that the Pauline letter corpus was recognized as canonical Scripture. Consequently, as long as a work such as Hebrews was regarded as part of the Pauline corpus, its canonical status was generally recognized. The only notable exception to this pattern is Revelation, a writing that did not circulate as part of a specific subcollection. Acts also appears to have circulated independently, but its canonical status was never seriously questioned. As noted above, there is also evidence that it later became closely associated with the Catholic Epistles.

The emergence of the canonical subcollections. The evidence explored in this chapter has also provided insight about the general state of each of the canonical subcollections in early Christianity. The first subcollection to develop would have likely been the Pauline corpus. It is possible that initial collections of Paul's writings were limited to ten epistles (the Pastorals and Hebrews omitted), and that editions containing thirteen or fourteen writings began to circulate soon thereafter. This would have been followed by the emergence of the fourfold Gospel, a collection that appears to have been well known by the second half of the second century and may have formed as early as the first half of the second century. The various witnesses to the early state of the canon make clear that there was an overwhelming consensus that the four canonical Gospels provide authoritative witness to the life and teaching of Christ. As a result, they quickly became closely linked to one another and began to circulate throughout the Christian world as a discrete unit. In addition to the Gospels and Pauline Epistles, the other major unit of literary texts that formed the core of the New Testament canon was the Catholic Epistles. The CE took longer to emerge as a canonical unit and do not appear to have circulated as widely as the Gospels and Pauline Epistles. It would seem that there was occasional reluctance to recognize the authenticity of some of the epistles and that some of the writings were not as widely known as others. By around the fourth century, however, a seven-letter collection of the CE appears to have been widely recognized. As the writings became more widely known and as questions related to their authenticity and background began to dissipate, recognition of the CE as a discrete collection become more common. Looking at the larger picture, it may be said that the formation of the CE was really the final major step in the formation of the

New Testament as a whole. As David Nienhuis and Robert Wall explain, "The Catholic Epistle collection can thus be seen to represent the final redactional act of the church's canon-constructing endeavor."[36] To these three primary subcollections, we may add the book of Acts, a writing that was often linked to the CE and shared a common author with the Gospel of Luke, as well as Revelation, a unique writing that provides a fitting conclusion to the canon.

---

[36]Nienhuis and Wall, *Reading the Epistles*, 17.

PART THREE

QUESTIONS RELATING to the AUTHORITY of the NEW TESTAMENT CANON

APOSTOLICITY AND THE FORMATION OF THE NEW TESTAMENT CANON

WHAT ROLE DID THE CRITERION OF APOSTOLICITY PLAY
IN THE FORMATION OF THE NEW TESTAMENT CANON?

*The church upheld the apostolic witness in its sacred literature
as a way of grounding its faith in Jesus, represented by the
apostles' teaching, and insuring that the church's tradition was
not severed from its historical roots and proximity to Jesus, the
primary authority of the church.*

LEE MARTIN McDONALD, *THE BIBLICAL CANON*

OUR FOCUS TO THIS POINT IN THE VOLUME has largely centered on historical matters related to the composition and formation of the New Testament. We have considered the unique contributions that certain types of individuals likely played in the compositional process of the New Testament writings, revisited concepts such as "original audience" and "original autographs," explored the possibility that an influential figure such as Marcion or Constantine or an ecclesiastical body of some kind may have played a significant role in the establishment of the canon, and considered how the emergence of the various canonical subcollections provides a plausible explanation for the formation of the larger canonical collection known as the New Testament. We will continue to treat a number of historical issues in the final two chapters, though our aim here is to address an important theological consideration—namely, the question of the canon's authority. As we reflect on the prominence and influence of these writings throughout church history, it is helpful to consider not only *how* they were written and eventually came together as a single collection, but *why* they were recognized as authoritative Scripture in the first place. We are dealing, after all, not simply with ancient artifacts but with writings that have exerted significant influence for two millennia and continue to be recognized as sacred Scripture by Christians around the world today.

In what follows, it will be suggested that apostolic authorship was regarded as the primary basis for the authority of the New Testament writings in the early church and that it remains foundational to its authority today. The New Testament is not simply a book of "classics" from the early church that have achieved popularity as a result of their appeal to readers. To be clear, the canonical writings were highly esteemed for their practical relevance and theological significance. The recognition of their status as authoritative Scripture, however, was closely linked to perceptions about their origin. While there were disputes about the background of certain writings, it became widely recognized that each of the New Testament writings were composed by those who were part of the small body of individuals that Christ had directly commissioned to continue his earthly mission.

Because of the number of complex subjects that relate to the issue of apostolic authorship and the basis of the canon's authority, we will take up the subject of apostolicity over the course of two chapters. In this chapter we will consider the role that the criterion of apostolicity appears to have played in the formation of the canon and why many contemporary readers are often reluctant to recognize a connection between a work's human author and its authority. In the following chapter we will take up the subject of the New Testament's ongoing authority more directly and consider how the subject of apostolic authorship might be understood in relation to other subjects such as inspiration, divine providence, and the role of the church.

THE CRITERION OF APOSTOLICITY AND
THE ESTABLISHMENT OF THE NEW TESTAMENT CANON

Before we address the possible basis of the New Testament's ongoing authority, it will be helpful to first consider several foundational historical questions relating to the subject of apostolic authorship. In what follows, we will briefly consider four particular subjects: (1) the affinity for apostolic instruction in the early church; (2) the manner in which perceptions about the authorship of early Christian writings may have impacted their reception; (3) the practice of pseudepigraphy; (4) and the scope of the apostolic community.

The affinity for apostolic instruction in early Christianity. A number of early sources reveal that the early church placed a significant emphasis on the importance of apostolic instruction.[1] We find in Luke's narrative that the early followers of Jesus "were continually devoting themselves to the apostles' teaching and to fellowship, to the breaking of bread and to prayer. Everyone kept feeling a sense of awe; and many wonders and signs were taking place through the apostles" (Acts 2:42-43). This brief passage provides a succinct yet valuable portrait of the first generation of Christians living in Jerusalem. Not to be overlooked, the first of the four activities Luke alludes to in this passage is the teaching of the apostles. As those who had lived and ministered alongside Jesus and had been personally appointed by him to carry out his mission, it was only natural for early believers to look to the apostles as the primary leaders of the fledgling movement. In a practical sense, the Twelve functioned as extensions of Jesus' earthly ministry. After his earthly life came to an end, the disciples continued to spread the good

---

[1]In addition to the major works on the New Testament canon, further treatment related to the subject of apostolic authority may be found in the following sources: Everett Ferguson, "The Appeal to Apostolic Authority in the Early Centuries," *ResQ* 50 (2008): 49-62; Hans von Campenhausen, *Ecclesiastical Authority and Spiritual Power in the Church of the First Three Centuries* (Peabody, MA: Hendrickson, 1997); John Howard Schütz, *Paul and the Anatomy of Apostolic Authority* (Louisville, KY: Westminster John Knox, 2007); A. Hilhorst, ed. *The Apostolic Age in Patristic Thought*, SVC 70 (Leiden: Brill, 2004); Lee Martin McDonald, "Identifying Scripture and Canon in the Early Church: The Criteria Question," in *The Canon Debate*, ed. Lee Martin McDonald and James A. Sanders (Peabody, MA: Hendrickson, 2002), 424-27; Daniel Castelo and Robert W. Wall, *The Marks of Scripture: Rethinking the Nature of the Bible* (Grand Rapids, MI: Baker Academic, 2019), 117-37.

news of the gospel and take part in his earthly work. In recognition of their close relationship with Christ, their teaching was widely regarded as part of the authoritative foundation of the church's doctrine (cf. Eph 2:20). In fact, those who challenged or rejected their authority and teaching were often portrayed as divisive (cf. 2 Thess 3:14). The apostles certainly had their personal limitations and shortcomings, yet the authority of their teaching was widely recognized throughout the Christian world.

As the Christian movement continued to expand, it became increasingly difficult for the apostles to play an active and direct role in the ever-expanding Christian communities throughout the Roman world. With each passing decade, the Christian faith continued to grow numerically as well as geographically, all while the number of active apostles steadily decreased. Because of their inability to provide personal instruction in each community, several of the apostles and their close associates composed a number of works for those living in distant locations. This practice was of benefit not only to the original readers, but to subsequent generations of believers who sought to remain, to use Luke's language once again, devoted to the apostles' teaching. The production of apostolic literature allowed the apostles to provide timely and useful instruction and encouragement to those they were unable to visit, while ensuring the preservation of their teaching and eyewitness testimony of the life of Jesus.[2]

This high regard for apostolic instruction was by no means limited to Jesus' initial followers in Jerusalem and elsewhere. In several of the writings of the church fathers we find further evidence of the foundational role that their teaching played in the life of Christian communities and in the formation of Christian doctrine. To cite but a few

---

[2]Written instruction was often regarded as a less than ideal substitute for in-person instruction and interaction. This would have been especially the case with the Epistles of the New Testament. Paul, for example, appears to have only penned letters when his circumstances did not allow for him to visit a particular community. Even with the Gospels, we find that there was a desire for living eyewitness testimony of the life of Christ. While many details of his account are disputed, Eusebius's discussion about Papias emphasizes this point. He observes that Papias desired "the living and abiding voice." *Hist. eccl.* 3.29.4 (*NPNF* 2.7).

examples, Ignatius famously wrote on his journey to martyrdom in Rome, "I do not give you orders like Peter and Paul: they were apostles, I am a convict; they were free, but I am even now still a slave" (*Rom.* 4.3).[3] Similarly, the author of *1 Clement* writes, "The apostles received the gospel for us from the Lord Jesus Christ; Jesus the Christ was sent forth from God. So then Christ is from God, and the apostles are from Christ. Both, therefore, came of the will of God in good order" (*1 Clem.* 42:1-2).[4] The second-century apologist Irenaeus emphasized the role that the apostles played in providing the church with authoritative teaching: "We have learned from none others the plan of our salvation, than from those through whom the Gospel has come down to us, which they did at one time proclaim in public, and, at a later period, by the will of God, handed down to us in the Scriptures, to be the ground and pillar of our faith" (*Haer.* 3.1.1).[5] Tertullian contended that true teaching finds its foundation in the teaching of the apostles and does not rest on the authority of modern teachers: "We, however, are not permitted to cherish any object after our own will, nor yet to make choice of that which another has introduced of his private fancy. In the Lord's apostles we possess our authority; for even they did not of themselves choose to introduce anything, but faithfully delivered to the nations (of mankind) the doctrine which they had received from Christ."[6] Eusebius emphasized the exclusive nature of the apostolic community when he explained that Jesus, ". . .not long after the beginning of his ministry, called the twelve apostles, and these alone of all his disciples he named apostles, as an especial honor."[7] Finally, Cyril of Jerusalem describes the instruction written by the leadership of the Jerusalem Council as "universal from the Holy Ghost" (*Lec.* 27.29).[8] Many additional passages could also be cited. This brief sampling of patristic

---

[3]Cited from Michael W. Holmes, ed, *The Apostolic Fathers: Greek Texts and English Translations*, 3rd ed. (Grand Rapids, MI: Baker Academic, 1999), 171.

[4]Holmes, *The Apostolic Fathers*, 75.

[5]Irenaeus, *Haer.* 3.1.1 (*ANF* 1).

[6]Tertullian, *Praescr.* 6 (*ANF* 3).

[7]Eusebius, *Hist. eccl.* 1.10.1 (*NPNF* 2.1)

[8]Cyril of Jerusalem, *Lec.* 27.29 (*NPNF* 2.7).

testimony is simply illustrative of the high esteem for apostolic instruction in the early church and the recognition of its authority. As the British scholar and clergyman B. F. Westcott stated many years ago:

> They [early Christian writers] attributed to them [the apostles] power and wisdom to which they themselves made no claim. Without having any exact sense of the completeness of the Christian Scriptures, they still drew a line between them and their own writings. As if by some providential instinct, each one of those teachers who stood nearest to the writers of the New Testament contrasted his writings with theirs, and definitely placed himself on a lower level.[9]

Apostolicity and the reception of the New Testament writings. In view of the high esteem of early Christians for the apostles and the importance that was placed on their instruction, it was only natural for writings that were linked to the apostles to become quickly and widely recognized as authoritative Scripture. Although a large body of Christian writings was produced in the decades and centuries following the establishment of the church, it was the relatively small number of writings linked to the apostles that circulated most frequently, that made the greatest impact on the life and teaching of the church, and which ultimately came to be recognized as canonical Scripture. In fact, each of the works of the New Testament was understood to be linked in one way or another to the apostolic ministry of Christ's early followers, and therefore indirectly connected to Christ himself.

We will consider the contemporary relevance of apostolic authorship more directly in the final chapter. For the present, it will be helpful to observe that as a historical matter, the works that were widely perceived to have been composed by the apostles or those with direct ties to the apostles were the works that were embraced as authoritative instruction and recognized as canonical Scripture. Conversely, the writings commonly understood to have been written after the lifetime of the apostles or by those outside the apostolic circle were not widely recognized as

---

[9]B. F. Westcott, *A General Survey of the History of the Canon of the New Testament*, 7th ed. (London: Macmillan, 1896), 57.

authoritative Scripture. To be clear, apostolicity was not the only factor influencing the reception of early Christian writings. We find evidence that the authoritative status of some works was questioned at least in part as a result of theological concerns (e.g., Hebrews and Revelation),[10] or because they did not appear to be as conducive to public reading in church gatherings (again, Revelation), or simply because they were not as well known to early Christians or thought to be of limited practical value (e.g., 2–3 John, Jude). Augustine explains in his famous *Christian Instruction*, for example, that preference should be given to works that were either affirmed by the majority of churches or by the churches with the most authority (*Doctr. chr.* 2.8).

Although it was clearly the case that a variety of factors influenced the reception of early Christian writings, the earliest witnesses to the canon strongly suggest that the perception of a work's authorship was the leading factor in whether it was ultimately recognized as canonical Scripture. Apostolicity, of course, was not unrelated to these other factors. If a work was regarded as apostolic, it was only natural for it to likewise be recognized as orthodox and of ancient origin. To put the matter a bit differently, we would not expect early readers to recognize a work as apostolic while rejecting its authoritative status, antiquity, and theological orthodoxy. As a consequence of the close connection between various attributes of Scripture, we might suspect that there would have been occasions in which early Christians assessed the possible apostolic status of a work by considering factors such as its reception and content. Augustine, for example, surely understood that the reception of a work by various Christian communities is a strong indication of its apostolic origin and authority.

The influential role that apostolicity played in the reception of early Christian writings may be observed in a number of early references to the canonical writings, only a few of which may be referenced here. The

---

[10]There is some evidence that the warning passages of Hebrews were a concern for some during the controversy over the lapsed which reached its peak during the third century. See Benjamin P. Laird, *The Pauline Corpus in Early Christianity: Its Formation, Publication, and Circulation* (Peabody, MA: Hendrickson, 2022), 209-14.

Muratorian Fragment, an important witness discussed in the fifth chapter, is especially noteworthy. The author of the canonical list contained in this manuscript states that the epistles written to the Laodiceans and the Alexandrians—writings that are no longer extant— were "[both] forged in Paul's name to [further] the heresy of Marcion."[11] Other unnamed writings "cannot be received into the catholic church," the author explains, as "it not fitting that gall be mixed with honey." The writer also refers to the *Shepherd of Hermas*, describing it as a work written "very recently, in our times, in the city of Rome." The work may be useful in certain respects, but it is not to be counted "among the apostles, for it is after [their] time."[12] As assertions such as these in-dicate, there was clearly an effort to distinguish between the writings that can legitimately be traced back to the apostles and those that were written later and were thus not to be regarded as part of the body of apostolic Scripture.

Similar explanations are offered in Eusebius's survey of early Christian writings in his *Ecclesiastical History*. In his enumerations of the works of Scripture (*Hist. eccl.* 3:3 and 3.25), he describes some works using terms such as "genuine," "undisputed," "accepted," and "acknowledged," while noting that the authenticity of other works was disputed.[13] With regard to the Pauline Epistles, Eusebius observes that fourteen epistles are to be recognized, though some in Rome disputed the canonical status of Hebrews on the basis of its uncertain Pauline authorship. We may finally note that similar language is used by Jerome in his *On Illustrious Men*. With regard to the Petrine Epistles, Jerome observed that 2 Peter was regarded by some as inauthentic, a

---

[11]Some scholars are of the persuasion that the *Epistle to the Laodiceans* was simply an epistle that Paul reworked from one of his other writings or that it was a lost pseudonymous writing de-signed to satisfy the curiosity of those familiar with the reference to Paul's correspondence in Col 4:16. Assuming the authenticity of Colossians, it would seem most likely that Paul did in fact write a letter to the Laodiceans, but that this writing was not included in initial collections of the corpus and is thus no longer extant.

[12]Translation adopted from Bruce Metzger, *The Canon of the New Testament: Its Origin, Develop-ment, and Significance* (Oxford: Clarendon, 1987), 307.

[13]See chap. 5 for further information regarding Eusebius's treatment of the canon and the catego-ries in which he lists the individuals works.

judgment that was based, at least in part, on the conclusion that its style differs from that of the first epistle (*Vir. ill.* 1). Jerome also reveals that some had rejected the Pauline authorship of Hebrews because of the opinion that its style and language are inconsistent with that of Paul. Additional examples could be cited but cannot be fully explored here. Suffice it to say that that when questions arose about the apostolic origin of a given work, the work tended to be rejected as Scripture or struggle for widespread canonical reception (e.g., Hebrews and several of the Catholic Epistles).

The practice of pseudonymity and the question of authority. As noted above, early Christian literature is replete with references and allusions to the works of the apostles and their lives and ministries, a reality that cannot be adequately explained apart from the widespread recognition of apostolic authority in early Christianity. It was common for apologetic works, theological treatises, homilies, catechetical instruction, epistolary literature, and other types of early Christian writings to make appeals and references to the works of the apostles in order to defend a particular theological belief or to provide instruction and encouragement to readers. These numerous references clearly indicate that the influence of the apostles was not limited to their lifetimes and that they were regarded as the primary witnesses to Christ's redemptive work and teaching. Noting the importance of the apostolic witness to Christ, John Webster explains that the canonical writings may be described as "an account of the extension of Christ's active, communicative presence in the Spirit's power through the commissioned apostolic testimony."[14]

Within the wider body of early Christian literature were several pseudonymous works attributed to members of the apostolic circle. Pseudepigraphy, it will be recalled, refers to the ancient practice of composing a work and falsely attributing it to another individual, usually one who was more widely known or influential. Put simply, pseudonymous writings are literary forgeries designed to deceive audiences into

---

[14]John Webster, *Holy Scripture: A Dogmatic Sketch* (Cambridge: Cambridge University Press, 2003), 59.

thinking that the text was written by someone other than the true author. The practice might be thought of as the opposite of plagiarism. Whereas plagiarism involves the presentation of another author's work as one's own, pseudepigraphy involves the attribution of one's work to another figure. Both practices involve deception, though the motivations tend to differ.

Among the large body of literature that has survived from early Christianity are several noncanonical gospels, acts, apocalyptic works, epistles, and other types of writings that were attributed to one of the apostles or other prominent Christians. As an example, we might point to the large number of clearly inauthentic works attributed to Peter and Paul. Early writings attributed to Peter include works such as *The Gospel of Peter*, *The Apocalypse of Peter*, and the lesser-known *Kerygma Petri* (the *Preaching of Peter*), while works attributed to Paul include works titled *The Epistle to the Laodiceans*, *The Apocalypse of Paul*, *Third Corinthians*, and a number of clearly fictious letters purported to have been written by Paul to Seneca, the famous Stoic philosopher and Roman statesman.[15]

Most of the pseudonymous works that have survived appear to have been written at some point after the lifetime of those to whom they are attributed, but this was not always the case. In his second canonical epistle to the Thessalonians, Paul, or, as some would have it, an unknown individual who composed the writing in Paul's name, instructs his readers to not be swayed by false teaching, even if it is contained in an epistle that purports to have been written by him or one of his

---

[15]Recent treatments of early Christian pseudepigraphy and other apocryphal writings include the following: J. K. Elliott, *The Apocryphal New Testament: A Collection of Apocryphal Christian Literature in an English Translation Based on M. R. James* (New York: Oxford University Press, 1993); Tony Burke and Brent Landau, eds., *New Testament Apocrypha: More Noncanonical Scriptures,* vol. 1 (Grand Rapids, MI: Eerdmans, 2016); Tony Burke, ed., *The New Testament Apocrypha: More Noncanonical Scriptures. Volume 2* (Grand Rapids, MI: Eerdmans, 2020); Tony Burke, ed., *The New Testament Apocrypha: More Noncanonical Scriptures. Volume 3* (Grand Rapids, MI: Eerdmans, 2023); Tony Burke, ed., *Fakes, Forgeries, and Fictions: Writing Ancient and Modern Christian Apocrypha* (Eugene, OR: Cascade, 2017); Bart D. Ehrman, *Forgery and Counterforgery: The Use of Literary Deceit in Early Christian Polemics* (New York: Oxford University Press, 2013); Wolfgang Speyer, *Die literarische Fälschung im heidnischen und christlichen Altertum: Ein Versuch ihrer Deutung* (München: Beck, 1971); David G. Meade, *Pseudonymity and Canon: An Investigation into the Relationship of Authorship and Authority in Jewish and Earliest Christian Tradition* (Grand Rapids, MI: Eerdmans, 1987).

companions (2 Thess 2:2).[16] As his reputation as a letter writer and as the "apostle to the Gentiles" continued to grow, the number of pseudonymous works written under his name appears to have only increased.

Some modern readers may find it difficult to understand why the practice of pseudepigraphy was so common and what would have motivated individuals to produce pseudonymous works in the first place. The circumstances that prompted the composition of each of the writings that were attributed to notable Christian writers such as Peter and Paul would have been unique, of course, but scholars generally recognize that many of these works were written for one or more of the following purposes: (1) to establish the writing's authority; (2) to enhance or preserve an individual's legacy; (3) to contextualize the teaching of a particular Christian leader for particular audiences; (4) to satisfy historical interests (e.g., a lost letter of Paul); or (5) to provide additional clarification or information regarding one or more subjects that are not fully addressed elsewhere. Once these objectives are recognized, it is not difficult to imagine why a number of writings were produced under the names of eminent figures such as the apostles, even long after their lifetimes. While each of these objectives appear to have had a role in prompting the creation of pseudonymous works, the most common purpose of these writings was to ensure its acceptance in Christian communities. By attributing a work to a known apostle or other prominent figure, a writer had a much better chance of his or her work being read and recognized as authoritative instruction. As Bart Ehrman rightly observes, writers often "assumed false names for one chief end: to provide for their views an authority that otherwise would have proved difficult to obtain had they written anonymously or in their own names."[17]

Because of the frequency in which pseudonymous works were produced, it is sometimes suggested that early Christians did not have an entirely negative perspective of the practice. In fact, some have

---

[16]For an alternative viewpoint on the language of 2 Thess 2:2, see Timothy A. Brookins, "The Alleged 'Letter Allegedly from Us': The Parallel Function of ὡς δι᾽ ἡμῶν in 2 Thessalonians 2.2," *JSNT* 45 (2021): 109-31.

[17]Ehrman, *Forgery and Counterforgery*, 150.

suggested that pseudonymous works often served as honorable tributes to the legacy of a given figure or that early Christians showed little interest in investigating the background of works attributed to the apostles and other prominent figures. The historian J. N. D. Kelly's reflections on the Pastoral Epistles serves as a fitting example of this perspective:

> Pseudonymity, or the practice of publishing one's own works under the name of some revered personage of the past, was fashionable in both Jewish and Christian circles about the beginning of our era. . . . The modern reader who feels an initial shock at what he takes to be fraud should reflect that the attitude, approach, and literary standards of that age were altogether different from those accepted today. The author who attributed his own work to an apostle was probably sincerely convinced that it faithfully reproduced the great man's teaching and point of view. It is also likely that, in the first and early second century at any rate, Christians had little or no interest in the personality of the human agent who wrote their sacred books. The Spirit who had spoken through the apostles was still active in prophetic men, and when they put pen to paper it was he who was the real author of their productions.[18]

It is certainly the case that a number of pseudonymous works circulated in early Christianity and that some of them were even recognized as authoritative Scripture, at least by those living in certain places and at certain times. The general posture of the church, however, was that pseudepigraphy was a deceptive and dishonorable practice and that it is only the works that can make a rightful claim to have derived from the apostles or members of their immediate circle that are to be recognized as authoritative Scripture. Evidence for this perspective is quite compelling and has been discussed in detail by a number of scholars. A couple of examples of how the church responded to certain pseudepigraphal works will illustrate this point.

In his instructional work *On Baptism*, Tertullian makes reference to a legendary writing known as *The Acts of Paul and Thecla*, a text that

---

[18]J. N. D. Kelly, *The Pastoral Epistles*, BNTC 14 (Peabody, MA: Hendrickson, 2009), 5.

was part of a larger apocryphal work known as *The Acts of Paul*. Patterned after the canonical work of Acts, this account includes several stories about Paul's ministry and travels, an excerpt of a sermon he supposedly delivered that is noticeably similar to Jesus' Sermon on the Mount, and his supposed conversations with various individuals, most notably a young aristocratic woman named Thecla. In his instruction on the practice of baptism (*De baptismo* 17), Tertullian observes that a certain presbyter in the province of Asia manufactured the account about Thecla "from his own materials under Paul's name . . . in support of women's freedom to teach and baptize."[19] Tertullian finds the act highly egregious, not simply because of its deceptive nature but because, in his estimation, it misrepresented Paul's teaching on the role of women in the life of the church. The individual who was responsible for the composition of the work was discovered, Tertullian records, and was promptly removed from his position. While some might argue that Tertullian and others were offended simply because of the content of the pseudonymous writing, the fact that the individual was forced to step down from his leadership role might suggest that the production of apocryphal and pseudepigraphal literature was regarded as a significant offense.

A second example concerns a pseudonymous work attributed to Paul's companion Timothy that was published during the fifth century by a presbyter in Marseilles named Serapion.[20] The text *Ad Ecclesiam* is presented as a letter from Timothy to a congregation that had grown lax in its commitment to its calling. In response to this development, "Timothy" encourages the church's members to embrace a more moderate and disciplined lifestyle and to care for the needs of those with little. It was later discovered that this letter was composed by Serapion's bishop Salvian, who defended his actions by contending that it is the content of a writing that is important, not the identity of its author. Ehrman is certainly correct to question this argument, noting

---

[19]Translation from *Tertullian's Treatises: Concerning Prayer, Concerning Baptism*, trans. Alexander Souter (New York: Macmillan, 1919).

[20]For relevant background on this writing, see Ehrman, *Forgery and Counterforgery*, 94-96.

that it would have been unnecessary to falsely write in the name of "Timothy" if the human author was inconsequential. "If he really thought that an author's name did not matter," Ehrman asks, "why would he write pseudonymously? Why not write in his own name? Or even better, if names do not matter, why not write the book anonymously?"[21] As Ehrman observes, the work was clearly written under the name of Timothy in order to enhance its credibility and thereby extend its influence.

These instances remind us that a number of pseudonymous works were indeed produced during the early centuries of Christianity. Contrary to what some have assumed, however, the practice was viewed unfavorably by the majority of Christians, and works that were not recognized as authentic were rarely recognized as authoritative Scripture. Despite ongoing debate about the extent to which pseudonymous works were received as canonical Scripture and whether there are pseudonymous writings in the New Testament canon, it is clear that one of the primary factors that prompted the creation of pseudepigraphal literature was the high value placed on apostolic literature. If apostolic authorship was not recognized as a foundational attribute of authoritative Scripture, it would be difficult to account for the large body of writings that circulated in early Christianity under the names of the apostles or those who were part of the wider apostolic circle.

The apostolic circle and the New Testament writings. Many readers find the concept of apostolic authority to be somewhat puzzling because of the fact that several works in the New Testament do not appear to have been written directly by apostles. Even if we were to affirm the traditional authorship of the anonymous writings and the authenticity of the others, we would still be left with several writings that were not written directly by one of the Twelve or by the apostle Paul. This would include the Gospels of Mark and Luke, the book of Acts, and the epistles of James and Jude. How important could apostolic authority be, it might be asked, if several writings were composed anonymously or by

---

[21]Ehrman, *Forgery and Counterforgery*, 95.

those who were not recognized as apostles?[22] Making the subject even more challenging is the distinction some have made between apostolicity and apostolic authorship. As C. Stephen Evans suggests, "The concept of apostolic authority must not be identified with the concept of apostolic authorship. Apostolic authorship certainly is an indicator of apostolic authority, but it is clear that the church, in making decisions about the New Testament canon, did not identify apostolic authority with apostolic authorship."[23] In this line of thinking, the works written by the apostles are certainly apostolic, though we need not conclude that all apostolic writings were composed directly by apostles.

So where does this leave us? What are we to make of the fact that the early church placed a significant emphasis on apostolic authority while simultaneously recognizing several works as Scripture that were not written by those directly commissioned by Christ as apostles? In order to address this thorny issue, we must first recognize that early Christian readers did not limit their recognition of apostolic authorship to the Twelve and the apostle Paul. In other words, there seems to have been a larger body of individuals who were associated with the apostolic community than what is typically recognized today. In one sense, the identity of the apostles is rather straightforward. Each of the Synoptic Gospels include a list of the individuals whom Jesus called as disciples and commissioned as apostles (Mt 10:2-4; Mk 3:16-19; Lk 6:13-16). While there is dispute regarding the identity of certain individuals in these lists (e.g., is the Bartholomew of the Synoptics to be identified as the Nathaniel of John's Gospel?), there clearly was a defined group of "the Twelve." To this rather exclusive and clearly defined group, we may also add Paul, an apostle who was "untimely born" (1 Cor 15:8) and who was occasionally compelled to defend his apostolic status. Each of these

---

[22]While many of the New Testament writings are formally anonymous, Gregory Goswell observes that each of these writings quickly became connected to specific members of the apostolic community. Gregory Goswell, "Authorship and Anonymity in the New Testament Writings," *JETS* 60 (2017): 733-49.

[23]C. Stephen Evans, "Canonicity, Apostolicity, and Biblical Authority: Some Kierkegaardian Reflections," in *Canon and Biblical Interpretation*, ed. Craig Bartholomew et al. (Grand Rapids, MI: Zondervan, 2006), 151.

men was directly called by Christ, whom they personally encountered in his resurrected state (1 Cor 15:5-9), and performed various "signs, wonders, and miracles," which served as evidence that they were "true apostle[s]" (2 Cor 12:12; see also, Acts 2:43; 5:12; 14:3; Rom 15:19; Heb 2:3-4). Interestingly, there are additional figures in the New Testament writings that appear to be recognized as part of the apostolic community, a reality that can make the subject of apostolicity rather difficult to navigate. In order to gain a clearer sense of how early Christians understood the extent of the apostolic community, it will be helpful to briefly consider the language that is used in the New Testament for various individuals and how early Christian writers distinguished between members of the apostolic community.

APOSTOLIC LANGUAGE IN THE NEW TESTAMENT

Many contemporary readers may be surprised to learn that a number of passages in the New Testament refer to individuals other than Paul or members of the Twelve using language that may suggest that they were part of the apostolic mission or part of the broader apostolic community. This would include none other than Jesus (Heb 3:1) as well as Barnabas (Acts 14:4, 14), Andronicus and Junia (Rom 16:7), Silas and Timothy (1 Thess 1:1; 2:6), and possibly James the brother of Jesus (Gal 1:19).[24] The language used to describe these individuals may seem a bit unexpected given that the Twelve are often referred to as a singular group, especially in Luke-Acts. On the other hand, it might be suggested that the use of this language is not all that remarkable given that the Greek noun ἀπόστολος (*apostolos*) and its verbal cognate ἀποστέλλω (*apostellō*) appear frequently in Greek literature in reference to those who have been commissioned to deliver some type of message or instruction (*apostolos*) or to the act of commissioning an individual to deliver a message (*apostellō*). Paul and the members of the Twelve were

---

[24]Epaphroditus is also referred to as an apostle in Phil 2:25, but not as an apostle of Christ. For further background relating to each of these individuals and a discussion of their possible apostolic role, see Benjamin P. Laird, "Apostolicity and the Formation of the New Testament Canon," in *The New Testament Canon in Contemporary Research*, ed. Stanley E. Porter and Benjamin P. Laird, TENTS (Leiden: Brill, forthcoming).

certainly not the only individuals who proclaimed the gospel message or who were commissioned to deliver an important message or proclamation! While it is certainly the case that these words were used in a variety of contexts, we also find that writers such as Luke and Paul often applied these terms to a clearly defined group of witnesses who were directly commissioned by Jesus.

Crucial to understanding the apostolic language used in early Christian writings is the recognition that those who served alongside the apostles often functioned as extensions of their ministries. This was most clearly evident in the ministry of the apostle Paul. As is clear from Acts as well as his extant writings, Paul often traveled with a number of companions (e.g., Barnabas, Silas, Timothy, Titus) who assisted him in his missionary work. Despite his commitment to passionately proclaim the gospel "from Jerusalem and round about as far as Illyricum" (Rom 15:19), there were many occasions in which he was not able to travel to a particular location to provide instruction or to personally visit with believers. On these occasions, he would often send one of his trusted companions to minister to them in order to provide additional instruction, encouragement, and guidance, and even to deliver his letters. When individuals such as Timothy or Titus took part in the work that Paul had assigned them, they served in a practical sense as extensions of his ministry.

Based on these factors, we might conclude that while there was a clearly defined group of disciples who served as the primary witnesses of the resurrected Christ and who were directly commissioned to lead the church, similar language was occasionally used in reference to individuals who assisted them or who otherwise took part in the proclamation of the gospel. It is often necessary, therefore, to carefully evaluate the immediate context of a given passage in order to determine the sense in which certain individuals were part of the apostolic mission. As we consider the language of the New Testament and its portrayal of various individuals, we might observe that there were three basic types of individuals who were described as apostles: (1) Christ, the most eminent apostle (Heb 3:1), who was sent directly by God the Father with a divine mission; (2) the twelve disciples and the apostle Paul, who were eyewitnesses of the resurrected Lord and were directly appointed by him to provide leadership and instruction for the newly founded church; and (3) individuals such as Barnabas and Silas, who worked directly with one or more of the apostles and served a prominent role in the early years of the Christian movement. Not all members of the apostolic community shared the same degree of notoriety or influence, but it does appear that the apostolic circle was generally understood to be much wider than is typically recognized by modern readers.

TERTULLIAN AND THE "APOSTOLIC MEN"

An interesting vignette that provides insight into how early Christians often understood the concept of the apostolic circle comes to us in Tertullian's polemical work attacking Marcion. Defending the recognition of four authoritative Gospels rather than only one, the position held by Marcion, Tertullian makes the following assertions:

> The documents of the gospel have the apostles for their authors, and . . . this task of promulgating the gospel was imposed upon them by our Lord himself. If they also have for their authors apostolic men, yet these stand not alone, but as companions of apostles or followers of apostles: because the preaching of disciples might be made suspect of the desire of vainglory, unless there stood by it the authority of their teachers, or rather the authority of Christ, which made the apostles teachers.[25]

Tertullian makes several interesting comments in his reflection on the four Gospels. We may first note his remark that the Gospels were written by apostles who were commissioned by "our Lord himself" as well as some who were "apostolic men." He seems to understand that each of the Gospel writers was part of the apostolic community even though their backgrounds and specific callings were different. Matthew and John were clearly numbered among the Twelve and were acknowledged by all as members of the apostolic community. Mark and Luke,

---

[25]*Marc.* 4.2. Translation from *Tertullian: Adversus Marcionem*, trans. Ernest Evans (Oxford: Clarendon, 1972).

on the other hand, are referred to as "apostolic men" who were "companions" and "followers of apostles." Elsewhere he describes Luke as "an apostolic man, not a master but a disciple, in any case less than his master, and assuredly even more of lesser account as being the follower of a later apostle, Paul, to be sure" (*Marc.* 4.2). References such as these would suggest that apostolic authority, at least from the perspective of Tertullian, was an attribute that belongs to writings composed directly by the apostles as well as to the works produced by individuals who served alongside them. This perspective on the scope of the apostolic circle may also be observed in Tertullian's treatment of Hebrews. Although he did not recognize its Pauline authorship, he nonetheless recognized its apostolic authority on the basis of his persuasion that it was written by Paul's companion Barnabas (*Pud.* 20.2). For Tertullian, the Gospels composed by Mark and Luke were to be regarded as apostolic Scripture, though it may have been the case that he did not regard their authority to be equal to that of Matthew and John, prominent figures who were numbered among the Twelve.

Tertullian does not seem to be alone in this viewpoint. As previously observed, the four canonical Gospels appear to have circulated independently for a relatively short period of time before they began to circulate almost exclusively in codices containing the fourfold Gospel. As was noted, the extant witnesses strongly indicate that Matthew and John's Gospels were read more frequently than those attributed to Mark and Luke. The popularity of Matthew and John's writings may be due to a variety of factors such as their unique material or perhaps the greater emphasis they place on Jesus' fulfillment of Old Testament Scripture and the various Jewish institutions. In addition to these general features, it may also have been the case that early Christians were drawn to these writings in large part because of the recognition that they were written directly by Christ's apostles.

The extant testimony of early Christian writers and early witnesses to the New Testament writings reveals that a close connection was often made between a work's perceived authorship and its assumed authority. The identity of a work's author was certainly not the only factor that influencing its early reception, though it was arguably the most consequential. Looking back at the development of the canon, we may conclude that there were no writings that were widely regarded as apostolic that were omitted from the canon. In addition, there does not appear to have been any writings that were widely considered to have been produced outside of the apostolic community that came to be recognized as canonical Scripture.

Contemporary Perspectives on the Relevance of Apostolic Authority

Interest in the background of the canonical writings is by no means unique to early Christians. Numerous textbooks, monographs, articles, and other types of literature continue to be published each year which treat one aspect or another of the composition or historical background of the biblical writings. Despite the continual interest in the background of the writings, there is often a degree of hesitancy to acknowledge the relevance of the human author of the canonical writings. When the subject of apostolic authorship is treated in contemporary studies on the canon, it is often presented simply as an explanation for why some early Christian writings were recognized as Scripture rather than as justification for their present authority. The hesitancy to recognize the relationship between a work's authorship and its status as authoritative Scripture is certainly not limited to experts in the field. It would seem that lay readers and students are increasingly reluctant to recognize the relevance of a work's human author, often viewing it as a largely irrelevant historical matter. Before we take up the ongoing relevance of apostolic authority in the next chapter, it will be helpful to briefly consider why many modern readers have become reluctant to recognize a possible connection between a work's authorship and its status as authoritative Scripture.

Biblical scholarship in the post-Enlightenment era. During the eighteenth century, major shifts took place in how the Bible was interpreted and studied. In many ways, these changes were the inevitable result of notable developments and events that took place in the world of the sciences and humanities from the fourteenth through the seventeenth centuries.[26] It was during these years that a *rinascita*—that is, a "renaissance" or "rebirth" of learning and exploration—occurred, resulting in significant advances in numerous fields of study. During these centuries, scholarship began to look both forward and backward: forward with a renewed focus on exploration and discovery, and backward with a greater appreciation for the great thinkers and works of antiquity. In the world of biblical scholarship, humanist thinkers such as Desiderius Erasmus (1466–1536) and William Tyndale (1494–1536) exemplified the progress taking place at this time. Both men drew on their expertise in classical and biblical languages and produced monumental works that promoted and advanced the study of the biblical text.

A notable development that took place during the Enlightenment period of the seventeenth and eighteenth centuries was the rise of philosophical systems of thought that called the reliability and authority of the biblical writings into question. Philosophical viewpoints and worldviews such as naturalism, rationalism, and empiricism resulted in an increased skepticism of the dogma of the church with many becoming convinced that the claims of Scripture were not to be uncritically accepted. Advocates of these approaches did not always agree on fundamental questions such as how knowledge is acquired or how ideas and beliefs are to be assessed or validated, but they were often in essential agreement that Scripture should not be treated as an authoritative source of absolute truth. Rather than uncritically embrace the claims of Scripture in toto with the assumption that the biblical writings are divinely inspired or that they were written by those who were the final authority on all matters they address, it became commonly assumed that all ideas, arguments, and propositions must be properly

---

[26]Several resources provide background related to the rise of historical criticism. See, for example, William Baird, *History of New Testament Research*, vol. 1: *From Deism to Tübingen* (Minneapolis, MN: Fortress, 1992); Stephen Neill and N. T. Wright. *The Interpretation of the New Testament 1861–1986*, rev. ed. (Oxford: Oxford University, 1988); Eldon J. Epp and George W. MacRae, eds. *The New Testament and Its Modern Interpreters* (Atlanta: Scholars, 1989); Gerald Bray, *Biblical Interpretation: Past & Present* (Downers Grove, IL: InterVarsity Press, 1996); Joel B. Green, ed. *Hearing the New Testament: Strategies for Interpretation* (Grand Rapids, MI: Eerdmans, 2013).

weighed and assessed regardless of the supposed source. In line with this thinking, many scholars during this time came to reject the plausibility of supernatural miracles, the immaterial nature of man, and the concept of life after death, regarding these beliefs as inconsistent with the fruits of scientific study, contrary to sound principles of logic, and as relics of primitive human thinking. In addition to the major paradigm shifts that took place in the world of the humanities and sciences during this time, we may briefly point to two important historical events that had a profound influence on the direction of biblical scholarship: the fall of Constantinople and the development of the printing press.

It was during the afternoon hours of May 29, 1453, that the young Sultan Mehmet II rode triumphantly through the St. Romanus gate of Constantinople after a bombardment of the Byzantine capital that had lasted nearly two months. After surveying the condition of the city, Mehmet headed to the Hagia Sophia where the Muslim prayers began to be offered in a city that had been a Christian stronghold since the rule of Constantine the Great. After more than a millennium, Constantinople was no longer a center of Christian worship, learning, and scholarship. Despite the undeniable setback that the fall of Constantinople was to the state of Christendom, it was, quite ironically, a catalyst for a significant resurgence of scholarly study and scientific exploration in Western Europe. In fact, the fall of the Byzantine Empire was a significant catalyst of the so-called Age of Discovery. Blocked from many of the traditional trade routes now under Ottoman control, those in the West were forced to discover alternative nautical routes to the traditional centers of trade in the East while searching for new economic opportunities in unexplored territories. It is perhaps no accident that within thirty-five years of the fall of Constantinople, the Portuguese explorer Bartholomeu Dias had sailed around the Cape of Good Hope, a feat that opened a new path to India. This was followed just four years later by the successful voyage to the Western Hemisphere by a little-known explorer from Genoa named Christopher Columbus.

In addition to these notable developments, the fall of Constantinople led to significant advancements in the study of the Greek New

Testament throughout Western Europe. Forced to migrate to the West as a result of the rapidly expanding Ottoman Empire, a number of scholars relocated to Italy and other locations throughout Europe, taking with them their expertise in the Greek language as well as valuable Greek literature and manuscripts. This migration of Greek scholarship to the West played no small role in the renewed scholarly interest throughout Europe in the study of the Greek New Testament, a development that helped fuel and shape several of the theological debates and ecclesiastical controversies that took place during the sixteenth century.

An interest in a subject is of little consequence, of course, if one does not have the means to engage in fruitful study or to share one's discoveries and ideas with others. It is for this reason that the development of the movable-type printing press by Johannes Gutenberg in the mid-fifteenth century was such a landmark event. Gutenberg's press did not simply make the publication of literature more convenient; it revolutionized the entire writing industry and the world of scholarship. In addition to quickly expanding the types of writings that were produced on a mass scale and the languages in which published works were typically composed, the availability of the printing press provided scholars with a more practical and economical means of disseminating their viewpoints to broader audiences. The influence of Gutenberg's movable-type press on the study and production of books is difficult to overstate. It is no coincidence that many Bibles, pamphlets on theological and biblical subjects, and other works of biblical or theological interest were produced during the sixteenth century, many of which were written in the language of local peoples.[27] What can easily be overlooked is the role that the printing press played in the historical and philological study of the New Testament writings. After the press became available, works relating to the background and language of the New Testament

---

[27]For further treatment of the role of the printing press, see Benjamin P. Laird, "The Legacy of the Printing Press for the Production and Study of the Bible" in *Celebrating the Legacy of the Reformation*, ed. Kevin King, Edward Hindson, and Benjamin Forrest (Nashville: Broadman & Holman, 2019), 27–44.

became more widely accessible and began to be produced much more frequently, playing no small role in the advancement of biblical scholarship.

The doctrine of inspiration in biblical scholarship. The revival of interest in the language and historical background of the New Testament and the various intellectual movements that took place during these centuries naturally led to what might be broadly described as the historical-critical study of the New Testament. By this we are not referring to a single method of biblical interpretation, but to a wide body of approaches related to the study of the biblical text that focus on historical and textual issues without a reliance on church dogma or tradition. The impact of these approaches has been nothing short of revolutionary. Our knowledge of the culture of the ancient Near East and the Greco-Roman world has been greatly enhanced, as has our knowledge of the Greek language and of important historical events and developments that took place in Judaism throughout the Second Temple period and within Christianity during the early period of its existence.

Among the more consequential results of biblical scholarship over the last few centuries has been the rejection of the authenticity and traditional authorship of several of the New Testament writings and the divine inspiration of Scripture. With regard to the former, many scholars have become skeptical of traditional viewpoints on the authorship of the New Testament writings and have come to reject the notion that one can blithely affirm traditional viewpoints solely on the basis of their internal attestation or early reception. It has become recognized that careful scrutiny of subjects such as the language and content of the biblical writings are essential to properly assess the viability of the traditional viewpoints of authorship. In addition, a large number of critical scholars have flatly rejected the notion of divine inspiration altogether. As an example, consider the perspective of the French biblical scholar Alfred Loisy, who wrote the following words near the end of the nineteenth century:

The idea of books entirely God-made, but written in the languages of men, in the native dialects of particular peoples and in the idiom of given times, an idea widely spread in the ancient world and retained in Christian orthodoxy, is inconsistent and self-contradictory. . . . In short, the idea of God as author of books is a myth, if ever there was one, and a myth redolent of magic. A book written by the hand of man and filled throughout with the light of God is inconceivable as a square circle. The books reputed all divine are simply not filled with truth from beginning to end—far from it! They contain as many errors as books of their kind, written when they were, could be made to hold. . . . To this notion of divine authorship, so artificial and fragile, the church committed her future and compromised it in so doing.[28]

Scholars such as Loisy who reject the notion of divine inspiration might argue that an attribute such as authority is something that can only be declared of a text, not something that is intrinsic to its nature. Understood in this light, the canonical writings are considered sacred today, not because they possess unique qualities that set them apart from all other writings, but for the simple reason that the majority of early Christian readers ultimately attributed to them a unique status that they did not afford to other writings. As unflattering as it may sound, scholars who hold this perspective might compare the authority attributed to the biblical writings to the authority ascribed to idols in ancient civilizations. There was clearly nothing inherently divine about the materials from which ancient idols were fashioned or from the circumstances surrounding their creation (i.e., construction). They were nothing more than objects built from wood, metal, or clay that were crafted by human hands. In light of this, it might be argued that their authority and divine status were merely assumed or declared by primitive civilizations. Surely no one in our enlightened age would affirm their divinity or authoritative status on the basis of their intrinsic properties or attributes!

---

[28]Alfred Loisy, *The Origins of the New Testament*, trans. L. P. Jacks (London: Allen and Unwin, 1950), 10-11.

Similarly, it has been argued that the authority of a writing is something that can only be declared or asserted, not something that is inherent and can merely be recognized.[29] According to this perspective, all literary compositions are nothing more than human inventions. They did not fall out of the sky from the heavens, so to speak, nor were they written by individuals who were somehow inspired by God in any direct sense. To use another illustration, those living in the Southern states during the American Civil War were under the authority of the Constitution of the Confederate States rather than the United States Constitution. There was nothing inherently authoritative about the Confederate Constitution, of course, but it bore authority for a time because it was ratified by several of the Confederate states and was enforced by the Confederate government until its eventual fall in May of 1865. At the conclusion of the war, those living in the South were suddenly no longer under the rule of the constitution written by "we, the people of the Confederate States" but were once again under the former constitution that was written by "we the People of the United States."

Like those who took part in the drafting of these historical documents, it might also be argued that the biblical authors were men of their age, not infallible writers who possessed a complete understanding of the subjects they addressed. Rather than conduits of divine revelation who faithfully passed along what they had received by supernatural means, it has become commonly assumed that the biblical authors were, like all of us, significantly influenced by their own experiences and culture and that they possessed limited knowledge, intelligence, and abilities. Some writers were certainly more articulate than others, some more compelling and persuasive, and some more sensitive to the concerns of their readers. What they are all thought to have in common, however, is that they were fallible human authors who

---

[29]Scholars do not share uniform opinions on these matters. It is certainly not the case that all who employ historical-critical approaches to the study of the New Testament reject the concept of divine inspiration or the plausibility of biblical claims of supernatural miracles such as the virgin birth and resurrection of Christ. Significant contributions have been made to the study of the canon by scholars who affirm both the divine nature of the biblical writings as well as the historical reliability of the New Testament.

sought to address matters they understood to be of importance. As might be expected, these types of assumptions have left many to question the relevance of apostolic authority. Even if a writing could be reasonably assumed to have derived directly from one of the apostles, why should it be regarded as authoritative to modern readers? Such a connection is difficult to make for those who reject the notion that God spoke in a unique way through specific individuals.

The impact of biblical scholarship on contemporary perspectives of the apostolicity. A significant consequence of these developments is that a growing number of contemporary readers have become uneasy about the aims and assumptions of critical scholarship and have responded by dismissing the relevance of the subject of authorship altogether. There seems to be a perception among many readers that interest in a work's authorship and other related issues is largely a preoccupation of critical scholars who approach their work with an antisupernatural and antirevelatory outlook. Rather than debate the findings of critical scholars—something few feel equipped to do—many simply discount the relevance of the subjects they address. As Herman Ridderbos explains,

> The objection to the historical-critical method is not that it is historical. In that respect it has brought to light many things that formerly were either unknown or too often neglected. The objection is that the origin of the historical method is secular, not revelatory. The historical-critical method thus misunderstands the absolutely unique character not only of the content of the New Testament message but also of the manner in which it has come to us.[30]

It is not uncommon for one's impression of a subject to be influenced by his or her perception of those who are most clearly associated with it. Because of the fact that many critical scholars hold perspectives that might be regarded as troubling, perplexing, or even antagonistic to their faith, contemporary readers are often inclined to dismiss the

---

[30]Herman N. Ridderbos, *Redemptive History and the New Testament Scriptures* (Phillipsburg, NJ: Presbyterian and Reformed, 1988), 49.

significance of the subject of authorship altogether, or at least to min-imize its importance. The fact that biblical scholars often disagree with one another on basic matters related to the background of the ca-nonical writings has only further diminished the confidence of some in the prospect of achieving reliable information about the basic back-ground of the New Testament. Despite several advancements that have been made in a number of fields of study, recent scholarship demon-strates that conclusions related to the composition and historical back-ground of the canonical writings are often difficult to achieve. Few lay readers find themselves prepared to engage in the scholarly study of the historical background of the New Testament, nor do they sense that their ability to arrive at certain conclusions regarding seemingly ob-scure historical matters is ultimately of great importance. If biblical scholars cannot reach a consensus on who wrote the books of the New Testament, one might ask, why should I be concerned? Sentiment such as this appears frequently in Christian literature and is often expressed in contemporary preaching. "We may not know who wrote this book," a pastor might explain to his congregation, "but we can be assured that God is the true author!"

While well-intended, such assertions often leave audiences with the impression that the subject of authorship is of little practical impor-tance and that it is simply a matter of historical curiosity that has a potential to distract from what is of real importance—namely, the spiritual truths contained in the biblical writings. In my personal inter-action with students over the years, I have found that an ambivalent attitude regarding the relevance of a work's authorship is not limited to the anonymous works of the New Testament such as the four Gospels or Hebrews but to the whole of the biblical canon. From one side, stu-dents are confronted with the perspective that the recognition of divine authorship renders the human author largely irrelevant, while from the other side they are confronted by the influence of historical-critical scholars, many of whom allege that the New Testament contains several pseudonymous works that were written after the lifetime of the apostles. These differing perspectives often lead students to conclude that the subject of authorship has little or no bearing on a work's relevance or authority. Even works judged to be pseudonymous, some would argue, should be recognized as authoritative Scripture. If the human author was merely an instrument that God used to communicate his will, why place so much emphasis on the author's identity? To do so, it might be thought, is to elevate the importance of the messenger over that of the message. Whether a work was written by the apostle Paul or by an unknown writer in the late first century, the ultimate author was God!

CONCLUSIONS

This chapter has considered the role that perspectives on the subject of apostolicity likely played in the formation of the canon and discussed some of the possible reasons that contemporary readers are often hesitant to recognize the importance of apostolic authority. With regard to the early reception of the canonical writings, it was demonstrated that the process of canonization was largely a protracted effort of the church to properly ascertain which writings can make a legitimate claim to have originated in the apostolic community. In some cases, the apostolic authorship of a work was immediately and widely recognized, while on other occasions there appears to have been a greater degree of uncertainty and dispute about its apostolic origin. This helps explain why some of the canonical writings appear to have been recognized very quickly as authoritative Scripture while other works were not consistently recognized or took much longer to achieve widespread recognition (e.g., several of the Catholic Epistles).

Now that we have considered how perspectives on the authorship of the canonical writings likely influenced their early reception, we may turn our attention to the possible relevance of apostolic authorship and how it may relate to other important subjects such as the doctrine of inspiration, the role of divine providence, and the influence of the church in the formation of the canon.

APOSTOLIC AUTHORSHIP
AND THE AUTHORITY OF THE
NEW TESTAMENT CANON

IS THERE A BASIS FOR THE CANON'S ONGOING AUTHORITY?

The story of the formation of what is known as the New Testament 'canon' is a story of the demand for authority. The Christian Church set out with a preposterously unlikely tale: that a person who had recently been executed by the Romans at the instigation of the Jewish religious authorities had been brought through death to an aliveness that brought life to others, and was the very corner-stone of the entire building 'Israel.' Where was their evidence for this, and what was their authority?

C. F. D. Moule, *The Birth of the New Testament*

IN ADDITION TO THE COMPLICATED HISTORICAL QUESTION of how the New Testament was formed, there is also the practical question whether the canonical works continue to bear authority, and what, if anything, serves as the basis of this authority. If the New Testament writings are to be regarded as authoritative, should we understand this authority to be based primarily on who wrote them, the truths they contain, their recognition by one or more ecclesiastical bodies, God's providence, or some other factor? The authority of the canon has been defended in a variety of ways. Some tend to emphasize one element of the canon over the others, while others have defended the authority of the canon by appealing to a number of factors, even if they are not entirely clear as to how they may relate to one another. Some might suppose, for example, that God led (an affirmation of God's providence) the early church to formally recognize a particular body of writings (an affirmation of the church's authority) that contain unique qualities and theological content (an affirmation of the divine nature of Scripture) and were written by those closely linked to Christ's earthly ministry (an affirmation of apostolic authority). Others may not have given the question of authority serious thought but have an innate sense that the works of the New Testament are ultimately from God and are therefore to be regarded as authoritative.

It is interesting to observe that the relevance of the human authors of Scripture is often dismissed by those who hold very different viewpoints on the nature of Scripture. Some might argue, for example, that if God ultimately led the early church to recognize a specific body of works that are divinely inspired, then the identity of those who were responsible for their composition is of little consequence. Understood in this manner, those who penned the writings of Scripture served merely as God's mouthpiece and did not write on their own authority. The authors of Scripture were nothing more than human instruments which God used to reveal himself to humanity. On the other end of the spectrum might be those who reject the doctrine of inspiration altogether and view the canon as little more than a collection of human works that merely reflect the viewpoints of certain religious authorities in ancient times. For those who reject the notion of inspiration, there are no writings that can claim divine origin. As a result, all written documents are to be regarded as human creations that lack intrinsic authority. Any authority that belongs to these writings is an authority that has simply been pronounced or conferred.

Complicating matters even further are the recent developments discussed in the previous chapter that have led many scholars and lay readers to place less emphasis on the importance of the human authors of the canonical writings. As a matter of observation, less emphasis tends to be placed on the relevance of the human authors of Scripture when factors such as divine providence, the role of the church, or divine inspiration are recognized as the primary basis of the canon's authority. It would seem as though some have adopted something like a zero-sum way of thinking about the basis of the canon's authority. In many cases, the more emphasis that is placed on one of these means of justifying the canonical status of the New Testament writings, the less emphasis that is placed on apostolic authorship. What are we to think of this? Does the recognition of divine inspiration diminish the relevance of the human authors of Scripture, at least with respect to its authority? To put the question a bit differently, does the affirmation that "all Scripture is inspired by God" (2 Tim 3:16) reduce the significance of the human author? These are the types of questions that will be helpful for us to consider as we draw our study of the canon to a close.

A treatment of the subject of apostolicity in a volume on the canon may not seem all that unusual or noteworthy. Most introductions to the canon include some type of discussion on the criterion of apostolicity and how perceptions about the authorship of the canonical writings influenced their reception. Many of these studies readily acknowledge that the early church was drawn to the apostolic writings and that there were often disputes over the subject of authorship. In many cases, however, the subject of apostolic authorship is treated merely as an explanation for why the early church recognized certain writings over others. What is often overlooked in these discussions is the possible relationship between a work's human author and its ongoing authority. In what follows, we will reflect on some of the common ways that contemporary readers have defended and understood the basis of the canon's authority. After discussing appeals to divine providence, divine inspiration, and the church's authority, we will consider the possible relationship between a work's apostolic authorship and its ongoing authoritative status. As a word of clarification, this closing chapter is not intended to serve as a comprehensive introduction to the doctrine of revelation in general or the doctrine of inspiration in particular. These important theological subjects are beyond the scope of this volume and have been taken up much more thoroughly elsewhere.[1] Our objective here is to consider the relevance of apostolicity in contemporary thought and some of the common ways that the authority of Scripture has been defended.

The Recognition of Divine Providence in the Canonical Process

A common perspective of many contemporary readers is that the canonical writings are to be regarded as authoritative Scripture on the basis of God's providence throughout human history. We could never have full assurance that certain works were authoritative, it might be argued, if the authority of a given writing is somehow related to the human author. There is simply much that we cannot know about the historical background of the canonical writings. Thankfully, we can trust that God has preserved the correct writings and that he has guided the church to recognize the specific body of works that he intended. Surely God does not require each individual to become a world-class historian to have assurance that he has revealed himself through the written Word. Even if we were to devote our lives to the study of the historical background of the biblical writings, would we not be severely misguided if our assurance of the canon's authority rests on our ability to arrive at definitive conclusions about obscure historical matters?

---

[1]One of the most extensive theological treatments of the doctrine of revelation, of course, is that of Karl Barth who devotes the first two volumes of his massive *Church Dogmatics* to a treatment of the subject. In addition to standard introductions to systematic theology, readers may also wish to consult the following studies: Paul J. Achtemeier, *Inspiration and Authority: Nature and Function of Christian Scripture* (Grand Rapids, MI: Baker Academic, 1999); B. B. Warfield, *The Inspiration and Authority of the Bible*, ed. Samuel G. Craig (Phillipsburg, NJ: Presbyterian and Reformed, 1948); Herman N. Ridderbos, *Redemptive History and the New Testament Scriptures* (Phillipsburg, NJ: Presbyterian and Reformed, 1988); Peter Jensen, *The Revelation of God*, CCT (Downers Grove, IL: InterVarsity Press, 2002); David S. Dockery, *Christian Scripture: An Evangelical Perspective on Inspiration, Authority and Interpretation* (Eugene, OR: Wipf & Stock, 1995); Vern Sheridan Polythress, *Inerrancy and Worldview: Answering Modern Challenges to the Bible* (Wheaton, IL: Crossway, 2012); John M. Frame, *The Doctrine of the Word of God*, vol. 4 of *A Theology of Lordship* (Phillipsburg, NJ: Presbyterian and Reformed, 2010); James Barr, *Holy Scripture: Canon, Authority, Criticism* (New York: Oxford University Press, 1983); Denis M. Farkasfalvy, *Inspiration & Interpretation: A Theological Introduction to Sacred Scripture* (Washington, DC: Catholic University of America Press, 2010).

Rather than base our recognition of a work's authority on our limited knowledge of its background, it might be argued that our confidence in the authority of the canonical writings is to be based on the conviction that God was sovereign over the process of the canon's formation and that he providentially guided his people to recognize the specific works that he intended. We can know that a work such as Hebrews is authoritative Scripture, not because we have complete knowledge about the circumstances surrounding its composition but because of the conviction that God has led his people to recognize its authority. Just as God used human agency in the composition of the New Testament, so too, it might be suggested, did he direct and guide human events in order to orchestrate the formation of the New Testament. Those who share this viewpoint may not always agree about the specific events that led to the recognition of the canonical writings or the specific role of the church in the process, but there seems to be a widespread recognition, or at least an intuitive assumption, that God played an active role in overseeing the lengthy process that eventually led to the canon's formation. If there is not even a single sparrow that falls to the ground apart from the will of God (Mt 10:29), is it unreasonable to assume that he was actively involved in directing the process of the canon's formation?

This viewpoint is often predicated on the conviction that God's involvement in the canonical process was not limited to the composition of the individual writings. The Spirit would not have inspired the composition of specific writings, it might be reasoned, only to leave the formation of the canon to the judgment of subsequent generations of Christians who lacked the means, insight, or in many cases the inclination to assess which writings were ultimately from God. As Wayne Grudem contends,

> The preservation and correct assembling of the canon of Scripture should ultimately be seen by believers, then, not as part of church history subsequent to God's great central acts of redemption for his people, but as an integral part of the history of redemption itself. Just as

God was at work in creation, in the calling of his people Israel, in the life, death, and resurrection of Christ, and in the early work and writings of the apostles, so too was God at work in the preservation and assembling together of the books of Scripture for the benefit of his people for the entire church age. Ultimately, then, we base our confidence in the correctness of our present canon on the faithfulness of God.[2]

The perspective that God's providence extended in some sense to the canonical development of the New Testament is thought to be a reasonable inference, even if the canonical development of the New Testament was a lengthy process. Despite the fact that there was not an immediate consensus on which writings were to be recognized as authoritative Scripture, it is widely understood that God ultimately guided his church to recognize the works that he intended. For many, the nearly universal recognition of a relatively small number of Christian writings is nothing short of miraculous. How are we to explain how a diverse group of Christians living throughout the Roman world ultimately came to regard a specific collection of writings as authoritative Scripture? For many, it is difficult to explain this consensus apart from the recognition of God's providential hand over the canonical process.

It is not difficult to understand why this viewpoint has proven to be attractive to many contemporary readers. By emphasizing God's providence, one is able, at least theoretically, to wash one's hands clean of several messy historical questions while still recognizing the authority of the New Testament writings. Because the canonical history of the New Testament has a reputation for being rather controversial and involves the study of several obscure events and witnesses, many find it reassuring to conclude that our confidence in the Bible's authority is not ultimately based on our ability to achieve a complete understanding of the compositional background and historical context of each writing (e.g., the authorship of Hebrews or 2 Peter) or the events that may have

---

[2] Wayne Grudem, *Systematic Theology: An Introduction to Biblical Doctrine*, rev. ed (Grand Rapids, MI: Zondervan, 2020), 54.

prompted the canon's formation. We may never know who wrote certain books, why some are no longer extant, or the precise role that particular events and circumstances may have played in the formation of the canon. What we can trust, it might be argued, is that God oversaw the canonical process and that the writings that have been handed down over the centuries are the writings that God in his infinite wisdom has determined to preserve for his people.

Canonical approaches to the study of the canon. Emphasis on God's providence in the formation of the canon is not limited to lay readers and nonspecialists. In fact, a number of contemporary scholars have come to favor viewpoints that assume God's providence in the formation of the canon. One particular approach that has gained notoriety in recent years is what has come to be known as the canonical approach to the biblical writings. Proponents of this approach often place less emphasis on the historical background of the individual writings and more emphasis on the canon's final shaping and the reception of the writings by the church. Although adherents of the canonical approach hold differing viewpoints on a number of subjects, there is widespread agreement that the canon itself serves as the context in which Scripture is to be read and interpreted. Naturally, those who favor this approach tend to emphasize that the works contained in the New Testament are not to be read in isolation but as part of an established body of writings, whether the entire canon or one of the canonical subcollections such as the Pauline Epistles or Catholic Epistles.[3]

One of the pioneers of this movement was the late Brevard Childs, a biblical scholar known primarily for his scholarship on the Old Testament.[4] Childs became disillusioned with the state of biblical scholarship, which he believed had unduly relegated certain canonical writings to secondary status. From his perspective, this development created a

---

[3]For an overview of this debate, see Ron Haydon, "A Survey and Analysis of Recent 'Canonical' Methods (2000–2015)," *JTI* 10 (2016): 145-55.

[4]See Brevard S. Childs, *The New Testament as Canon: An Introduction* (Philadelphia: Fortress, 1985). For Childs's most extensive treatment of the canonical formation of the Pauline Epistles, see his posthumously published work, *The Church's Guide for Reading Paul: The Canonical Shaping of the Pauline Corpus* (Grand Rapids, MI: Eerdmans, 2008).

number of unnecessary and unfortunate hermeneutical challenges. He did not dispute many of the conclusions of critical scholars that relate to the background of the New Testament. In fact, he agreed that many writings are inauthentic or written later than traditionally assumed. Rather than dispute the conclusions critical scholars made about the background of the writings, Childs challenged prevailing perspectives on the role of Scripture and articulated a particular approach that places value on each writing in the canon. He thus spent much of his lengthy career considering how the church is to read and apply Scripture in the current intellectual environment.

Because the authenticity of several of the New Testament writings has been challenged, it has become increasingly difficult to explore the theological perspectives of certain authors or to develop a well-informed perspective on various theological subjects. The "canon within the canon" approach, it might be suggested, has relegated several works to secondary status, depriving readers of the full benefit of the biblical canon. When exploring Paul's perspective on a given subject, for example, scholars often limit their attention to the undisputed writings, while treating the "Deutero-Pauline" letters merely for what they reveal about the ways that early Christians understood or sought to apply Paul's teaching in their particular contexts. As an alternative to this approach, Childs postulated that the relevance of a work was not to be assessed solely on the basis of what might be determined about its historical background but on its established place in the canon. As he emphasizes throughout his writings, the canon provides a unified witness to the life and teachings of Christ, regardless of what might be inferred about the origin of the individual works.

For Childs and those who have adopted a similar approach, it is helpful to think of the New Testament not so much as a collection of authoritative writings but as an authoritative collection of writings.[5] In other words, proponents of the canonical approach tend to emphasize

---

[5]For further reflections of the difference between these two perspectives, see Bruce Metzger, *The Canon of the New Testament: Its Origin, Development, and Significance* (Oxford: Clarendon, 1987), 282-88.

the authoritative nature of the collection itself more than they do the authoritative nature of the individual writings. The difference between the two perspectives may seem very subtle, but the implications are significant. Rather than basing the authority of a writing on what might be determined about its background, proponents of the canonical approach are inclined to affirm the authority of each of the canonical writings because they are part of the authoritative collection. As a practical consequence, the individual works of the canon are not to be read in isolation but as part of an established body of texts that provides a holistic witness to the person and work of Christ. Further, proponents of the canonical approach often contend that the shaping and arrangement of the collection are of hermeneutical relevance and that they provide the appropriate context in which the individual writings are to be read and studied. Even the various paratextual features present in the biblical writings are thought to serve as an authoritative guide to modern readers.[6]

Although Childs was primarily concerned about the role of the church in forming and shaping the canon, many of those who have adopted his viewpoints have emphasized the providential hand of God during the process of canonization. As Stephen Chapman has suggested:

> A canonically oriented view of inspiration, one that is suggested and even warranted by the historical study of canon formation, retains for the transcendent but sees the divine-human encounter as occurring over a lengthier period of time and as including more people than just one author alone. In this view, inspiration would extend throughout the entirety of the process of the Bible's formation and focus as much on the community that transmitted the text as on the role of the text's putative author.[7]

---

[6]For treatment of paratextual features of the New Testament, see Gregory Goswell, *Text and Paratext: Book Order, Title, and Division as Keys to Biblical Interpretation* (Bellingham, WA: Lexham Academic, 2022); Stanley E. Porter, David I. Yoon, and Chris Stevens, eds., *Studies on the Paratextual Features of Early New Testament Manuscripts*, TENTS (Leiden: Brill, 2023).

[7]Stephen B. Chapman, "Reclaiming Inspiration for the Bible," in *Canon and Biblical Interpretation*, ed. Craig Bartholomew et al. (Grand Rapids, MI: Zondervan, 2006), 172.

As Chapman contends, we need not limit inspiration to the specific occasions in which the individual writings were composed. In addition to
the inspiration of the individual writings, Chapman suggests that God's
hand was on the church throughout the entire canonical process. In this
line of thinking, the canon itself might be regarded as authoritative.[8]

The reception of canonical approaches. While many scholars have
a favorable perspective of the canonical approaches, some have dismissed them on hermeneutical or theological grounds. A work cannot
be properly studied, some might argue, without careful consideration
of the circumstances related to its composition. For some, the approach of Childs and others is little more than a feeble attempt to
preserve the value of Scripture in our postmodern age. It is not just
critical scholars who have found fault with the canonical approach,
however. Evangelical scholars and theologians such as Carl F. H. Henry
have also voiced concerns. According to Henry, the canonical approach (1) elevates the role of the church's authority while placing less
emphasis on apostolic authority, (2) overstates the significance of the
historical reception of the writings, a history that is not always clear,
and (3) diminishes the importance of authorial intent in biblical interpretation.[9] Some of Henry's criticisms have resonated with scholars
more than others and there have been a number of attempts by proponents of the canonical approach to assuage these concerns. Although
a significant number of scholars are now convinced that the canonical
approach to the study of Scripture is wholly appropriate, even demanded, and that it does not diminish authorial intent or undermine
the importance of sound hermeneutical principles, a number of
scholars remain skeptical of its assumptions or points of emphasis. In
reference to Childs's treatment of the Pauline corpus, for example,
Jeffrey Kloha contends,

---

[8]In his interaction with Chapman, Darian Lockett suggests that it may be more appropriate to
relate God's involvement in the canonical process to divine providence rather than divine inspiration. Darian R. Lockett, "A Conservative Evangelical Perspective on the New Testament Canon,"
in *Five Views on the New Testament Canon*, ed. Stanley E. Porter and Benjamin P. Laird (Grand
Rapids, MI: Kregel, 2022), 60.

[9]Carl F. H. Henry, "Canonical Theology: An Evangelical Appraisal," *SBET* 8 (1990): 76-108.

Childs removes the authority of the Pauline writings from their apostolic voice and vests it in the community (or communities) that ultimately determined "the canon." . . . Rather than their authority being found in Christ himself ("you have heard it said . . . but I say") and intrinsic to the texts written by those who taught by his same authority, the authority of the text is located in the church, potentially several generations removed from the apostles.[10]

Despite these and other objections, the canonical approach continues to be regarded by many contemporary scholars and theologians as an effective solution to the divide between biblical scholarship and theological engagement with the text that has significantly widened in recent decades. It is also commonly recognized as a useful way to affirm the canon's authority without arriving at specific conclusions about the historical background of the writings (e.g., the authorship of disputed works).

DIVINE INSPIRATION AS THE BASIS OF THE CANON'S AUTHORITY

In addition to an emphasis on divine providence, many have argued that the writings of the New Testament are to be recognized as authoritative Scripture on the basis of their divine nature. The emphasis on the divine origin of Scripture is certainly not a recent development. This has been emphasized by pastors, theologians, and scholars throughout church history. In recent years, the implications of this conviction for our understanding of the canon have been addressed by scholars such as Michael Kruger, who argues that a work's authoritative status is something that may be recognized but not something that can be conferred or determined. "Books do not become canonical," he explains. "They are canonical because they are the books God has given as a permanent guide for his church. Thus, from this perspective, it is the existence of the canonical books that is determinative, not

---

[10]Jeffrey Kloha, "The Problem of Paul's Letters: Loss of Authority and Meaning in the 'Canonical Approach' of Brevard Childs," *ConJ* 35 (2009), 165.

their function or reception."[11] Kruger recognizes that there was a process by which books came to be regarded as authoritative Scripture, yet he emphasizes that an awareness of a work's authoritative status is not to be confused with its inherent and unchangeable qualities. Because the canonical writings are of divine origin, they bear authoritative status regardless of what type of opinion we may have about them, he argues. Kruger is thus inclined to conclude that the church played what some might describe as a more passive role in the establishment of the canon. Rather than the leadership of the church playing an active role in determining which writings were to be included or excluded from the Christian canon, Kruger finds it more appropriate to describe the church as the heir of Scripture. We may speak of the church as handing down the Scriptures from one generation to the next but not of the church creating the canon on a particular occasion in response to particular concerns or controversies at some point in church history. Although there was clearly a historical process that led to the recognition of particular writings as authoritative Scripture, the authority of these writings is ultimately based on their divine qualities rather than their reception.

The intrinsic authority of the canonical writings. Because the New Testament writings are divinely inspired, the notion that their authority resides in something extrinsic to the text itself must be rejected, some might argue. Understood in this manner, the authority of the canonical writings does not derive from its reception in early Christian communities, the decree of an ecclesiastical body, or the judgments that biblical scholars and historians have made about their compositional background, but instead on the basis of their divine origin.[12] As divine revelation that is inspired by the Spirit

---

[11]Michael J. Kruger, *The Question of Canon: Challenging the Status Quo in the New Testament Debate* (Downers Grove, IL: IVP Academic, 2013), 40.

[12]To be clear, Kruger does not dismiss the relevance of apostolic authority or the value of historical investigation relating to the background of the New Testament. As he clarifies, "While we certainly agree that [the New Testament] books do bear internal marks of their divinity. . . . this does not mean that outside information has no place in how the canon is authenticated." *Canon Revisited: Establishing the Origins and Authority of the New Testament Books* (Wheaton, IL: Crossway, 2012), 90. Kruger's recognition of historical matters is evidenced by the fact that he includes

for the benefit of God's people, we may then look to the "self-authen-ticating" qualities of Scripture as evidence of their divine nature.[13] As Kruger has suggested, there are various qualities, attributes, and fea-tures of the canonical writings that bear witness to their divine nature. These self-authenticating qualities, it is understood, provide contemporary readers with the assurance that each of the writings in the New Testament were inspired by the Spirit and that they are thus fully authoritative and have a rightful place in the Christian canon. Similar to the viewpoint that we can be confident in the le-gitimacy of the canon because of God's providential role in the process, it might be argued that we can be assured of the authority of the Scriptures not because we possess full knowledge of every historical matter or because of our trust in the judgment of the early church but because each of the canonical writings exudes qualities and attributes that are consistent with their divine nature. It is Christ's disciples who know his voice and follow him (Jn 10:27), it might be reasoned, not the scholar or historian who concerns himself with obscure and speculative historical matters, many of which cannot be fully known or verified.

Limitations of the "self-authenticating" model. In Kruger's esti-mation, modern readers can be assured that the correct writings have been recognized as part of the canon in large part because of the various ways they bear witness to their divine origin. Although Kruger affirms the importance of accounting for the historical development of the canon, he calls for a decidedly greater emphasis on the internal qual-ities of Scripture than on historical criteria when addressing the legit-imacy and authority of the canon. From my perspective, Kruger makes

---

an entire chapter on the importance of apostolic authority in *Canon Revisited*. Although Kruger affirms the relevance of apostolic authority and the value of historical study, he contends that our assurance of the authority of the canonical writings is not ultimately based on their recep-tion in early Christianity or on our complete knowledge of historical matters such as authorship. As he explains, an "unequivocal emphasis on the role of historical investigation can unwittingly communicate that there are no other God-given means by which Christians can have assurance about the boundaries of the canon" (86).

[13]Kruger describes and discusses what he regards as the divine qualities of the canonical writings in *Canon Revisited*, 125-59.

a valuable contribution to the study of the canon with his treatment of the inherent qualities and attributes of Scripture that are consistent with their divine origin. As important as the internal criteria are for evaluating the authoritative status of early Christian writings, I would suggest that there are some limitations to the self-authenticating model that should be kept in mind.

Among the apparent limitations of the self-authenticating model is the subjective nature of the internal criteria upon which it is largely based and the fact that some of the attributes that are emphasized could arguably be shared by some noncanonical works. In view of the fact that early Christians were in essential agreement over a core body of doctrines, we might expect for there to have been a number of early Christian writings that share similar theological perspectives and other features. The authors of the canonical writings were certainly not alone in their theological convictions, nor were they the only individuals to compose works that were found to be edifying or practically relevant. While some works were clearly at odds with the teaching of the apostles and the prevailing beliefs of the early church, we may assume that there was a large body of Christian writings that were in essential theological agreement. Early works such as *1 Clement, Polycarp's Epistle to the Philippians*, and the Ignatian epistles are a few possible examples. Texts have been produced throughout church history that emphasize spiritual truths, provide instruction on subjects of theological importance, encourage greater devotion to Christ, confront sin, and contain edifying material. In light of this, determining which writings have a rightful place in the canon is certainly not as straightforward as simply identifying the works that might be regarded as theologically sound, spiritually edifying, practically relevant, or share some other quality that relates to its content.

The lengthy process of canonization also poses a challenge. If there are specific qualities or attributes that bear witness to the writings of divine origin, why was the canonical status of some writings quickly affirmed while other works took much longer to become widely recognized? Might the disagreement over the status of certain writings suggest that certain self-authenticating qualities are not as evident as might be assumed? Just how confident can we be in our ability to accurately identify the works that were inspired by the Spirit if the early church struggled to find agreement over the scope of writings that are of divine origin? Are we somehow better positioned to assess whether works such as Hebrews, James, 2 Peter, and Jude should be recognized as authoritative Scripture than readers during the second, third, and fourth centuries?[14] I certainly agree with Kruger that early disputes about the canonical status of certain writings do not preclude the legitimacy of the canon, or the authoritative nature of the canonical writings, or that there are certain characteristics of divine Scripture. It is helpful to recognize, however, that the internal criteria is often subjective in nature and that there are often a number of similarities between early Christian writings, canonical and noncanonical alike. Because of this, we must consider if there are one or more attributes that are exclusive to the writings that were recognized by the early church. We will consider if this is indeed the case after observing some of the additional ways that the canon's authority has been defended.

Inspired inauthentic works? What may come as a surprise to some is that it is not just evangelical scholars such as Kruger who have recognized the inspiration of Scripture, at least in some sense and to some degree. Some would argue that the New Testament includes a number of inauthentic works that were likely written after the age of the apostles but that this should not dissuade us from recognizing the divine origin of their composition, or at least of their message. If the works in the canon are ultimately from God, then the circumstances relating to their composition are of little significance, it might be argued, at least with respect to their status and authority. Whatever we may think about the practice of pseudepigraphy, and whatever conclusions we may draw about the background of each writing, we can trust that the Spirit of God used a number of authors—some

---

[14]Kruger addresses these questions at length in *Canon Revisited*. See pages 197-202 for a concise summary.

known and some unknown—to reveal his will to the church. Consider, for example, the perspective of the well-known German text-critic Kurt Aland:

> None may find fault if in the process of canonization some pseudonymous writings were accepted as what they claimed to be. In any instance, however, where the Church knew or thought it knew that a document had to be attributed to a different author, it answered this by excluding such writings from the canon. . . . The unknown men, by whom they were composed, not only believed themselves to be under the sign of the Holy Spirit; *they really were*.[15]

Aland rightly affirms that the early readers of the New Testament took the matter of authorship seriously, though he seems to suggest that they often made errors of judgment. Despite mistaken perspectives related to the background of some writings, we can be assured, Aland contends, that each of the works of the canon bear authority. The reason for this, he explains, is that each of the authors of the New Testament—regardless of who they may have been—wrote "under the sign of the Holy Spirit." In other words, divine inspiration is not attributed only to the works that were written by certain individuals (e.g., members of the apostolic community). Such a viewpoint allows one to recognize the conclusions of critical scholars while grounding the authority of the canonical writings on their divine status rather than on something external to the text itself such as the decision of an ecclesiastical body.

THE CHURCH'S RECEPTION AS THE BASIS OF THE CANON'S AUTHORITY

A third perspective is that the authority of the canon is to be affirmed on the basis of its acceptance by the church. The canon is not an object that was simply discovered in its present state, it might be argued, but is instead a collection of writings that were composed, collected, and

---

[15]Kurt Aland, "The Problem of Anonymity and Pseudonymity in Christian Literature of the First Two Centuries," *JTS* 12 (1961), 49, italics added.

shaped by the church. One cannot account for the emergence of the canon or the consensus that eventually was achieved with respect to its content without recognizing the active role of the church in the process. Simply put, without the church, there would be no canon. The individual writings were produced by members of the church, and it is within the context of the Christian community that the canonical writings have been recognized, read, studied, and interpreted.

An example of this type of perspective may be observed in the recent work of Craig Allert, who emphasizes that there were many writings in early Christianity that share similar theological perspectives and provide edifying and useful material. According to Allert, "inspiration was not seen to be the unique possession of only the documents that later came to be part of the New Testament canon. The Spirit was seen as living and active in the entire community of the faithful and therefore inspiring it. Historically speaking, inspiration functioned in a very broad way in the early church."[16] Many works outside the canon were treated as Scripture in early Christianity, Allert contends, at least on certain occasions.[17] In keeping with his understanding that the early church regarded the Spirit as active and that God spoke through a variety of individuals, Allert concludes that it would be misguided to suggest that early Christians only regarded the canonical works as inspired. Put succinctly, "canonical/noncanonical was not synonymous with inspired/noninspired."[18] This raises the question, of course, of whether there is anything that might separate the canonical and noncanonical works. If inspiration is not an attribute of the canonical writings alone, why were certain works ultimately recognized as authoritative Scripture? For Allert, it is the church's reception of the canonical writings that serves as the basis of their canonical status, not the notion of divine inspiration. We should not understand the canon

---

[16]Craig Allert, *A High View of Scripture? The Authority of the Bible and the Formation of the New Testament Canon* (Grand Rapids, MI: Baker Academic, 2007), 148.

[17]Allert provides a substantial appendix with citations from several early Christian writings in order to demonstrate that certain works were sometimes treated as inspired or authoritative Scripture. See Allert, *A High View of Scripture?* 177-88.

[18]Allert, *A High View of Scripture?* 60.

as something independent of the church, Allert insists, but as a creation of the church. "The Bible both grew in and was mediated through the church," he writes, "hence, the Bible is the church's book." He further posits that "by accepting the Bible as authoritative, we must also accept the process and means through which it came to be."[19]

So while Kruger argues that the authority of the biblical writings is grounded in their divine origin, Allert places an emphasis on the church's reception. Both scholars address central issues at the heart of the canon debate and offer a perspective on the canon that many readers will undoubtedly find compelling, even when disagreeing with some of their specific assumptions. Many will surely resonate, for example, with Kruger's argument that the canonical writings bear intrinsic authority and are in a sense "canonical" regardless of whether their authority is recognized. Others will resonate with Allert's conclusion that the recognition of inspiration is not as straightforward as we might assume and that the early church played an active role in ascertaining which writings are to be recognized as authoritative Scripture.

So how are we to navigate these thorny issues? If we are to affirm divine inspiration, are there reasonable grounds to conclude that it is only the New Testament writings that are inspired, and how might we even assess whether a work is of divine origin in the first place? With regard to the role of the church, we might ask if the establishment of the canon was a divinely appointed task. If so, what "church" took the leading role? Who or what ecclesiastical body had the right to establish the contours of the canon, and what was the basis of this authority? Also, how can we be assured that the church's decisions about the canon were appropriate and justified and that the "right" books were selected? Given the difficulties of these questions, it is little wonder that many contemporary readers find it difficult to account for the authority and legitimacy of the canon. As a needed solution to these issues, it will be helpful for us to consider an overlooked yet foundational attribute of the canon—namely, its apostolic authorship.

---

[19] Allert, *A High View of Scripture?* 84-85.

Apostolic Authorship as the Basis
of the Canon's Authority

As we observed in the previous chapter, the early recognition of the canonical writings does not appear to have been based primarily on their reception by certain churches, their practical value, or the insight they provided on various theological matters, but on the basis of their apostolic origin. To be clear, the recognition of apostolic authorship was certainly not the only factor that influenced the reception of the canonical writings, but it was arguably the most consequential. As the historical evidence makes plain, the works of the canon were not recognized as authoritative Scripture despite widespread doubts about their apostolic origin, but in large part because they were recognized to have been written by members of the apostolic community. There were several early Christian writings that were theologically sound and included material that was edifying, instructive, or practically valuable. However, only a small number of writings were understood to have originated within the apostolic community, a small body of first-century believers that functioned as an extension of Christ's earthly ministry. Entrusted by Christ with the responsibility of continuing and expanding his earthly mission, the apostles and their close companions devoted themselves earnestly to this work, proclaiming the good news of their resurrected Lord in both oral and written form. This high regard for the apostles and their teaching naturally resulted in the recognition of the authority of the apostolic writings and prompted their circulation throughout the Christian world.

As a result of the importance that was placed on apostolic authority, disputes related to the canonical status of early Christian writings tended to center around the subject of authorship. It was certainly not unusual for early Christians to weigh and assess the value of a work's teaching, universal relevance, antiquity, language, and many other attributes and subjects, but these discussions tended to take place when its apostolic authorship was in question. If a work was largely unknown, for example, its claim to have been written by a member of the apostolic community might be called into question. Similarly, we find early writers drawing attention to the language and style of works such as Hebrews and 2 Peter. Early readers seem to have understood that there may be reason to question the apostolic origin of a writing if it lacks sound instruction, does not exude a sense of authority, does not have a history of use in the church, does not appear to have ancient roots, or was written in a manner that was thought to be inconsistent with that of its supposed author.

The diminished emphasis on apostolic authorship in contemporary thought. As discussed in the previous chapter, a number of contemporary readers are hesitant to attribute the ongoing authority of the canonical writings to their supposed apostolic authorship. If God is the true author of Scripture and the human authors simply functioned as the instruments he used to reveal himself to his people, why would it matter who he used for this task? If God could speak through the mouth of Balaam's donkey (see Num 22:21-39), could he not likewise speak through any number of individuals? If so, would it not be misguided to determine which works are authoritative on the sole basis of our ability to discern who may have composed them? In addition, if we recognize a connection between a work's human author and its authoritative status, have we not overlooked the importance of a work's divine nature or denied either divine providence in the canonical process or the authority of the church?

Perhaps an illustration will enable us to better understand the crux of the problem. Suppose for a moment that a score for the much beloved *The Four Seasons*, a piece traditionally attributed to the Italian composer Antonio Vivaldi, was suddenly discovered among a collection of compositions that could be positively dated to the mid-seventeenth century. While the composer of the piece could not be determined, let us assume for the sake of the argument that the recently uncovered evidence is irrefutable that the piece was composed much earlier than originally assumed—earlier, in fact, than Vivaldi's birth in 1678. What might be the implications of this discovery for those who enjoy classical music, particularly those who esteem Vivaldi as one of their favorite composers? Would musicians suddenly ignore the piece simply because it could no longer be recognized as one of Vivaldi's authentic works? The quality of the work would clearly not be diminished. The same features of the piece that ensured its popularity before the discovery—its creative brilliance, emotional appeal, and memorable melodies—would obviously remain unchanged even if the piece could no longer be attributed to the famous baroque composer. Because of its proven ability to please audiences, we would expect the work to continue to be played in concert halls around the world. While there is certainly a natural interest in the works composed by the more well-known composers, history has shown that the reception of a piece often has much more to do with its ability to please and inspire listeners than with the specific individual who may have been responsible for its composition.

In a similar vein, one might question why the human authorship of the canonical writings is of significance as long as the work is of practical value to modern Christians, provides meaningful instruction on matters of theological importance, or has a long and established history of use in the church. A writing such as Hebrews might serve as a fitting example. Widely esteemed for its unique theological significance, Hebrews has been recognized as authoritative Scripture for many centuries despite the lack of universal agreement regarding the identity of its author. While a strong case could be made that its early circulation as part of the Pauline letter corpus was the decisive factor in its initial recognition as canonical Scripture, many contemporary readers seem more inclined to assume that its authority today stems largely from its theological significance, its practical relevance, or simply its placement in the canon (i.e., reception), factors that, at best, are only loosely tied to the subject of authorship. Just how important could the authorship of this writing be if the author did not even bother to cite his or her name and if the early church eventually came to recognize its canonical status despite uncertainty about its background? In light of its rich theological instruction and clear ability to encourage Christians and point them to greater devotion to Christ, why would it really matter if it was written by Paul, Luke, Timothy, Apollos, or some unknown first-century figure? Just as a piece of music by an unknown composer might provide enjoyment and inspiration for contemporary audiences, so too, one might reason, is it possible for an ancient writing such as Hebrews to provide meaningful encouragement and instruction for modern Christians, regardless of who may have been directly responsible for its composition. To return to the illustration above, would not the rejection of Hebrews on the basis of its questionable apostolic authorship be similar to the decision to no longer listen to *The Four Seasons* simply because it could no longer be attributed to Vivaldi?

Divine inspiration and the relevance of apostolic authorship. I would submit that rather than an inconsequential historical matter of little relevance, the recognition of apostolic authorship is foundational to our understanding of why the early church recognized certain writings as authoritative Scripture and why they should be recognized as authoritative Scripture today. By affirming that each of the canonical writings were produced by members of the apostolic community, we are able to tie each work either directly or indirectly to those who were commissioned by Christ to build his church and to establish an objective basis for the canon's ongoing authority. We may regard the writings linked to the apostles as authoritative not simply because they personally walked with Christ and were eyewitnesses of his resurrection—there were indeed many earthly witnesses (cf. 1 Cor 15:3-8)—but because they were the conduits through whom God chose to speak and because they were the individuals he entrusted to serve as the pillars of the church.

As we read in 2 Peter, apostolic testimony did not derive from "human will" but from "men moved by the Holy Spirit [who] spoke from God" (2 Pet 1:21). To answer a key question that was raised earlier in the chapter, it is apostolic authorship that serves as the distinguishing attribute of each of the canonical writings. While a number of early Christian writings were regarded as profitable, edifying, instructive, or valuable in some way, it is only the canonical writings that were widely recognized by the early church to have originated from the apostolic community. Remarkably, there were no writings that were rejected as canonical Scripture despite having been commonly understood to have derived from the apostolic community and no writings that were ultimately recognized as Scripture that were widely assumed to have been written by individuals outside of the apostolic circle.

It is important to bear in mind that this understanding of the canon's authority does not conflict with the notion of divine inspiration, as it has long been recognized that the apostles were guided by the Holy Spirit. In fact, the recognition of apostolic authorship enables us to account for the divine inspiration of the canonical writings and to ascertain why they came to be regarded as authoritative by the early church. As Christ's directly appointed representatives, it was understood that the apostles possessed a unique status that was not shared by other early writers and Christian leaders. Because of their role as Christ's representatives, it was only natural for early Christians to regard their written works as authoritative. For readers in the early church, the canonical writings do not simply contain authoritative instruction or testify to inspired spiritual truths. More importantly, they derive from the authoritative representatives of Christ. As noted above, there were many writings that elucidated and emphasized key doctrines and provided useful instruction and encouragement. It is only the canonical writings, however, that were understood to have derived from the apostolic community. Consequently, there is both a theological and historical basis to the canon's authority.

Some might object that the apostles were not the only individuals God used to reveal his will. As the New Testament writings make plain, there were several individuals who served as prophets or prophetesses during the time of the apostles. Reference is made, for example, to individuals such as Zechariah (Lk 1:67-79), Anna (Lk 2:36-38), and Agabus and the daughters of Philip (Acts 21:7-14). Paul even refers to the gift of prophecy in his first epistle to the Corinthians (see 1 Cor 14). Because we find several examples in the New Testament of individuals who were engaged in prophetic activity, the instruction and testimony of the apostles may not seem all that significant. If God was impartial and spoke through numerous individuals, many of whom are no longer even known, was there anything truly unique about the canonical writings in the first place? The age inaugurated by Christ, it is often observed, is an age in which the Spirit of the Lord has been poured out on all his people (cf. Joel 2:28; Acts 2:17). Are we therefore to assume that the apostles were used in a unique way or that God's revelation was limited to this exclusive community? Some may find no conflict in recognizing the apostolic works as divinely inspired but find it difficult to attribute divine inspiration exclusively to the works linked to the apostles. As a result, the notion of a closed canon of Scripture becomes tenuous unless it is based on another factor such as the authority of the church, an argument that has been made by scholars such as Allert. What would be the basis for a closed canon if God spoke through many individuals throughout church history? As we have seen, there are grounds to conclude that apostolic authority is the primary attribute that sets the canonical writings apart from other early Christian writings, regardless of the specific convictions we may have about the doctrine of divine inspiration. Even if one were to affirm that certain noncanonical writings were inspired in some sense or degree, it would still be difficult to argue for their apostolic origin.

The persuasion that the Holy Spirit spoke through a number of individuals outside of the original apostolic community is certainly not a new idea. One group, for example, that was known for this conviction in the early church was the Montanists, a group that reached the height of its influence in the latter half of the second century. The Montanists maintained that the Spirit continued to speak through their founder, Montanus, and the prophetesses Prisca (or Priscilla) and Maximilla. Those associated with this movement were often regarded as outliers or as part of an aberrant movement, not so much because they espoused a particular doctrine that ran counter to the core doctrines of the faith but because of their understanding that fresh revelation continued to be delivered to God's people through specific individuals in their community. Members of this community came to understand that the revelation they received was fully authoritative and that strict obedience was therefore demanded. Such a conviction, of course, makes it difficult to affirm the unique status of apostolic instruction. Rather than viewing the apostolic writings as an exclusive body of authoritative instruction, the viewpoint that the Holy Spirit has spoken directly through a large body of individuals throughout church history makes the basis of a closed canon difficult to justify, that is, unless there is an appeal to the church's authority or to the role of divine providence.

Contemporary perspectives on the concept of apostolicity. For some, it is not so much the concept of inspiration that is problematic but rather the notion that the New Testament contains a number of works that are unlikely to have been written by members of the apostolic circle. As discussed previously, a common assumption in biblical scholarship is that the New Testament contains several writings that are pseudonymous or were not written by the traditional authors. The notion of apostolic authorship as the basis of the canon's authority becomes difficult to affirm if one denies the concept of inspiration altogether or concludes that some of the canonical writings were not written by members of the apostolic circle. It obviously becomes difficult to recognize the importance of apostolic authorship if one is not even convinced that each of the canonical writings can be traced back to the apostolic community!

One way that some have affirmed the authority of the New Testament writings without affirming their apostolic authorship is by separating the concept of apostolicity from apostolic authorship altogether. In recent years it has become increasingly common to understand apostolicity merely as a quality or attribute of a writing or some other form of communication and to not limit it to the works that were supposedly written by apostles. As some would suggest, the canonical writings are certainly apostolic, but not in an exclusive sense. A recent example of this perspective may be observed in the work of Daniel Castelo and Robert Wall. As they explain, "Apostolicity refers to the undying witness of the triune God in and through human media."[20]

---

[20]Daniel Castelo and Robert W. Wall, *The Marks of Scripture: Rethinking the Nature of the Bible* (Grand Rapids, MI: Baker Academic, 2019), 121-22.

Scripture certainly plays an important role in the life of the church, Castelo and Wall argue, but it is not the words of Scripture alone that are to be recognized as apostolic. Apostolicity, they explain, "has to do with the culture or ethos of the Christian community, which is inhabited and animated by the presence of the living God. While it is true that part of that culture involves the reading and use of text, that is only one part."[21]

To be clear, it is certainly legitimate to use terms such as *apostolic* and *apostolicity* in reference to the core body of established Christian doctrine and practices that were proclaimed and taught by Christ and the apostles and have been affirmed by the church over the centuries. Beliefs and teachings such as the bodily resurrection of Christ or his status as the eternal Son of God may certainly be described as apostolic teachings. We might also refer to the practice of baptism or the observance of the Lord's Supper as apostolic practices of the church. With regard to written texts, however, there appears to be an inclination in contemporary scholarship to distance the concept of apostolicity from apostolic authorship altogether. One cannot help but think that this may have been encouraged, at least in some cases, by objections to the authenticity of certain canonical works. By separating the concept of apostolicity from particular human authors, one may object to the authenticity of one or more of the canonical writings while still affirming their apostolic status. There would be no contradiction, it might be argued, in recognizing 2 Peter as an apostolic writing while concluding that it was likely composed by an unknown writer several decades after Peter's death.

It is certainly understandable why some have been drawn to this broader understanding of the concept of apostolicity, though it is not without its own complications. Rather than attributing the apostolic authority of the canonical writings to their apostolic authors, one must base their authority on alternative factors such as the church's reception or God's providence. One of the challenges of this perspective is that it

---

[21]Castelo and Wall, *The Marks of Scripture*, 122.

places the basis of the canon's authority on something that was not as widely emphasized by the early church. Looking back at history, one might argue that God's providential hand was indeed involved in the canonical process and that he used the church to form and establish the canon. But these convictions alone do not explain why the canonical writings were recognized as sacred Scripture in the first place or why they should continue to be recognized as such today. It is only by affirming the apostolic authorship of the New Testament writings that one is able to establish a basis for the canon's authority that has been strongly emphasized by the church from its very inception.

Another consequence of separating apostolicity from apostolic authorship is that it becomes much more difficult to justify the exclusion of certain works from the canon. Are we to assume that only twenty-seven works are apostolic in the broader sense described above? Were there really only twenty-seven writings that accurately articulate the Christian gospel, testify to the work of Christ, provide edifying instruction to the church, or call for God's people to carry out the church's mission? If not, what sets the canonical writings apart? If we are to recognize that many early Christian works outside of the canon were apostolic in one sense or another, what would be the basis for their exclusion from the canon? By broadening the concept of apostolicity, scholars have found a way to attribute apostolicity to works that they suspect may not be authentic. On the other hand, a new problem is created: the basis for a closed canon. By recognizing a broader concept of apostolicity, it becomes difficult to ascertain what sets the canonical works apart from any number of Christian writings that have also benefited God's people in one way or another.

Scholars such as Allert are certainly correct that early Christians often described or treated a number of writings as inspired in one sense or another. As noted above, the New Testament itself even refers to a number of individuals as prophets. This leads to an important question: If God's revelation was not imparted or delivered exclusively through the apostles, what is the justification for recognizing only a relatively small body of works as authoritative Scripture? Why did the early church not recognize a wider body of writings, and what makes the canonical writings more authoritative than other works? To answer these questions we must recognize that it was the apostles alone who were commissioned with the unique task of leading the church and serving as Christ's representatives. On the basis of this conviction, the writings that may be traced back to the apostolic community have rightly been regarded by Christians over the centuries as authoritative Scripture.

Whereas prophets such as Agabus appear to have received prophetic revelation on specific occasions for the benefit of specific individuals in specific contexts, the apostles were directly commissioned by Christ to continue his earthly work and to lead and guide the church in the early years of its existence. As Ridderbos helpfully writes, "Because [the apostles] not only received revelation but were also the bearers and organs of revelation, their primary and most important task was to function as the foundation of the church. To that revelation Christ binds His church for all time; upon it He founds and builds his church."[22] The New Testament, therefore, is not merely the sum of the writings that the early church regarded as inspired in some sense, but is instead a collection of works that the early church believed to bear apostolic authority. By establishing the apostolic authorship of the canonical writings, we are able to draw a link to Christ himself. Rather than products of the church that simply reveal what the church came to believe after much discussion and dispute, the canonical writings are the fruit of the apostolic witnesses who were entrusted by Christ to continue his earthly work.

Conclusions

As we have observed in this final chapter, there is often a marked difference in how ancient and contemporary readers perceive the relevance of apostolic authorship. In the early church, the works understood to have been produced by members of the apostolic community were highly valued and were widely recognized as authoritative Scripture.

---

[22]Ridderbos, *Redemptive History*, 13.

Although there were a number of issues that influenced the reception of the canonical writings, the recognition of a work's apostolic authorship was arguably the most consequential factor that ensured its placement in one of the canonical subcollections, a placement that ultimately led to its inclusion in the greater canon. There may not have been universal agreement about the authorship of each writing or the historical circumstances that gave rise to each work, yet it is clear that the reception of the canonical writings involved careful attention to these matters. As the ancient church sought clarity regarding the scope of the apostolic body of witnesses to the life and teaching of Christ, a consensus eventually emerged concerning the works that may be traced back to the apostolic witnesses of Christ. Thus, the canon was not formed irrespective of historical concerns but instead as a means of preserving the instruction that was understood to have derived from the apostles and their companions. Because of the importance of apostolic authority, we may conclude that the canonical writings are not to be regarded as authoritative simply because they are in the Bible. Rather, they are in the Bible because they are authoritative. As we have suggested, this authority is not ultimately based on their reception in church history, their affirmation by a particular ecclesiastical body, or from our recognition of their unique content and features. Ultimately, the works of the New Testament may be regarded as authoritative because of the conviction that they were composed by members of the apostolic community who wrote under the guidance of the Holy Spirit.

Although apostolic authorship played an unmistakable role in the reception of the canonical writings, its importance is not always emphasized in contemporary scholarship. Many have determined that definitive conclusions related to the compositional background of the New Testament writings are simply untenable or that traditional viewpoints cannot stand up under scrutiny, a conclusion that has prompted a variety of arguments for the canon's enduring authority. Rather than viewing the New Testament as a collection of authoritative writings— writings that possess inherent authority regardless of their recognition—a greater emphasis has been placed in recent years on the authoritative status of the collection itself. The canonical collection may be regarded as authoritative, some might suggest, not because we are able to reach definitive conclusions related to the historical origin of each individual writing, but because God's providential hand was involved in the canonical process or perhaps because of the conviction that the church was granted the authority to shape and form the canon.

Only time will tell what lies in the future of biblical scholarship, especially as it pertains to the study of the canon's origin, function, and significance. Much has been published in recent years on numerous aspects of the background of the individual canonical writings and the early reception of the canonical collection, yet it is clear that much work remains. Looking ahead, I am hopeful that a growing number of scholars will continue to investigate what may be determined regarding the early state of the New Testament canon and that our understanding of the process that gave rise to the formation of the canon will continue to advance. Because of the importance that was placed on apostolic authorship in the early church, it would seem that there is also a need for continued examination of the historical background of the individual writings. As an observation, it would appear that perceptions about the process of canonization are often shaped by assumptions about the historical background of the individual writings. When a number of the canonical writings are regarded as inauthentic, for example, it becomes only natural to understand the process that gave rise to the canon in a particular way or even to question the canon's legitimacy. What is needed in my view is a fresh evaluation of the evidence for the early state of the canon and a renewed focus on the possible basis for the apostolic authorship of the canonical writings.

Despite all that has been published on a number of subjects related to the historical background of the canonical writings and the formation of the canon, I believe that the final word has yet to be written. There is certainly more to be said regarding a number of historical-critical issues relating to the background of the canonical writings, and their reception in early Christianity, how our knowledge of ancient literary conventions might enhance our understanding of the manner in which the canonical writings were composed and collected, and a host of related issues. Ultimately, my hope is that the subjects we have explored in this volume will encourage further reflection, discussion, and investigation of the canonical writings and that this will result in fresh insights related to this ancient collection of texts that, in the words of Athanasius, have been "handed down, and accredited as Divine."[23]

---

[23] *Ep. fest.* 39 (NPNF 2.4).

BIBLIOGRAPHY

Achtemeier, Paul J. *Inspiration and Authority: Nature and Function of Christian Scripture.* Grand Rapids, MI: Baker Academic, 1999.

Adams, Sean A. "Paul's Letter Opening and Greek Epistolography: A Matter of Relationship." In *Paul and the Ancient Letter Form*, edited by Stanley E. Porter and Sean A. Adams, 33-55. PAST 6. Leiden: Brill, 2010.

Aland, Barbara. "Marcion/Marcioniten." *TRE* 22 (1992): 89-101.

———. "Sünde und Erlösung bei Marcion und die Konsequenz für die sogennante beiden Götter Marcions." In *Marcion und siene kirchengeschichtliche Wirkung*, edited by Gerhard May and Katharina Greschat, 147-58. TU 150. Berlin: de Gruyter, 2002.

Aland, Kurt. "The Problem of Anonymity and Pseudonymity in Christian Literature of the First Two Centuries." *JTS* 12 (1961): 39-49.

Alexander, Loveday. "Ancient Book Production and the Circulation of the Gospels." In *The Gospels for All Christians: Rethinking the Gospel Audiences*, edited by Richard Bauckham, 77-111. Grand Rapids, MI: Eerdmans, 1998.

———. *The Preface to Luke's Gospel.* SNTSMS 78. Cambridge: Cambridge University Press, 1993.

Allen, Ronald. *Missionary Methods: St. Paul's or Ours?* Grand Rapids, MI: Eerdmans, 1962.

Allert, Craig. *A High View of Scripture? The Authority of the Bible and the Formation of the New Testament Canon.* Grand Rapids, MI: Baker Academic, 2007.

The Ante-Nicene Fathers. Edited by Alexander Roberts and James Donaldson. 1885–1887. 10 vols. Repr., Peabody, MA: Hendrickson, 1994.

Aune, David E. *The New Testament in its Literary Environment.* LEC 8. Philadelphia: Westminster, 1987.

Bagnall, Roger S. *Early Christian Books in Egypt.* Princeton, NJ: Princeton University Press, 2009.

Baird, William. *History of New Testament Research Volume One: From Deism to Tübingen.* Minneapolis, MN: Fortress, 1992.

Barr, James. *Holy Scripture: Canon, Authority, Criticism.* New York: Oxford University Press, 1983.

Barton, John. *Holy Writings, Sacred Text: The Canon in Early Christianity*. Louisville, KY: Westminster John Knox Press, 1997.

———. "Marcion Revisited." In *The Canon Debate*, edited by Lee Martin McDonald and James A. Sanders, 341-54. Peabody, MA: Hendrickson, 2002.

Bauckham, Richard. *Jesus and the Eyewitnesses*. Rev. ed. Grand Rapids, MI: Eerdmans, 2017.

———. *Jesus and the God of Israel: God Crucified and Other Studies on the New Testament's Christology of Divine Identity*. Grand Rapids, MI: Eerdmans, 2008.

———, ed. *The Gospel for All Christians: Rethinking the Gospel Audiences*. Grand Rapids, MI: Eerdmans, 1998.

Bauer, Walter. *Orthodoxy and Heresy in Earliest Christianity*. Edited by Robert Kraft and Gerhard Krodel. Translated by Paul Achtemeier. Philadelphia: Fortress, 1971.

BeDuhn, Jason. *The First New Testament: Marcion's Scriptural Canon*. Salem, OR: Polebridge, 2013.

Bird, Michael F. *Jesus Among the Gods: Early Christology in the Greco-Roman World*. Waco, TX: Baylor University Press, 2022.

Bird, Michael F. and Joseph R. Dodson, eds. *Paul and the Second Century*. LNTS 412. London: T&T Clark, 2011.

Blackman, E. C. *Marcion and his Influence*. London: SPCK, 1948.

Bock, Darrell L. *The Missing Gospels: Unearthing the Truth behind Alternative Christianities*. Nashville: Thomas Nelson, 2006.

Bokedal, Tomas. *The Formation and Significance of the Christian Biblical Canon: A Study in Text, Ritual and Interpretation*. London: T&T Clark, 2014.

Borgman, Paul and Kelly James Clark. *Written to be Heard: Recovering the Messages of the Gospels*. Grand Rapids, MI: Eerdmans, 2019.

Botha, Pieter J. J. *Orality and Literacy in Early Christianity*. BPC 5. Eugene, OR: Cascade, 2012.

Bray, Gerald. *Biblical Interpretation: Past & Present*. Downers Grove, IL: InterVarsity Press, 1996.

———. *How the Church Fathers Read the Bible: A Short Introduction*. Bellingham, WA: Lexham, 2022.

Brookins, Timothy A. "The Alleged 'Letter Allegedly from Us': The Parallel Function of ὡς δι' ἡμῶν in 2 Thessalonians 2.2." *JSNT* 45 (2021): 109-31.

Brown, Dan. *The Da Vinci Code*. New York: Anchor, 2009.

Bruce, F. F. *The Canon of Scripture*. Downers Grove, IL: InterVarsity Press, 1988.

———. *The Epistles to the Colossians, to Philemon, and to the Ephesians*. NICNT. Grand Rapids, MI: Eerdmans, 1984.

———. *The Pauline Circle*. Eugene, OR: Wipf & Stock, 2006.

Bultmann, Rudolf. *The History of the Synoptic Tradition*. Rev. ed. Peabody, MA: Hendrickson, 1994.

Burke, Tony, ed. *Fakes, Forgeries, and Fictions: Writing Ancient and Modern Christian Apocrypha*. Eugene, OR: Cascade Books, 2017.

———. *The New Testament Apocrypha: More Noncanonical Scriptures. Volume 2*. Grand Rapids, MI: Eerdmans, 2020.

———. *The New Testament Apocrypha: More Noncanonical Scriptures. Volume 3*. Grand Rapids, MI: Eerdmans, 2023.

Burke, Tony and Brent Landau, eds. *New Testament Apocrypha: More Noncanonical Scriptures*, vol. 1. Grand Rapids, MI: Eerdmans, 2016.

Burridge, Richard. "Who Writes, Why, and for Whom?" In *The Written Gospel*, edited by Markus Bockmuehl and Donald Hagner, 99-115. Cambridge: Cambridge University Press, 2005.

Byrskog, Samuel. *Story as History—History as Story: The Gospel Tradition in the Context of Ancient Oral History*. WUNT 123. Tübingen: Mohr Siebeck, 2000.

Campbell, Douglas. *Framing Paul: An Epistolary Biography*. Grand Rapids, MI: Eerdmans, 2014.

Campenhausen, Hans von. *Ecclesiastical Authority and Spiritual Power in the Church of the First Three Centuries*. Peabody, MA: Hendrickson, 1997.

Castelo, Daniel and Robert W. Wall. *The Marks of Scripture: Rethinking the Nature of the Bible*. Grand Rapids, MI: Baker Academic, 2019.

Chapman, Stephen B. "Reclaiming Inspiration for the Bible." In *Canon and Biblical Interpretation*, edited by Craig Bartholomew et al, 167-206. Grand Rapids, MI: Zondervan, 2006.

Childs, Brevard S. *The Church's Guide for Reading Paul: The Canonical Shaping of the Pauline Corpus*. Grand Rapids, MI: Eerdmans, 2008.

———. *The New Testament as Canon: An Introduction*. Philadelphia: Fortress, 1985.

Cicero. *Letters of Cicero: The Whole Extant Correspondence in Chronological Order*. Translated by Evelyn S. Shuckburgh. London: George Bell and Sons, 1908–1909.

Clabeaux, John James. *The Lost Edition of the Letters of Paul: A Reassessment of the Text of the Pauline Corpus Attested by Marcion*. CBQMS 21. Washington, DC: Catholic Biblical Association of America, 1989.

Copenhaver, Adam. *Reconstructing the Historical Background of Paul's Rhetoric in the Letter to the Colossians*. LNTS 585. London: T&T Clark, 2018.

Cullmann, Oscar. *The Christology of the New Testament*. Translated by Shirley Guthrie and Charles Hall. Rev. ed. London: SCM Press, 1959.

Dahl, Nils A. "The Particularity of the Pauline Epistles as a Problem in the Ancient Church." In *Eine Freundesgabe Herrn Professor Dr. Oscar Cullmann zu seinem 60. Geburtstag überreicht. Neotestamentica et Patristica*, 261-71. NovTSup 6. Leiden: Brill, 1962.

Dassmann, Ernst. *Der Stachel im Fleisch: Paulus in der frühchristlichen Literatur bis Irenäus*. Münster: Aschendorff, 1979.

Davis, Leo Donald. *The First Seven Ecumenical Councils (325–787): Their History and Theology*. Collegeville, MN: Liturgical, 1990.

"Dei Verbum." http://www.vatican.va/archive/hist_councils/ii_vatican_council/documents /vat-ii_const_19651118_dei-verbum_en.html.

Deissmann, Adolf. *Light from the Ancient East: The New Testament Illustrated by Recently Discovered Texts of the Graeco-Roman World*. Translated by Lionel Strachan. New York: George H. Doran Co., 1927.

———. *Paul: A Study in Social and Religious History*. Translated by W. E. Wilson. New York: Harper & Brothers, 1957.

Dibelius, Martin. *Die Formgeschichte des Evangelium*. Edited by Günter Bornkamm. 3rd ed. Tübingen: J. C. B. Mohr, 1919.

Dockery, David S. *Christian Scripture: An Evangelical Perspective on Inspiration, Authority and Interpretation*. Eugene, OR: Wipf & Stock, 1995.

Doty, William. *Letters in Primitive Christianity*. Minneapolis, MN: Fortress, 1973.

Doval, Alexis James. "The Date of Cyril of Jerusalem's Catecheses." *JTS* 48 (1997): 129-32.

Downs, David J. *The Offering of the Gentiles: Paul's Collection for Jerusalem in Its Chronological, Cultural, and Cultic Contexts*. Grand Rapids, MI: Eerdmans, 2016.

Drake, H. A. *Constantine and the Bishops: The Politics of Intolerance*. Baltimore, MD: Johns Hopkins University Press, 2000.

Duff, Jeremy. "$\mathfrak{P}^{46}$ and the Pastorals: A Misleading Consensus?" *NTS* 44 (1998): 578-90.

Duffy, John and John Parker. *The Synodicon Vetus*. Corpus Fontium Historiae Byzantine XV. Washington, DC: Dumbarton Oaks, 1979.

Dungan, David. *Constantine's Bible: Politics and the Making of the New Testament*. Minneapolis, MN: Fortress, 2006.

Dunn, James D. G. *Christology in the Making: A New Testament Inquiry into the Origins of the Doctrine of the Incarnation*. Rev. ed. Grand Rapids, MI: Eerdmans, 1996.

———. *Did the First Christians Worship Jesus? The New Testament Evidence*. Louisville, KY: Westminster John Knox, 2010.

———. *The Oral Gospel Tradition*. Grand Rapids, MI: Eerdmans, 2013.

———. *Romans 9–16*. WBC 38B. Grand Rapids, MI: Word, 1988.

Edwards, Mark. "What Influence Did Church Councils and Theological Disputes Play in the Formation of the New Testament Canon?" In *The New Testament Canon in Contemporary Research*, edited by Stanley E. Porter and Benjamin P. Laird. TENTS. Leiden: Brill, forthcoming.

Ehrman, Bart D. *Forgery and Counterforgery: The Use of Literary Deceit in Early Christian Polemics*. New York: Oxford University Press, 2013.

———. *Lost Christianities: The Battles for Scripture and the Faiths We Never Knew*. New York: Oxford University Press, 2003.

———. "The Text as Window: New Testament Manuscripts and the Social History of Early Christianity." In *The Text of the New Testament in Contemporary Research*, edited by Bart D. Ehrman and Michael W. Holmes, 803-30. Rev. ed. NTTSD 42. Leiden: Brill, 2013.

———. *Truth and Fiction in* The Da Vinci Code. New York: Oxford University Press, 2004.

Elliott, J. K. *The Apocryphal New Testament: A Collection of Apocryphal Christian Literature in an English Translation Based on M. R. James.* New York: Oxford University Press, 1993.

Epp, Eldon J. "Issues in the Interrelation of New Testament Textual Criticism and Canon." In *The Canon Debate,* edited by Lee Martin McDonald and James A. Sanders, 485-515. Peabody, MA: Hendrickson, 2002.

———. "New Testament Papyrus Manuscripts and Letter Carrying in Greco-Roman Times." In *The Future of Early Christianity: Essays in Honor of Helmut Koester,* edited by B. A. Pearson et al, 35-56. Minneapolis, MN: Fortress, 1991.

———. "The Multivalence of the Term 'Original Text.'" In *Perspectives on New Testament Textual Criticism: Collected Essays, 1962–2004,* 551-93. NovTSup 116. Leiden: Brill, 2005.

Epp, Eldon J. and George W. MacRae, eds. *The New Testament and its Modern Interpreters.* Atlanta: Scholars, 1989.

Eusebius. *Life of Constantine: Translated with Introduction and Commentary.* Translated by Averil Cameron and Stuart Hall. Oxford: Clarendon, 1999.

Evangelical Free Church of America. "Statement of Faith." https://www.efca.org /resources/document/efca-statement-faith.

Evangelical Theological Society. "Doctrinal Basis." https://www.etsjets.org/about /constitution#A3.

Evans, C. Stephen. "Canonicity, Apostolicity, and Biblical Authority: Some Kierkegaardian Reflections." In *Canon and Biblical Interpretation,* edited by Craig Bartholomew et al, 146-66. Grand Rapids, MI: Zondervan, 2006.

Evans, Craig A. "How Long Were Late Antique Books in Use? Possible Implications for New Testament Textual Criticism." *BBR* 25 (2015): 23-37.

———. *Jesus and His World: The Archaeological Evidence.* Louisville, KY: Westminster John Knox, 2012.

Eve, Eric. *Behind the Gospels: Understanding the Oral Tradition.* Minneapolis, MN: Fortress, 2014.

Farkasfalvy, Denis M. *Inspiration & Interpretation: A Theological Introduction to Sacred Scripture.* Washington, DC: Catholic University of America Press, 2010.

———. "Irenaeus's First Reference to the Four Gospels and the Formation of the Fourfold Gospel Canon." *PRSt* 43 (2016): 415-27.

Farmer, William R. and Denis M. Farkasfalvy. *The Formation of the New Testament Canon: An Ecumenical Approach.* Ramsey, NJ: Paulist, 1983.

Fellowship of Evangelical Churches. "Articles of Faith." https://fecministries.org/about /our-beliefs/articles-faith/.

Ferguson, Everett. "The Appeal to Apostolic Authority in the Early Centuries." *ResQ* 50 (2008): 49-62.

———. "Canon Muratori: Date and Provenance." StPatr 17 (1982): 677-83.

———. "Factors Leading to the Selection and Closure of the New Testament." In *The Canon Debate*, edited by Lee Martin McDonald and James A. Sanders, 295-320. Peabody, MA: Hendrickson, 2002.

Fiore, Benjamin. *The Function of Personal Example in the Socratic and Pastoral Epistles.* AnBib 105. Rome: Pontifical Biblical Institute, 1986.

Foster, Lewis. "The Earliest Collection of Paul's Epistles." *BETS* 10 (1967): 44-55.

Frame, John M. *The Doctrine of the Word of God.* Vol. 4 of *A Theology of Lordship*. Phillipsburg, NJ: Presbyterian and Reformed, 2010.

Fredriksen, Paula. "Apocalypse and Redemption in Early Christianity: From John of Patmos to Augustine of Hippo." *VC* 45 (1991): 151-83.

Gallagher, Edmon. "Origen via Rufinus on the New Testament Canon." *NTS* 62 (2016): 461-76.

Gallagher, Edmon and John Meade. *The Biblical Canon Lists from Early Christianity: Texts and Analysis.* New York: Oxford University Press, 2017.

Gamble, Harry Y. *Books and Readers in the Early Church.* New Haven, CT: Yale University Press, 1995.

———. *The New Testament Canon: Its Making and Meaning.* Philadelphia: Fortress, 1985.

———. *The Textual History of the Letter to the Romans.* SD 42. Grand Rapids, MI: Eerdmans, 1979.

Gathercole, Simon. *The Gospel and the Gospels: Christian Proclamation and Early Jesus Books.* Grand Rapids, MI: Eerdmans, 2022.

———. "The Titles of the Gospels in the Earliest New Testament Manuscripts." *ZNW* 104 (2012): 33-76.

Gerhardsson, Birger. *The Reliability of the Gospel Tradition.* Grand Rapids, MI: Baker Academic, 2001.

Gibson, Roy. "On the Nature of Ancient Letter Collection." *JRS* 102 (2012): 56-78.

Glenny, W. Edward and Darian R. Lockett, eds. *Canon Formation: Tracing the Role of Sub-Collections in the Biblical Canon.* London: Bloomsbury, 2023.

Goodspeed, Edgar J. *The Formation of the New Testament.* Chicago: University of Chicago Press, 1926.

Gospel Coalition. "Confessional Statement." https://www.thegospelcoalition.org/about /foundation-documents/#confessional-statement.

Goswell, Gregory. "Authorship and Anonymity in the New Testament Writings." *JETS* 60 (2017): 733-49.

———. *Text and Paratext: Book Order, Title, and Division as Keys to Biblical Interpretation.* Bellingham, WA: Lexham Academic, 2022.

Green, Joel B. ed. *Hearing the New Testament: Strategies for Interpretation*. Grand Rapids, MI: Eerdmans, 2013.

Greer, Rowan A. *The Captain of Our Salvation: A Study in the Patristic Exegesis of Hebrews*. BGBE 15. Tübingen: Mohr Siebeck, 1973.

Gregory, Andrew and Christopher Tuckett, eds. *The Reception of the New Testament in the Apostolic Fathers*. New York: Oxford University Press, 2005.

Grudem, Wayne. *Systematic Theology: An Introduction to Biblical Doctrine*. Rev. ed. Grand Rapids, MI: Zondervan, 2020.

Guignard, Christophe. "The Muratorian Fragment as a Late Antique Fake? An Answer to C. K. Rothschild." *RevScRel* 93 (2019): 73-90.

Hahneman, Geoffrey M. "More on Redating the Muratorian Fragment." StPatr 19 (1989): 359-65.

———. *The Muratorian Fragment and the Development of the Canon*. Oxford: Clarendon, 1992.

———. "The Muratorian Fragment and the Origins of the New Testament Canon." In *The Canon Debate*, edited by Lee Martin McDonald and James A. Sanders, 405-15. Peabody, MA: Hendrickson, 2002.

Harmon, Matthew S. "Letter Carriers and Paul's Use of Scripture." *JSPL* 4 (2014): 129-48.

Harmon, Steven R. "Hebrews in Patristic Perspective." *RevExp* 102 (2005): 215-33.

von Harnack, Adolf. *The Origin of the New Testament and the Most Important Consequences of the New Creation*. Translated by J. R. Wilkinson. New York: Macmillan, 1925.

Harris, William. *Ancient Literacy*. Cambridge, MA: Harvard University Press, 1991.

Hartog, Paul, ed. *Orthodoxy and Heresy in Early Christian Contexts: Reconsidering the Bauer Thesis*. Eugene, OR: Pickwick, 2015.

Hartwig, Charlotte. "Die korinthische Gemeinde als Nebenadressat des Römerbriefes. Eine Untersuchung zur Wiederaufnahme von Themen aus dem 1. Korintherbrief im Römerbrief." PhD diss., University of Heidelberg, 2001.

Hartwig, Charlotte and Gerd Theissen. "Die Korinthische Gemeinde als Nebenadressat des Römerbriefs." *NovT* 46 (2004): 229-52.

Haydon, Ron. "A Survey and Analysis of Recent 'Canonical' Methods (2000–2015)." *JTI* 10 (2016): 145-55.

Head, Peter M. "Letter Carriers in the Ancient Jewish Epistolary Material." In *Jewish and Christian Scripture as Artifact and Canon*, edited by Craig A. Evans and H. D. Zacharias, 203-19. SSEJC 13. London: T&T Clark, 2009.

———. "Named Letter-Carriers Among the Oxyrhynchus Papyri." *JSNT* 31 (2009): 279-99.

Hefele, Charles Joseph. *A History of the Christian Councils From the Original Documents*. 5 vols. Translated and edited by William Clark. London: T&T Clark, 1871–1896.

Hengel, Martin. *The Four Gospels and the One Gospel of Jesus Christ*. Norcross, GA: Trinity Press International, 2000.

———. *Studies in Early Christology*. Translated by Rollin Kearns. Edinburgh: T&T Clark, 1995.

Henry, Carl F. H. "Canonical Theology: An Evangelical Appraisal." *SBET* 8 (1990): 76-108.

Hezser, Catherine. *Jewish Literacy in Roman Palestine*. TSAJ 81. Tübingen: Mohr Siebeck, 2001.

Hilhorst, A., ed. *The Apostolic Age in Patristic Thought*. SVC 70. Leiden: Brill, 2004.

Hill, Charles E. "The Book of Revelation in Early Christianity." In *The Oxford Handbook of the Book of Revelation*, edited by Craig R. Koester, 396-411. New York: Oxford University Press, 2020.

———. "The Debate over the Muratorian Fragment and the Development of the Canon." *WTJ* 57 (1995): 437-52.

———. *Who Chose the Gospels? Probing the Great Gospel Conspiracy*. New York: Oxford University Press, 2010.

Hollerich, Michael. *Making Christian History: Eusebius of Caesarea and His Readers*. CLA 11. Berkeley: University of California Press, 2021.

Holmes, Michael W. "From 'Original Text' to 'Initial Text': The Traditional Goal of New Testament Textual Criticism in Contemporary Discussion." In *The Text of the New Testament in Contemporary Research*, edited by Bart D. Ehrman and Michael W. Holmes, 637-88. Rev. ed. NTTSD 42. Leiden: Brill, 2013.

———, ed. *The Apostolic Fathers: Greek Texts and English Translations*. 3rd ed. Grand Rapids, MI: Baker Academic, 1999.

Houghton, H. A. G. *The Latin New Testament: A Guide to its Early History, Texts, and Manuscripts*. New York: Oxford University Press, 2018.

Houston, George W. *Inside Roman Libraries: Book Collections and Their Management in Antiquity*. Chapel Hill: University of North Carolina Press, 2014.

Huggins, Ronald. "Did Constantine Decide the New Testament Canon?" *MJT* 8 (2010): 102-14.

Hurtado, Larry W. *Destroyer of the Gods: Early Christian Distinctiveness in the Roman World*. Waco, TX: Baylor University Press, 2016.

———. "The Doxology at the End of Romans." In *New Testament Textual Criticism: Its Significance for Exegesis. Essays in Honor of Bruce M. Metzger*, edited by Eldon J. Epp and Gordon Fee, 185-99. Oxford: Clarendon, 1981.

———. *The Earliest Christian Artifacts: Manuscripts and Christian Origins*. Grand Rapids, MI: Eerdmans, 2006.

———. *Lord Jesus Christ: Devotion to Jesus in Earliest Christianity*. Grand Rapids, MI: Eerdmans, 2005.

Jensen, Peter. *The Revelation of God*. CCT. Downers Grove, IL: InterVarsity Press, 2002.

Jewett, Robert. "Fourth Sunday of Advent, Year B." In *The Lectionary Commentary: Theological Exegesis for Sunday's Texts, the Second Readings: Acts and the Epistles*, edited by Roger E. Van Harn, 142-45. Grand Rapids, MI: Eerdmans, 2001.

———. *Romans: A Commentary*. Hermeneia. Minneapolis, MN: Fortress, 2006.

Johnson, Luke Timothy. *The First and Second Letters to Timothy*. AB 35A. New York: Doubleday, 2001.

Johnson, William A. "The Ancient Book." In *The Oxford Handbook of Papyrology*, edited by Roger S. Bagnall, 256-81. New York: Oxford University Press, 2009.

———. *Readers and Reading Culture in the High Roman Empire: A Study of Elite Communities*. New York: Oxford University Press, 2010.

———. *Bookrolls and Scribes in Oxyrhynchus*. Toronto: University of Toronto Press, 2004.

Kalin, Everett R. "The New Testament Canon of Eusebius." In *The Canon Debate*, edited by Lee Martin McDonald and James A. Sanders, 383-404. Peabody, MA: Hendrickson, 2002.

Kelber, Werner and Samuel Byrskog, eds. *Jesus in Memory: Traditions in Oral and Scribal Perspectives*. Waco, TX: Baylor University Press, 2018.

Kelly, J. N. D. *The Pastoral Epistles*. BNTC 14. Peabody: MA: Hendrickson, 2009.

Kelly, Joseph F. *The Ecumenical Councils of the Catholic Church: A History*. Collegeville, MN: Liturgical, 2009.

Kinzig, Wolfram. "Καινὴ διαθήκη: The Title of the New Testament in the Second and Third Centuries." *JTS* 45 (1994): 519-44.

Klauck, Hans-Josef. *Ancient Letters and the New Testament: A Guide to Context and Exegesis*. Waco, TX: Baylor University Press, 2006.

Klein, William, Craig Blomberg, and Robert Hubbard. *Introducing Biblical Interpretation*. 3rd ed. Grand Rapids, MI: Zondervan, 2017.

Klinghardt, Matthias. *The Oldest Gospel and the Formation of the Canonical Gospels*. 2 vols. Leuven: Peeters, 2021.

Kloha, Jeffrey. "The Problem of Paul's Letters: Loss of Authority and Meaning in the 'Canonical Approach' of Brevard Childs." *ConJ* 35 (2009): 156-69.

Koester, Helmut. *Introduction to the New Testament. Volume Two: History and Literature of Early Christianity*. Philadelphia: Fortress, 1982.

Kraft, Robert A. "The Codex and Canon Consciousness." In *The Canon Debate*, edited by Lee Martin McDonald and James A. Sanders, 229-33. Peabody, MA: Hendrickson, 2002.

Kruger, Michael J. *Canon Revisited: Establishing the Origins and Authority of the New Testament Books*. Wheaton, IL: Crossway, 2012.

———. "Origen's List of New Testament Books in *Homiliae in Josuam* 7.1: A Fresh Look." In *Mark, Manuscripts, and Monotheism*, edited by Chris Keith and Dieter T. Roth, 99-117. LNTS 528. London: T&T Clark, 2015.

———. *The Question of Canon: Challenging the Status Quo in the New Testament Debate*. Downers Grove, IL: IVP Academic, 2013.

———. "The Reception of the Book of Revelation in the Early Church." In *Book of Seven Seals: The Peculiarity of Revelation, its Manuscripts, Attestation, and Transmission*, edited by Thomas Kraus and Michael Sommer, 159-74. WUNT 363. Tübingen: Mohr Siebeck, 2016.

Kruger, Michael J. and Andreas Köstenberger. *The Heresy of Orthodoxy: How Contemporary Culture's Fascination with Diversity Has Reshaped Our Understanding of Early Christianity*. Downers Grove, IL: InterVarsity Press, 2010.

Laird, Benjamin P. "Apostolicity and the Formation of the New Testament Canon." In *The New Testament Canon in Contemporary Research*, edited by Stanley E. Porter and Benjamin P. Laird. TENTS. Leiden: Brill, forthcoming.

——. "Early Titles of the Pauline Letters and the Publication of the Pauline Corpus." *BN* 175 (2017): 55-81.

——. "The Legacy of the Printing Press for the Production and Study of the Bible." In *Celebrating the Legacy of the Reformation*, edited by Kevin King, Edward Hindson, and Benjamin Forrest, 27-44. Nashville: Broadman & Holman, 2019.

——. *The Pauline Corpus in Early Christianity: Its Formation, Publication, and Circulation*. Peabody, MA: Hendrickson, 2022.

Laird, Benjamin P. and Miguel Echevarria. *40 Questions about the Apostle Paul*. Grand Rapids, MI: Kregel, 2023.

Lake, Kirsopp. *The Earlier Epistles of St. Paul: Their Motive and Origin*. London: Rivingtons, 1919.

Lampe, Peter. *From Paul to Valentinus: Christians at Rome in the First Two Centuries*. Minneapolis, MN: Fortress, 2003.

Lanier, Gregory R. *Corpus Christologicum: Texts and Translations for the Study of Jewish Messianism and Early Christology*. Peabody, MA: Hendrickson, 2021.

Larsen, Matthew. "Accidental Publication, Unfinished Texts and the Traditional Goals of New Testament Textual Criticism." *JSNT* 39 (2017): 362-87.

Lieu, Judith. *Marcion and the Making of a Heretic: God and Scripture in the Second Century*. Cambridge: Cambridge University Press, 2015.

Lightfoot, J. B. *Biblical Essays*. London: Macmillan, 1893.

Liljeström, Kenneth, ed. *The Early Reception of Paul*. PFES 99. Helsinki: Finish Exegetical Society, 2011.

Lindemann, Andreas. *Paulus im ältesten Christentum: Das Bild des Apostels und die Rezeption der paulinischen Theologie in der frühchristlichen Literatur bis Marcion*. Tübingen: Mohr Siebeck, 1979.

Lingelbach, John. "The Date of the Muratorian Fragment: An Inference to the Best Explanation." PhD diss., Liberty University, 2019.

Llewelyn, Stephen. "Sending Letters in the Ancient World: Paul and the Philippians." *TynBul* 46 (1995): 337-56.

Lockett, Darian R. "A Conservative Evangelical Perspective on the New Testament Canon." In *Five Views on the New Testament Canon*, edited by Stanley E. Porter and Benjamin P. Laird, 41-71. Grand Rapids, MI: Kregel, 2022.

———. *Letters from the Pillar Apostles: The Formation of the Catholic Epistles as a Canonical Collection*. Eugene, OR: Pickwick, 2017.

Loisy, Alfred. *The Origins of the New Testament*. Translation by L. P. Jacks. London: Allen and Unwin, 1950.

Longenecker, Richard N. "Ancient Amanuenses and the Pauline Epistles." In *New Dimensions in New Testament Study*, edited by Richard N. Longenecker and Merrill C. Tenney, 281-97. Grand Rapids, MI: Zondervan, 1974.

Mack, Burton. *Who Wrote the New Testament? The Making of the Christian Myth*. New York: Harper One, 1996.

Manson, T. W. "St. Paul's Letter to the Romans." In *The Romans Debate*, edited by Karl Donfried, 3-15. Grand Rapids, MI: Baker Academic, 1991.

Marshall, I. Howard. *A Critical and Exegetical Commentary on the Pastoral Epistles*. ICC. London: T&T Clark, 1999.

———. "Romans 16:25-27: An Apt Conclusion." In *Romans & the People of God: Essays in Honor of Gordon D. Fee on the Occasion of His 65th Birthday*, edited by Sven Soderlund and N. T. Wright, 170-84. Grand Rapids, MI: Eerdmans, 1999.

May, Jordan D. "The Four Pillars: The Fourfold Gospel before the Time of Irenaeus." *TJ* 30 (2009): 67-79.

McDonald, Lee Martin. *The Biblical Canon: Its Origin, Transmission and Authority*. Peabody, MA: Hendrickson, 2007.

———. *The Formation of the Biblical Canon*, vol. 2: *The New Testament Canon: Its Authority and Canonicity*. London: T&T Clark, 2021.

———. "Identifying Scripture and Canon in the Early Church: The Criteria Question." In *The Canon Debate*, edited by Lee Martin McDonald and James A. Sanders, 416-39. Peabody, MA: Hendrickson, 2002.

Meade, David G. *Pseudonymity and Canon: An Investigation into the Relationship of Authorship and Authority in Jewish and Earliest Christian Tradition*. Grand Rapids, MI: Eerdmans, 1987.

Metzger, Bruce. *The Canon of the New Testament: Its Origin, Development, and Significance*. Oxford: Clarendon, 1987.

Mitchell, Margaret M. "The New Testament Envoys in the Context of Greco-Roman Diplomatic and Epistolary Conventions: The Example of Timothy and Titus." *JBL* 111 (1992): 641-62.

Mitchell, Timothy. "Exposing Textual Corruption: Community as a Stabilizing Aspect in the Circulation of the New Testament Writings during the Greco-Roman Era." *JSNT* 43 (2020): 266-98.

———. "Myths about Autographs: What They Were and How Long They May Have Survived." In *Myths and Mistakes in New Testament Textual Criticism*, edited by Elijah Hixson and Peter Gurry, 26-47. Downers Grove, IL: InterVarsity Press, 2019.

———. "What are the NT Autographs? An Examination of the Doctrine of Inspiration and Inerrancy in Light of Greco-Roman Publication." *JETS* 59 (2016): 287-308.

———. "Where Inspiration is Found: Putting the New Testament Autographs in Context." *SBJT* 24 (2020): 83-101.

Mitton, C. Leslie. *The Formation of the Pauline Corpus of Letters*. Eugene, OR: Wipf & Stock, 2009.

Moll, Sebastian. *The Arch-Heretic Marcion*. WUNT 250. Tübingen: Mohr Siebeck, 2010.

———. "Three Against Tertullian: The Second Tradition about Marcion's Life." *JTS* 59 (2008): 169-80.

Moule, C. F. D. *The Birth of the New Testament*. BNTC. 3rd ed. London: Adam & Charles Black, 1981.

———. *The Origin of Christology*. Cambridge: Cambridge University Press, 1977.

Murphy-O'Connor, Jerome. "Co-Authorship in the Corinthian Correspondence." *RB* 100 (1993): 562-79.

———. *Paul the Letter Writer*. Collegeville, MN: Liturgical, 1995.

Need, Stephen. *Truly Divine and Truly Human: The Story of Christ and the Seven Ecumenical Councils*. Peabody, MA: Hendrickson, 2008.

Neil, Bronwen and Pauline Allen, eds. *Collecting Early Christian Letters: From the Apostle Paul to Late Antiquity*. Cambridge: Cambridge University Press, 2015.

Neill, Stephen and N. T. Wright. *The Interpretation of the New Testament 1861–1986*. Rev. ed. Oxford: Oxford University Press, 1988.

Newman, Carey C. "Jude 22, Apostolic Theology, and the Canonical Role of the Catholic Epistles." *PRSt* 41 (2014): 367-78.

The Nicene and Post-Nicene Fathers, Series 1. Edited by Philip Schaff. 1886–1889. 14 vols. Repr., Peabody, MA: Hendrickson, 1994.

The Nicene and Post-Nicene Fathers, Series 2. Edited by Philip Schaff and Henry Wace. 1890–1889. 14 vols. Repr., Peabody, MA: Hendrickson, 1994.

Nicklas, Tobias. "The Book of Revelation in the New Testament Canon." In *The Oxford Handbook of the Book of Revelation*, edited by Craig R. Koester, 361-72. New York: Oxford University Press, 2020.

Niebuhr, Karl-Wilhelm and Robert W. Wall, eds. *The Catholic Epistles and Apostolic Tradition: A New Perspective on James to Jude*. Waco, TX: Baylor University Press, 2009.

Nienhuis, David. *Not by Paul Alone: The Formation of the Catholic Epistle Collection and the Christian Canon*. Waco, TX: Baylor University Press, 2007.

Nienhuis, David and Robert W. Wall. *Reading the Epistles of James, Peter, John & Jude as Scripture: The Shaping & Shape of a Canonical Collection*. Grand Rapids, MI: Eerdmans, 2013.

Nongbri, Brent. *God's Library: The Archaeology of the Earliest Christian Manuscripts*. New Haven, CT: Yale University Press, 2018.

———. "Reconsidering the Place of Papyrus Bodmer XIV-VI ($\mathfrak{P}^{75}$) in the Textual Criticism of the New Testament." *JBL* 135 (2016): 405-37.

Origen. *Homilies on the Gospel of Luke* 1.1-3. Translation from Vol. 94 of *Fathers of the Church: A New Translation*. Washington, DC: Catholic University of America Press, 2009.

Oxford Society of Historical Theology. *The New Testament in the Apostolic Fathers*. Oxford: Clarendon, 1905.

Padilla, Osvaldo. *The Acts of the Apostles: Interpretation, History and Theology*. Downers Grove, IL: InterVarsity Press, 2016.

Parvis, Sara. "Christology in the Early Arian Controversy: The Exegetical War." In *Christology and Scripture: Interdisciplinary Perspectives*, edited by Angus Paddison and Andrew Lincoln, 120-37. LNTS 348. London: T&T Clark, 2007.

Patzia, Arthur G. *The Making of the New Testament*. Downers Grove, IL: InterVarsity Press, 1995.

Piper, Ronald. "The One, the Four and the Many." In *The Written Gospel*, edited by Markus Bockmuehl and Donald Hagner, 254-73. Cambridge: Cambridge University Press, 2005.

Plummer, Robert L and John Mark Terry, eds. *Paul's Missionary Methods: In His Time and Ours*. Downers Grove, IL: InterVarsity Press, 2012.

Polythress, Vern Sheridan. *Inerrancy and Worldview: Answering Modern Challenges to the Bible*. Wheaton, IL: Crossway, 2012.

Porter, Stanley E. ed. *The Pauline Canon*. PAST 1. Leiden: Brill, 2001.

Porter, Stanley E. and Bryan Dyer, eds. *The Synoptic Problem: Four Views*. Grand Rapids, MI: Baker Academic, 2016.

Porter, Stanley E. and Benjamin P. Laird, eds. *The New Testament Canon in Contemporary Research*. TENTS. Leiden: Brill, forthcoming.

Porter, Stanley E., David I. Yoon, and Chris Stevens, eds. *Studies on the Paratextual Features of Early New Testament Manuscripts*. TENTS. Leiden: Brill, 2023.

Räisänen, Heikki. "Marcion." In *The Blackwell Companion to Paul*, edited by Stephen Westerholm, 305-15. Chichester, UK: Wiley Blackwell, 2011.

Reece, Steve. *Paul's Large Letters: Paul's Autographic Subscriptions in the Light of Ancient Epistolary Conventions*. LNTS 561. London: T&T Clark, 2017.

Richards, E. Randolph. *Paul and First-Century Letter Writing: Secretaries, Composition and Collection*. Downers Grove, IL: InterVarsity Press, 2004.

———. "Reading, Writing, and Manuscripts." In *The World of the New Testament: Cultural, Social, and Historical Contexts*, edited by Joel B. Green and Lee Martin McDonald, 345-66. Grand Rapids, MI: Baker Academic, 2013.

Ridderbos, Herman N. *Redemptive History and the New Testament Scriptures*. Phillipsburg, NJ: Presbyterian and Reformed, 1988.

Roberts, Colin H. and T. C. Skeat. *The Birth of the Codex*. Oxford: Oxford University Press, 1983.

Roth, Dieter T. "Marcion and the Early New Testament Text." In *The Early Text of the New Testament*, edited by Charles E. Hill and Michael J. Kruger, 302-12. New York: Oxford University Press, 2012.

———. *The Text of Marcion's Gospel*. NTTSD 49. Leiden: Brill, 2015.

Rothschild, Clare K. "The Muratorian Fragment as Roman Fake." *NovT* 60 (2018): 55-82.

———. *The Muratorian Fragment: Text, Translation, Commentary*. STAC 132. Tübingen: Mohr Siebeck, 2022.

Rowland, Christopher. "The Reception of the Book of Revelation: An Overview." In *The Book of Revelation and its Interpreters*, edited by Ian Boxall and Richard Tresley, 1-25. London: Rowman and Littlefield, 2016.

Salzman, Michele Renee. "Latin Letter Collections before Late Antiquity." In *Late Antique Letter Collections: A Critical Introduction and Reference Guide*, edited by Cristiana Sogno, Bradley Storin, and Edward Watts, 13-37. Oakland: University of California Press, 2017.

Schmid, Ulrich. *Marcion und sein Apostolos: Rekonstrucktion und historische Einordnung der Marcionitischen Paulusbriefausgabe*. ANTF 25. Berlin: de Gruyer, 1995.

Schmidt, Daryl D. "The Greek New Testament as a Codex." In *The Canon Debate*, edited by Lee Martin McDonald and James A. Sanders, 469-84. Peabody, MA: Hendrickson, 2002.

Schnabel, Eckhard. "The Muratorian Fragment: The State of Research." *JETS* 57 (2014): 231-64.

———. *Paul the Missionary: Realities, Strategies and Methods*. Downers Grove, IL: InterVarsity Press, 2008.

Schröter, Jens. *From Jesus to the New Testament: Early Christian Theology and the Origin of the New Testament Canon*. Translated by Wayne Coppins. BMSEC. Waco, TX: Baylor University Press, 2013.

Schröter, Jens, Simon Butticaz, and Andreas Dettwiler, eds. *Receptions of Paul in Early Christianity: The Person of Paul and His Writings through the Eyes of his Early Interpreters*. BZNW 234. Berlin: de Gruyter, 2018.

Schütz, John Howard. *Paul and the Anatomy of Apostolic Authority*. Louisville, KY: Westminster John Knox, 2007.

Shah, Abidan Paul. *Changing the Goalpost of New Testament Textual Criticism*. Eugene, OR: Wipf & Stock, 2020.

Skeat, T. C. "The Codex Sinaiticus, The Codex Vaticanus and Constantine." *JTS* 50 (1999): 583-625.

Sogno, Cristiana, Bradley Storin, and Edward Watts, eds. *Late Antique Letter Collections: A Critical Introduction and Reference Guide*. Oakland: University of California Press, 2017.

Speyer, Wolfgang. *Die literarische Fälschung im heidnischen und christlichen Altertum: Ein Versuch ihrer Deutung.* München: Beck, 1971.

Stanton, Graham. "The Fourfold Gospel." *NTS* 43 (1997): 317-46.

Starr, Raymond J. "The Circulation of Literary Texts in the Roman World." *ClQ* 37 (1987): 213-23.

Stirewalt, M. Luther. *Paul, the Letter Writer.* Grand Rapids, MI: Eerdmans, 2003.

Stowers, Stanley K. *Letter Writing in Greco-Roman Antiquity.* LEC 5. Philadelphia: Westminster, 1986.

Strawbridge, Jennifer R. *The Pauline Effect: The Use of the Pauline Epistles by Early Christian Writers.* SBR 5. Berlin: de Gruyter, 2015.

Sundberg, Albert. "The Biblical Canon and the Christian Doctrine of Inspiration." *Int* 29 (1975): 352-71.

———. "Canon Muratori: A Fourth-Century List." *HTR* 66 (1973): 1-41.

Tanner, Norman P. *The Councils of the Church: A Short History.* New York: Crossroad, 2001.

Tertullian. *Tertullian: Adversus Marcionem.* Translated by Ernest Evans. Oxford: Clarendon, 1972.

———. *Tertullian's Treatises: Concerning Prayer, Concerning Baptism.* Translated by Alexander Souter. New York: Macmillan, 1919.

Theissen, Gerd. *The New Testament: A Literary History.* Minneapolis, MN: Fortress, 2012.

Thomas, Robert, ed. *Three Views on the Origins of the Synoptic Gospels.* Grand Rapids, MI: Kregel, 2002.

Thomassen, Einar. "Orthodoxy and Heresy in Second-Century Rome." *HTR* 97 (2004): 241-56.

Towner, Philip H. *The Letters to Timothy and Titus.* NICNT. Grand Rapids, MI: Eerdmans, 2006.

Tregelles, Samuel P. *Canon Muratorianus: The Earliest Catalogue of the Books of the New Testament.* Oxford: Clarendon, 1867.

Trobisch, David. *The First Edition of the New Testament.* New York: Oxford University Press, 2000.

———. *Paul's Letter Collection: Tracing the Origins.* Minneapolis, MN: Fortress, 1994.

Turner, Eric G. *Greek Papyri: An Introduction.* Oxford: Oxford University Press, 1968.

———. *The Typology of the Early Codex.* Eugene, OR: Wipf & Stock, 1977.

Verheyden, Joseph. "The Canon Muratori: A Matter of Dispute." In *Biblical Canons*, edited by J.-M. Auwers and H. J. de Jonge, 487-556. Leuven: Leuven University Press, 2003.

Vinzent, Markus. "The Influence of Marcion on the Formation of the New Testament Canon." In *The New Testament Canon in Contemporary Research*, edited by Stanley E. Porter and Benjamin P. Laird. TENTS. Leiden: Brill, forthcoming.

———. "Marcion's Gospel and the Beginnings of Early Christianity." *ASE* 32 (2015): 55-87.

Wallace, Daniel. "Challenges in New Testament Textual Criticism for the Twenty-First Century." *JETS* 52 (2009): 79-100.

Walton, John H. and D. Brent Sandy. *The Lost World of Scripture: Ancient Literary Culture and Biblical Authority.* Downers Grove, IL: InterVarsity Press, 2013.

Warfield, B. B. *The Inspiration and Authority of the Bible.* Edited by Samuel G. Craig. Phillipsburg, NJ: Presbyterian and Reformed, 1948.

Watson, Francis. *Gospel Writing: A Canonical Perspective.* Grand Rapids, MI: Eerdmans, 2013.

Webster, John. *Holy Scripture: A Dogmatic Sketch.* Cambridge: Cambridge University Press, 2003.

Westcott, B. F. *A General Survey of the History of the Canon of the New Testament.* 7th ed. London: Macmillan, 1896.

Williams, David. "Reconsidering Marcion's Gospel." *JBL* 108 (1989): 477-96.

Williams, Peter J. *Can We Trust the Gospels?* Wheaton, IL: Crossway, 2018.

Wiseman, T. P. *The Roman Audience: Classical Literature as Social History.* New York: Oxford University Press, 2015.

Wolter, Michael. *Die Pastoralbriefe als Paulustradition.* FRLANT 146. Göttingen: Vandenhoeck & Ruprecht, 1988.

Wright, Brian. *Communal Reading in the Time of Jesus: A Window into Early Christian Practices.* Minneapolis, MN: Fortress, 2017.

Young, David. *The Concept of Canon in the Reception of the Epistle to the Hebrews.* LNTS 658. London: T&T Clark, 2021.

——. "The Revelation of John in Eusebius' Catalogue of Scriptures." *WesTJ* 55 (2020): 134-47.

Zahn, Theodor. *Geschichte des Neutestamentlichen Kanons,* 2 vols. Erlangen: Deichert, 1888–1892.

——. *Grundriss der Geschichte des Neutestamentlichen Kanons.* Leipzig: Deichert, 1901.

NAME INDEX

Bauer, Walter, 89
BeDuhn, Jason, 92, 94, 96-97
Bird, Michael F., 90, 159
Blackman, E. C., 92
Blomberg, Craig, 66
Bock, Darrell L., 147
Bokedal, Tomas, 78, 141, 151
Borgman, Paul, 33
Bray, Gerald, 116, 197
Brookins, Timothy A., 187
Brown, Dan, 3, 110
Bruce, F. F., 4, 35-36, 67, 104, 121
Bultmann, Rudolf, 25
Burke, Tony, 186
Burridge, Richard, 66
Butticaz, Simon, 159
Byrskog, Samuel, 29
Campbell, Douglas, 65, 69-70, 74-75
von Campenhausen, Hans, 179
Castelo, Daniel, 179, 230-31
Chapman, Stephen B., 214-15
Childs, Brevard S., 212-16
Clabeaux, John James, 94
Clark, Kelly James, 33
Copenhaver, Adam, 77
Cullmann, Oscar, 90
Dahl, Nils A., 60, 79-80
Dassmann, Ernst, 159
Davis, Leo Donald, 108
Deissman, Adolf, 11, 76-80, 82
Dettwiler, Andreas, 159
Dibelius, Martin, 25
Dockery, David S., 209
Dodson, Joseph R., 159
Doty, William, 21, 79

Doval, Alexis James, 128
Downs, David J., 72
Drake, H. A., 101
Duff, Jeremy, 157
Duffy, John, 111
Dungan, David, 103-6
Dunn, James D. G., 29, 60-61, 90
Dyer, Bryan, 24
Edwards, Mark, 118-19
Ehrman, Bart D., 43, 88-92, 110-11, 116, 186-87, 189-90
Elliott, J. K., 186
Epp, Eldon J., 19, 42, 44-45, 48, 56, 136, 143, 197
Evans, C. Stephen, 191
Evans, Craig A., 16, 42-43
Eve, Eric, 29
Farkasfalvy, Denis M., 88, 150, 209
Farmer, William R., 88
Ferguson, Everett, 104, 124, 179
Fiore, Benjamin, 78
Foster, Lewis, 162
Frame, John M., 209
Fredriksen, Paula, 169
Gallagher, Edmon, 121, 123, 126
Gamble, Harry Y., 4, 14, 31, 37-38, 49, 55-57, 60-61, 63, 87, 106, 108, 151
Gathercole, Simon, 26, 68, 147
Gerhardsson, Birger, 29
Gibson, Roy, 50
Glenny, W. Edward, 145
Goodspeed, Edgar J., 1, 79, 153

Goswell, Gregory, 191, 214
Green, Joel B., 197
Greer, Rowan A., 160
Gregory, Andrew, 125
Grudem, Wayne, 46, 210-11
Guignard, Christophe, 124
Hahneman, Geoffrey M., 123-24
Harmon, Matthew S., 19
Harmon, Steven R., 160
Harnack, Adolf von, 4
Harris, William, 16
Hartog, Paul, 91
Hartwig, Charlotte, 69-72, 74
Haydon, Ron, 212
Head, Peter M., 19, 21
Hefele, Charles Joseph, 108
Hengel, Martin, 90, 145
Henry, Carl F. H., 215
Hezser, Catherine, 16
Hilhorst, A., 179
Hill, Charles E., 124, 145, 169
Hodge, Archibald, 45
Hodge, Charles, 45
Hollerich, Michael, 127
Holmes, Michael W., 45, 181
Houghton, H. A. G., 166
Houston, George W., 14, 34, 50
Hubbard, Robert, 66
Huggins, Ronald, 111
Hurtado, Larry W., 13, 56, 90, 151-52
Jensen, Peter, 209
Jewett, Robert, 59-61
Johnson, Luke Timothy, 77-78
Johnson, William A., 16, 20, 152

de Jonge, H. J., 123
Kähler, Martin, 25
Kalin, Everett R., 171
Kelber, Werner, 29
Kelly, J. N. D., 188
Kelly, Joseph F., 108
Kinzig, Wolfram, 144
Klauck, Hans-Josef, 14-15, 19
Klein, William, 66
Klinghardt, Matthias, 94
Kloha, Jeffrey, 215-16
Koester, Helmut, 96
Knox, John, 79, 153
Köstenberger, Andreas, 91
Kraft, Robert A., 152
Kruger, Michael J., 81, 91, 120,
  126, 169, 216-20, 223
Laird, Benjamin P., 68,
  80, 145, 153, 159, 183,
  192, 199
Lake, Kirsopp, 58-59
Lampe, Peter, 70
Landau, Brent, 186
Lanier, Gregory R., 90
Lieu, Judith, 92
Lightfoot, J. B., 60
Liljeström, Kenneth, 159
Lindemann, Andreas, 159
Lingelbach, John, 123
Llewelyn, Stephen, 19
Lockett, Darian R., 145, 162,
  165, 215
Loisy, Alfred, 200-201
Longenecker, Richard N., 15
Mack, Burton, 101
MacRae, George W., 197
Manson, T. W., 58-59
Marshall, I. Howard,
  56, 82-83
May, Jordan D., 145, 150
McDonald, Lee Martin, 4,
  104, 108, 177, 179
Meade, David G., 186
Meade, John, 121, 123

Metzger, Bruce, 4, 79-80, 124,
  184, 213
Mitchell, Margaret M., 19
Mitchell, Timothy, 20, 32,
  45, 49
Mitton, C. Leslie, 79, 153
Moll, Sebastian, 92
Moule, C. F. D., 90, 206
Murphy-O'Connor, Jerome,
  15, 19, 37, 40
Need, Stephen, 117
Neil, Bronwen, 50
Neill, Stephen, 197
Newman, Carey C., 162
Nicklas, Tobias, 169
Niebuhr, Karl-Wilhelm, 162
Nienhuis, David, 162, 165,
  168, 174
Nongbri, Brent, 12, 148
Padilla, Osvaldo, 27
Parker, John, 111
Parvis, Sara, 117
Patzia, Arthur G., 4
Piper, Ronald, 146
Plummer, Robert L., 35
Polythress, Vern
  Sheridan, 209
Porter, Stanley E., 24, 145, 153
Räisänen, Heikki, 92
Reece, Steve, 15
Richards, E. Randolph, 14-15,
  19, 37-38
Ridderbos, Herman N., 203,
  209, 233
Roberts, Colin H., 151
Roth, Dieter T., 94
Rothschild, Clare K., 123-24
Rowland, Christopher, 169
Salzman, Michele
  Renee, 51-52
Sandy, D. Brent, 45-46
Schmid, Ulrich, 94
Schmidt, Daryl D., 136, 142
Schnabel, Eckhard, 35, 123

Schröter, Jens, 145, 159
Schütz, John Howard, 179
Shah, Abidan Paul, 43
Skeat, T. C., 103, 151
Sogno, Cristiana, 50
Speyer, Wolfgang, 186
Stanton, Graham, 145
Starr, Raymond J., 31
Strawbridge, Jennifer R., 159
Stevens, Chris, 214
Stirewalt, M. Luther, 14, 19, 21
Storin, Bradley, 50
Stowers, Stanley K., 14
Sundberg, Albert, 123-24
Tanner, Norman P., 108
Terry, John Mark, 35
Theissen, Gerd, 69, 78
Thomas, Robert, 24
Thomassen, Einar, 93
Towner, Philip H., 78
Tregelles, Samuel P., 123
Trobisch, David, 14, 68, 153
Tuckett, Christopher, 125
Turner, Eric G., 32, 152
Verheyden, Joseph, 123-24
Vinzent, Markus, 92, 94
Wall, Robert W., 162, 174,
  179, 230-31
Wallace, Daniel, 43
Walton, John H., 45-46
Warfield, B. B., 45, 209
Watson, Francis, 24, 145
Watts, Edward, 50
Webster, John, 185
Westcott, B. F., 4, 182
Williams, David, 94
Williams, Peter J., 145
Wiseman, T. P., 20
Wolter, Michael, 78
Wright, Brian, 20
Wright, N. T., 197
Yoon, David I., 214
Young, David, 160, 171
Zahn, Theodor, 4, 123

SCRIPTURE INDEX

OLD TESTAMENT

Numbers
22:21-39, *225*

Proverbs
8, *117*
8:22-25, *117*

Joel
2:28, *229*

NEW TESTAMENT

Matthew
5:17, *66*
5:21, *16*
5:27, *16*
5:33, *16*
5:38, *16*
5:43, *16*
10:2-4, *191*
10:29, *210*
12:3, *16*
21:16, *16*
22:31, *16*

Mark
3:16-19, *191*
7:13, *28*
16:9-20, *55*

Luke
1:1, *27*
1:1-4, *27, 146*
1:2, *27*
1:3, *29, 34*
1:5–2:52, *30*
1:67-79, *228*

2:36-38, *228*
4:14-30, *20*
6:13-16, *191*
10:26, *16*
19:1-10, *30*
24:13-49, *30*

John
1:1-18, *117*
7:53–8:11, *55*
10:27, *218*
14:28, *117*

Acts
1:1, *34*
2:17, *229*
2:42-43, *179*
2:43, *192*
5:12, *192*
6:14, *28*
14:3, *192*
14:4, *192*
14:14, *192*
15, *108*
15:21, *20*
17:14, *39*
18:5, *39*
18:17, *39*
21:7-14, *228*

Romans
1–15, *58*
1–16, *58*
1:4, *117*
1:7, *58*
1:14, *71*
1:18–2:16, *71*
2, *71*
4, *181*

6:1-11, *71*
6:17, *28*
7, *71*
9–16, *60*
14, *57, 59, 61*
14–15, *71*
14:23, *57*
15, *56, 57, 59*
15–16, *61, 62*
15:8, *59*
15:19, *192, 193*
15:25-32, *72*
15:26, *72*
16, *58, 59*
16:1-2, *73*
16:7, *192*
16:20, *61*
16:22, *18, 73, 155*
16:23, *73*
16:24, *57, 61, 62*
16:25-27, *56, 57*

1 Corinthians
1:2, *78*
1:11, *36*
1:11-17, *71, 75*
1:18–2:5, *71*
1:20-21, *71*
2:6, *71*
6:9, *71*
8–9, *71*
11:2, *28*
12:12-26, *75*
14, *228*
15:3, *28*
15:3-8, *227*
15:5-9, *192*
15:6, *28*
15:8, *191*
16:1-4, *72*

2 Corinthians
3:15, *20*
8–9, *72*
10:10, *78*
12:12, *192*

Galatians
1:19, *192*
3:26-29, *75*
5:19-21, *74*

Ephesians
1:1, *67*
2:20, *180*
14, *159*

Philippians
2:25, *192*
3:2-3, *67*
3:18-19, *67*
4, *159*
4:2, *68*

Colossians
1:15, *117*
1:18, *117*
4:7-9, *21*
4:16, *16, 20, 78, 184*

1 Thessalonians
1:1, *192*
2:6, *192*
5:27, *16, 20, 78*

2 Thessalonians
2, *187*
2:2, *40, 187*
2:15, *40*
3:14, *40, 180*

1 Timothy
4:13, *16, 20*
6:9, *129*

2 Timothy
3:16, *208*

Hebrews
1:5-6, *117*
1:6, *117*
2:3-4, *192*
3:1, *192, 193*

2 Peter
1:21, *227*
2:21, *28*
3:15-16, *78, 160*
3:16, *21*

1 John
1:1, *28*

Jude
3, *28*
22, *162*

ANCIENT WRITINGS INDEX

Aelius Donatus
Life of Virgil, 32-33

Amphilochius of Iconium
Iambics for Seleucus,
80, 132-33

The Apocalypse of Paul, 186

The Apocalypse of Peter, 186

Athanasius
Festal Letters, 104, 129-30, 236

Athenagoras
*Supplication for the
Christians*, 159

Augustine
Christian Instruction, 134, 183

Cicero
Epistles of, 17-18, 37,
50-51, 155

Clement of Alexandria
Christ the Educator, 170
Exhortation to the Greeks, 159
Miscellanies, 159, 170

Clement of Rome
1 Clement, 138, 159-61, 181, 219

Cyprian
Epistles of, 51, 80

Cyril of Jerusalem
Catechetical Lectures, 128-29,
170, 181

Epiphanius
Panarion (*Refutation of All
Heresies*), 95, 117,
130-31, 134

Epistle of Barnabas, 138

Epistle to the Laodiceans,
184, 186

Eusebius
Ecclesiastical History, 27, 51,
103-4, 125-28, 165, 170-71,
180-81, 184
Life of Constantine, 100-103

Gospel of Judas, 151

Gospel of Peter, 88, 151, 186

Gospel of Philip, 151

Gospel of Thomas, 12, 26, 88,
146, 151

Gregory of Nazianzus
Carmina, 131-32, 170-71

Hippolytus of Rome
Refutation of All Heresies, 170

Ignatius
Epistles of, 51, 159, 181

Irenaeus
Against Heresies, 27, 80,
149-50, 159, 170-71,
181

Jerome
Epistles of, 80, 133-34
On Illustrious Men, 93,
133, 184-85

Josephus
Against Apion, 27
Jewish Antiquities, 27
Jewish War, 27

Justin Martyr
Dialogue with Trypho,
27, 170-71

Origen
Commentary on Romans, 62
*Commentary on the Gospel of
Matthew*, 38
Homily on Joshua, 125-27,
165
Homily on Luke, 150

Pliny the Younger
Epistles of, 17, 236

Polybius
The Histories, 27

Polycarp
Epistle to the Philippians, 159,
165, 219

The Preaching of Peter, 186

Rufinus of Aquileia
*Exposition of the
Creed*, 134-35

Second Clement, 138

Seneca
Epistles of, 51-52, 55, 155

Shepherd of Hermas, 124, 135, 138, 184

Tertullian
Against Marcion, 62, 67, 81, 93-95, 117, 150, 194-95
Baptism, 188-89
Modesty, 195
Prescription against Heresies, 181

Theophilus
To Autolycus, 159

Third Corinthians, 186

Victorinus of Pettau
Commentary on the Apocalypse, 80

Virgil
Aeneid, 32-33